D1447209

GRINGOLANDIA

Globalization and Community

Susan E. Clarke, Series Editor

Dennis R. Judd, Founding Editor

(continued on page 267)

GRINGOLANDIA

Lifestyle Migration under Late Capitalism

MATTHEW HAYES

Globalization and Community, Volume 29

University of Minnesota Press
Minneapolis
London

Portions of chapter 1 were previously published in a different form in "Moving South: The Economic Motives and Structural Context of North America's Emigrants in Cuenca, Ecuador," *Mobilities* 10, no. 2 (2015): 267–84; available online at http://www.tandfonline.com/. Portions of chapter 3 were previously published in a different form in "'It Is Hard Being the Different One All the Time': Gringos and Racialized Identity in Lifestyle Migration to Ecuador," *Ethnic and Racial Studies* 38, no. 6 (2014): 943–58; available online at http://www.tandfonline.com/. Portions of chapter 5 were previously published in a different form in "Into the Universe of the Hacienda: Lifestyle Migration, Individualism, and Social Dislocation in Vilcabamba, Ecuador," *Journal of Latin American Geography* 14, no. 1 (2015): 79–100; available online at http://www.tandfonline.com/.

Copyright 2018 by the Regents of the University of Minnesota

All rights reserved. No part of this publication may be reproduced, stored in a retrieval system, or transmitted, in any form or by any means, electronic, mechanical, photocopying, recording, or otherwise, without the prior written permission of the publisher.

Published by the University of Minnesota Press
111 Third Avenue South, Suite 290
Minneapolis, MN 55401-2520
http://www.upress.umn.edu

The University of Minnesota is an equal-opportunity educator and employer.

Library of Congress Cataloging-in-Publication Data
Names: Hayes, Matthew F. (Matthew Frederick), author.
Title: Gringolandia : lifestyle migration under late capitalism / Matthew Hayes.
Description: Minneapolis : University of Minnesota Press, [2018] | Series: Globalization and community ; Volume 29 | Includes bibliographical references and index.
Identifiers: LCCN 2018008955 (print) | ISBN 978-1-5179-0491-3 (hc) |
    ISBN 978-1-5179-0492-0 (pb)
Subjects: LCSH: Emigration and immigration–Social aspects. | Transnationalism. |
    Lifestyles–Economic aspects.
Classification: LCC JV6225 .H39 2018 (print) | DDC 304.8/86624—dc23
LC record available at https://lccn.loc.gov/2018008955

For Linda Freeman, whose Comparative Politics and Development class disabused me of some liberal truisms I took to be self-evident

Contents

Introduction

Lifestyle Migration and Global Sociology

Diana's hearty smile stood out immediately in the café where we had arranged to meet, across the street from her apartment in Cuenca, Ecuador.[1] She lived in a neighborhood that has come to be called "Gringolandia"– a backhanded reference to the growing number of "gringo" foreigners residing in the area's condo blocks. Diana was a sixty-year-old retiree from Eastern Canada who had left her husband of twenty-five years at home and moved to Ecuador in search of adventure. She was a vibrant, outgoing woman, with expectations of the future that seemed to mark a break with those she had previously had about this phase of her life. Diana had decided to live out her retirement half a world away from home, her husband, her family, and her friends.

Diana's decision to move to Ecuador's third largest city, twenty-five hundred meters above sea level, seemed both exciting and out of the ordinary to me. The city is not well known in Canada or the United States, and Diana had little familiarity with the language or culture—though she did have a desire to learn more. Moreover, it is a city marked by deep inequalities and an average household income of about $700 a month, well below Diana's Canadian pension. These were to be the themes of our conversation in the café, which abutted a four-lane, concrete artery that runs through the center of Gringolandia. Racing traffic and passing blue public transit buses, spewing plumes of thick black smoke, punctuated our discussion. We drank weak Ecuadorian coffee as great gobs of rain smacked against the plastic awning. We both wore sweaters, because the altitude makes daytime temperatures rather cool. Diana had lived in Cuenca for more than a year at that point and was still excited to share her story.

Like many Canadians, Diana was keen to escape the snow after years of working through the winters. But unlike many of her
compatriots, the beach was not her thing. Desiring an affordable
location in a steady climate without too much heat, she typed
"temperate climate" into Google. "Ecuador was one of the first
places [that came up]," she said. "And I'd never heard of Ecuador.
I mean, you hear about it in the back of your mind, you know,
but I had never done any research. And so from there I started researching." Diana wasn't just thinking of a vacation. She wanted
to move permanently and was able to tap a large online network
of other North Americans who had already taken the plunge. "I
started emailing people cold: 'look, this is what I'm looking for,'"
she recounted. "Safety, as an older single woman, obviously, that
was a really big one for me. . . . And I had to start narrowing
down."

"I figure I've got another ten years of good health," Diana told
me. "Ten years, maybe fifteen years if I'm really, really careful,
and very lucky. And that's not very long, in the wider scheme of
things, you know, ten years is one-seventh of my life. That's what
I have left. And so there was the recognition, and my, my mother
had just died, recently, and there's just the recognition that, if
I'm going to do anything, it needs to be *now*." Instead of aging
in ways familiar to her from past experience, Diana wanted an
adventure, she said. "Anything where I have to take a risk, you
know? Like, this was a big risk, for me, coming down here and,
and yeah, this was the most risk-taking thing I've ever done in
my life." She was moving to a country where she did not know the
language and where she had no friends prior to an initial visit.
For Diana, taking a risk meant "moving out of my comfort zone,
and doing something, experiencing something that frightens me,
that unnerves me, that makes me anxious. And especially doing
it alone. Especially doing it alone." Though Diana could return to
Canada, she had sold her home. Furthermore, though she was
still legally married, she did not seem interested in going back to
her relationship and spoke about feeling bored with her routine
there. She said she had done more in the last year and a half than
she had done in her entire life, immersing herself in the more in-

tense experiences associated with this risk taking. When I asked her to explain her fascination with moving out of her comfort zone, she explained matter-of-factly that it was about "growth. Just personal growth."

Once Diana got to Cuenca, a welcoming and sociable group of fellow North Americans drew her in, as it had so many others. She was nearly ecstatic at how much more active her social life was. Other "expats," as they call themselves, told me again and again that their experience was akin to going back to college. There were many parties and lots of eating and drinking out—events that rarely happened in their social circles back home. Everyone was more or less the same age, and they all wanted to hang out with one another and settle into a new life. Many had even arrived in Cuenca at the same time. But why pursue this project in Cuenca, an unfamiliar city on another continent, where incomes are lower and inequality much greater than at home?

Diana's experience of transnational mobility is typical of the experiences of many of the North Americans living in Cuenca with whom I spoke. Like Diana, nearly all North Americans who have relocated to Ecuador are racialized as white.[2] Their experiences and ideals illustrate the cultural beliefs and imaginaries that underpin the growing popularity of moving abroad, or "expatriating," as many of the self-declared expats called it. These beliefs and ideals are socially situated: they underscore the experiences of white, middle-class North Americans, whose aspirations for active living and material well-being have been a constant hallmark

Figure 1. Gringolandia, 2012. Photograph by the author.

of their cultural upbringing (Gilleard and Higgs 2011). Diana seemed to be living out a utilitarian life project, where she experienced aging through the accumulation of intense experiences in a bid to "grow" as much as possible. Defining her decision to move to Ecuador as an adventure and a risk, Diana also saw her move as a particular type of project of self-fulfillment. Furthermore, "doing it alone" made it an autonomous and individualistic self-project for her—a particularly gendered one in this instance, in which she asserted herself against traditional obligations to her relationship. Diana's notion of adventure involved expressing and fulfilling her own desires and interests and thereby moving further away from her comfort zone, a zone of familiarity that perhaps included painful knowledge of posttraditional, market-driven aging and dying in North America. In a bid to escape the inevitability of aging and decline in Canada, Diana, like many others, had decided to go for "another adventure." This adventure, of course, required economic resources, making a lower-cost location like Cuenca useful for other reasons.

Not all lifestyle migrants to Cuenca are like Diana. Many refer to themselves as "economic refugees." They express the same cultural ideals as Diana but are also clear that what enables them to live out the ideals of an active, adventurous retirement is the lower cost of living. North American migrants to Cuenca narrate their experience there as a kind of risk that has the potential to deliver personal growth in an aging process that they conceive of as a challenge, one where they can age successfully by showing signs of adventurousness and flexibility in the face of living in a new culture. Lana, age sixty-six, moved from Oakland, California, almost a year prior to our meeting in a café in central Cuenca. She also thought of her experience as an adventure and articulated it in terms similar to Diana's explanation. "Every day I learn something," she said. "And that's exciting. Whereas at home, I know where to go and everything. It became much harder to have an adventure [there], to see someone different." Every day, she said, was an adventure because she was always learning in a new culture, a culture that itself became a kind of stimulating game offering new experiences. "I'd be much more closed in [back in Oakland]. And here, I just feel much more alive." In Cuenca, she said, even going to the market was an adventure, and she didn't have to worry about spending too much to get the best-quality food, stating, "I don't have to worry about spending money. At home, I would always torture myself."

Other lifestyle migrants, who were enjoying new social occasions, new experiences, and the ability to spend money freely, echoed this point. An Australian woman in her late sixties, Joan,[3] who was contemplating a move to Cuenca, declared, "I just find it more interesting to be here, than I do living in Sydney, where I don't know why this is happening, but my life seems to be narrowing, and I'm getting into an age group where my friends die." Speaking with some weight and solemnity, she was describing her attempt to avoid a world that she saw closing down around her as she aged alone as a single woman. By contrast, she saw a potential move to Cuenca as an "expansionary thing to do."

Rick offered another example of this cultural phenomenon. Rick was seventy-five, had worked part time in advertising, and had relocated from Houston, Texas, almost a year before we met at his home in Cuenca's historic El Centro neighborhood. He wore glasses, had a thick mustache, and smiled a lot. "Money," he said, "was never my main objective [in life]; having fun was." As a consequence, Rick had not saved up a lot of money and was in financial difficulty. He felt his inner suburban neighborhood was in decline, something he narrated in terms of a rise in crime. Rick was white and said he was concerned about the "wrong kind of blacks" moving in, illustrating the racialized perceptions of crime and social decline many white people have in the United States. Given his savings and the value of his home, he could not easily move elsewhere within Houston. The city was about to build an expressway nearby, bringing a long period of noise and pollution. Rather than see his quality of life fade away, he decided to "pull the trigger" and move to Cuenca after an initial visit. Like Diana, he conceived of his trip as an adventure.

"I have been playing golf with the same guys for 28 years," he said. "We know where every blade of grass is on two courses." Like Diana and Lana, Rick found the familiarity of the known increasingly giving way to a desire for something new. "I mean, sometimes you gotta get out of your comfort zone." Rick could not achieve a new experience by staying closer to home or by moving to, say, St. Louis. There were economic factors that sent him to a lower-cost country, reasons that are integral to North American migration to Ecuador. It is not that North American retirees moving to Ecuador are poor—most are not. Rather, it is that ideals about retirement and aging appear too costly to pursue in the United States, and thus the chances of accumulating experiences that symbolize successful aging seem fewer there. Rick's self-understanding of his relocation also drew on ideals of aging and how to age properly. He had contemplated living in Florida. "But I couldn't live there," he said, with a deep laugh and wide grin, "you know, with all those old people! You know? God! I mean, they overwhelm you. You go in the grocery store and, you know, they're puttering along and pushing you out of the way." Rick's ageist stereotypes informed his desire to do something different and experiment with apparently more adventurous and independent ways of living and aging. The notion of aging as a decline was something that this seventy-five-year-old could not fathom for himself, as he sat on a rooftop in a city he had never heard about until just two years prior. Tending lovingly to his jalapeño and habanero peppers, he told me about his plans to establish a commercial garden and sell his hot peppers, joking around with potential marketing labels: "Rick's Rockets," he called them.[4] "This appeals," he said. "It's a challenge, you know, it's totally different, you know? And it's fun." Rather than an aging process in which Rick's world began turning in on him, Rick saw his life expanding outward, much as Joan wished for her own life. "This garden is the beginning of my New Deal," he said, echoing the sentiments of previous generations, who sought to build something new, something that might offer a brighter future.

Rick's New Deal, like other instances of lifestyle migration, is an individual, personal project of self-fulfillment through migration (Korpela 2014; Oliver 2007), a New Deal quite different from the collective projects that sought social welfare reforms and a new deal for American workers in the twentieth century. While individualistic, Rick's New Deal remains embedded in social relations, specifically the unequal relations of the global division of labor, such that it requires lower-income groups whose lives are, in many ways, even more precarious. These unequal relations enable migrants like Diana, Joan, and Lana to move to lower-cost locations, where savings accrued during their working lives can stretch further and facilitate new experiments in aging. They enable people like Joan, who felt stuck in an urban environment that diminished her opportunities for sociability, to live more fulfilling lives. They also allow people like Rick, who may have internalized ageist stereotypes about aging, to avoid confronting the contradictions of a materialist culture that avoids thinking about care, infirmity, and death. The social consequences of these cultural narratives of aging are the topic of this book. North Americans think of their relocations mostly in terms of their own lives, even as they continue to be rooted in unequal global social relations.

An Ethnography of Global Inequality

These unequal global social relations are most evident in the disparity of income and wealth between North Americans migrating to Ecuador, on one hand, and the migrations of Ecuadorians and other Latin Americans moving north, on the other. The asymmetries of rights and experiences in receiving communities demand further reflection at a moment in history characterized by intense transnational mobility—of tourists and lifestyle migrants as well as refugees and labor migrants. North–South migrations, or lifestyle migrations, differ from those that are the object of most mainstream migration scholarship. However, if considered within the frame of global migration and transnationalism, they draw attention to the colonial legacies of contemporary migration and the international rules that govern them. The life projects and retirement adventures of Diana and Rick play out in an unequal and increasingly interconnected global society, and their relocations say something important about it. Starting from the reflections of North Americans in Cuenca, this book explores global inequality and the transnational social relations that occur in a context marked by a history of colonial exploitation. North Americans in Ecuador interact with this legacy and attempt to reckon with it. This book begins from their motivations, imaginaries, and experiences, noting how their movements and ideals embody, in many respects, an unequal global society, a product of historical, colonial social relations of exploitation and unequal accumulation. But these transnationalized lives also connect to the existing social relations of Ecuador, ones steeped in their own traditions of epistemic and "internal colonialism" (Grosfoguel 2007; Quijano 2000; Santos 2014). The settlement of North Americans in the condos of Gringolandia (see Figures 1 and 2) are an example of the unequal social relations that mark the coloniality of contemporary Ecuadorian society. The book is based on data collected through thirty-four weeks of fieldwork conducted between 2011 and 2016, using methods outlined in the appendix.

This ethnographic project is in dialogue with other global sociologists who grapple with the colonial continuities of global society that shape contemporary forms of inequality, especially in transnational contexts (Beck 2011; Bhambra 2014; Boatcă 2016; Go 2009; Levitt and Glick Schiller 2004; Weiß 2005). Our contemporary global society is built on a foundation of colonial domination, oppression, slavery, and violent appropriation, the consequences of which continue to play out long "after the event" (Bhambra 2014, 138). Building on the reflections of white, mostly middle-class North Americans who occupy relatively privileged global social positions, this book provides some ethnographic muscle to "cartographic" and skeletal theories of global inequality that attempt to come to grips with coloniality—or the remainder of colonial social relations and worldviews after the end of formal colonial administration.[5] As the decolonial social theorist Walter Mignolo (2011) suggests, a global sociology must attempt to reckon fully with the real consequences of the colonial experience, without which modernity remains a compromised project, reproducing epistemic colonialism and Eurocentric domination. The stakes are clear: a fuller understanding of how coloniality plays out in quotidian situations of inequality in transnational perspective helps to clarify and visualize the full consequences of colonialism, as its violence ripples through time. It forces us to face certain truths, the sources of existing injustices, and— potentially—draws attention to the need for a global movement

Figure 2. Looking up at the condos of Gringolandia from the western edge of
Cuenca. Photograph by the author.

of reconciliation, built on greater material and symbolic justice
and egalitarian ideals rooted in a shared human condition. What
we currently call "globalization," or even "modernity," is a product
of a colonial integration of the globe, a process that includes slavery, violent appropriation of land, and exploitation of colonized
people. While many lifestyle migrants in a variety of global locations may find that this colonial legacy is far in the past, closer
scrutiny reveals its constant presence in the lives of "white migrants" (Lundström 2017) in places like southern Ecuador, where
few people identify as white.

   No topic more clearly illustrates global structures of coloniality than transnational migration—especially when we include
the transnational relocations of North Americans to Latin American destinations. In particular, transnational migration is imbri-
cated in what Aníbal Quijano (2000) refers to as the coloniality of
power, or modes of representing human social diversity in ways
that justify unequal treatment and asymmetrical appropriation
of a globally produced social surplus. Ideologies that justify an

arbitrary and false evolutionary hierarchy of "races," and disparage the corrosive impact of nonwhite people on supposedly homogeneous "white" or "European" groups, continue to mark global social relations. Furthermore, in the geographic expression of global inequalities in local spaces of the Global South, we can also come to a fuller understanding of the coloniality of urban "revitalization" and heritage restoration, especially in contexts marked by transnational mobility from the Global North. North American migrants in Ecuador usually want to find ways to bridge inequalities and shun ethnocentric displays of superiority. But this does not mean that their presence is not contiguous in important ways with modes of colonial occupation and displacement (see also Peraldi and Terrazzoni 2016). This book uncovers some of these contiguities and draws attention to how a stratified global society reproduces spatial and social injustices.

Latitudes of the Global Division of Labor

What made Rick's New Deal possible, and what allowed Diana to experience personal growth, was the existence of a low-cost country, Ecuador, that was willing to embrace the arrival of several thousand North Americans (perhaps as many as twelve thousand in Cuenca alone)[6] over a relatively short period of time, and even openly promoted some of its towns and cities for further settlement. Once they arrived, newcomers found that the municipality of Cuenca and other state institutions offered classes and services to facilitate their integration. Local businesses promoted products and services to them. Their experiences are in sharp contrast with other migrants moving north with the same hope of improving their lives and say a great deal about the remainders of a colonial global order white North Americans often associate with a distant past. Yet, the experiences of North American lifestyle migrants in Ecuador appear, at least sometimes, to play out in circumstances marked by these remainders and are visible in the meanings they give to their transnational mobility and the material motivations that spur them. As discussed earlier in the examples of Diana and Rick, North Americans in Ecuador often narrate their relocations in terms of an adventure. In part, this narrative helps to make sense of their relocation. Moreover, it fits the cultural ideal of a generation that seeks to define the aging process in opposition to traditional ideas of aging, emphasizing continued activity and consumer identities (Allain and Marshall 2017; Gilleard and Higgs 2011; Marshall 2015; McHugh 2000). Given that these ideals require incomes that often depend on working, many may feel they need a low-cost safe haven to preserve culturally significant notions of "successful" aging (Dillaway and Byrnes 2009), particularly those who lack sufficient savings, either due to financial losses or lower incomes during their working lives. In a global division of labor, marked by a history of colonial domination that centered social processes of accumulation mostly in Northern European cities and parts of North America, the existence of high- and low-cost regions is a product of an unequal political economy that stratifies regions and labor forces along shifting territorial lines. Drawing on the work of Aihwa Ong (2006), I suggest thinking about these territorial inequalities as "latitudes" of a global division of labor, a concept that captures the unequal accrual of privileges and rewards from a global system of production and accumulation. These latitudes are, as I suggest throughout, a by-product of an exploitative and often very violent appropriation of wealth in the colonies that was later expressed in the European metropoles in both cultural and material forms.

The exploitative practices of colonialism that led to an unequal global economy seem a long way away from the contemporary experiences of North American retirees in southern Ecuador. But they are entangled in many ways, as this book will point out. At an economic level, Diana and Rick are able to relocate to Ecuador because they inherited positions at higher latitudes of the global division of labor—they were born into citizenship in Canada and the United States, where racialized white workers like them have historically benefited from better working conditions, higher incomes, and a greater distribution of social surpluses in the form of health care, education, and social rights. These social rights may now be entering a period of decline, but they were hard-fought victories for the working classes in the twentieth century, who sought a better distribution of accumulated surpluses in the "developed" countries at the core of a global and colonial division of labor. Higher incomes and more generous social programs were made possible in part by the unequal way that the global surplus was divided. It is not merely that local and national inequalities marked the global system but that on a global scale, some regions were centers of accumulation, while others were primarily spaces of raw materials exploitation and extraction (Furtado [1959] 2006; Galeano [1971] 2010; Prasad 2012; Prebisch 1962). The resulting uneven terms of trade produced lasting global geographies of difference and inequality. The historically higher incomes accrued to higher latitudes of the global division of labor—the centers of colonial and global accumulation—reproduce these regions' ability to lay claim to the labor power of workers from lower latitudes. Wealthier regions, often former centers of colonial power, benefit from and perpetuate extractive activities that "trickle up," leaving fewer surpluses for redistribution at lower latitudes. These claims to labor power are also claims to the capitalist uses of local space, as communities in the Global South—or regions colonized by Europe—are connected to a global system of accumulation in which most of the surplus flows to core regions of the world economy. Diana and Rick did not choose this legacy, and they did not directly participate in its elaboration for the most part. But they did benefit from it. The structure of this system, held together first by colony–metropole trade patterns and more recently by international free trade and a global market for raw materials and manufactured goods, facilitates North–South relocation and enables migrants like Diana and Rick to accumulate some of the cultural symbols of a successful aging process.

The benefits Diana and Rick and others draw from historically produced, global inequalities contrast with the experiences of other transnational migrants, many of them refugees fleeing war, persecution, climate change, and economic stagnation in their home countries. Aihwa Ong (2006) discusses this stratification in terms of latitudes of citizenship, whereby some populations are included and others excluded from citizenship rights, rights increasingly disarticulated from territorial spaces in a globalizing world. Diana and Rick provide interesting examples of the portability of citizenship, and even the consumption of global spaces, since both selected Cuenca after having first researched a variety of different locations. Other lifestyle migrants in Latin America discuss "checking out" or visiting different locations before relocating to ensure prospective locations will suit their needs. For Ong, the concept of "latitudes" describes the hierarchical gradients of labor discipline, instilled by states applying neoliberal forms of "governance at a distance," which shape the lives of workers' "self-projects" in relation to global processes of surplus accumulation (Ong 2006). At upper latitudes, mobile citizens who are able to abide by the rules of the labor market are also rewarded for their skills, which can be transferred across borders. At lower latitudes, however, a labor incarceration regime operates, whereby the lack of citizenship rights (including labor standards, welfare benefits, etc.) that occurs in many low-income countries enforces participation in the deterritorialized production of goods for the benefit of distant export markets. The inability of most workers to legally cross borders to seek labor rights in other countries seals a labor incarceration regime. The differences between latitudes are the product of a politically enforced differentiation of rights, or what Glick Schiller and Salazar (2013) refer to as mobility regimes, which police some bodies differently than others, racializing the global division of labor and often framing nonwhite bodies as threats to the social cohesion and security of northern states. The differences between individuals across these latitudes are arbitrary. They do not reflect the abilities of individuals, or their talents for internalizing neoliberal labor market discipline, because even development and consolidation of talent and discipline are a reflection of unequal accumulation within the global division of labor, its institutional expression within territorial bounded nation-states, and its unequal redistribution. In other words, the inequalities the concept of latitudes expresses are the result of a colonial difference that has historically assigned certain populations to tasks and modes of labor that have asymmetrically benefited wealthy, core regions of the global economy. Thus the historical enslavement and indenture of nonwhite populations in European colonies continue to mark contemporary global society and its inequalities, both within and between nation-states.

Rick and Diana had little to do with configuring this uneven global division of labor. Yet they also benefit from it, because their racialized whiteness and their citizenship at higher latitudes of the global division of labor enable them to lay claim to rights and benefits in Ecuador that facilitate their projects of personal growth and self-discovery. In Ecuador, their savings go further and permit them to experiment with new forms of aging, where they have the illusion of greater control and the possibility of staving off what Joan referred to as a "narrowing" of their social worlds. These more expansive lifestyles sometimes enable North–South migrants to help expand the lives of others with whom they have come to live. For example, they often seek to help poorer Ecuadorian individuals and families, sometimes episodically, sometimes through long-lasting paternalistic bonds. However, in many cases, they end up participating in unequal social relations and in processes of appropriation of local places, which limit the lives of local Ecuadorians.

Lifestyle Migration and Global Inequality

The experiences of lifestyle migrants like Diana and Rick offer a good window into the permutations of our increasingly global society, its growing interconnectedness, and its accompanying injustices. Many North Americans say that they moved less to pursue lifestyle ideals and more out of economic necessity, as we will see in chapter 1. In most cases, these migrants could not attain their lifestyle ideals—especially those associated with active aging—without transnational relocation to a lower-income country. The experiences of many of my research participants both confirm the cultural ideal of "third age" (Gilleard and Higgs 2011; Katz 2005) and demonstrate how achieving this ideal is dependent on material conditions that were historically specific to the post–World War II period. Indeed, even the very notion of a "third age," that is, of a life stage marked by postproductive activity that precedes infirmity and old age (sometimes referred to as an "age of personal fulfillment" as opposed to an "age of decline"), emerges only in the 1950s in Great Britain and the United States

(Laslett 1991). For a growing number of North Americans, achieving these culturally and historically specific ideals of personal fulfillment and active leisure in postproductive years is dependent on access to low-cost labor or even transnational relocation to a low-income country. Lifestyle migration, thus, has an overlooked relationship to global inequality, one that helps frame the field of transnational migration broadly in relation to colonial continuities with respect to mobility rights, citizenship, and claims to labor and space. It is not coincidental that relocation in retirement from high-income to lower-income countries has gained substantial popularity at the same historical moment that millions of refugees have sought to escape the deteriorating social, political, and economic conditions of their home countries, spawning the so-called migrant crisis, which several political movements have sought to exploit to justify further austerity reforms that mostly punish workers and pensioners.

Decolonial sociology helps frame these diverse migrations within a global political economy of human mobility. This framework transcends a more limited focus on migration as primarily involving people moving from the Global South to the Global North, motivated by hopes for better job opportunities or protection of basic citizenship rights. As Fechter and Walsh (2010, 1198) point out, a postcolonial approach to migration that integrates the experiences of people in relatively privileged social positions helps "reveal how racial hierarchies and power inequalities persist, as well as how they are being reconfigured and challenged." One of the ways that global inequality is reproduced is through the unequal experiences of global mobility of North–South migrants relative to those of refugees and labor migrants from lower-income countries moving north (cf. Álvarez Velasco 2016; Glick Schiller and Salazar 2013; Gómez Martín 2016; Hansen and Jonsson 2011; Vaughan-Williams 2015). At the same time, North American lifestyle migrants are often aware of these imbalances, and it is not rare that they see them as injustices too. As Pauline Leonard (2008, 1248) notes with respect to the British in Hong Kong, changing political environments also require "personal shifts to new subject positions." This requires that migrants work to make sense of their own privileges and to find ways to compensate for them, or to adjust their outlooks and interactions with local populations.

Yet despite challenging and disrupting inequalities in some aspects of their emplacement in Ecuador, North Americans also often reinforce inequalities in others. For example, North Americans are not always fully aware of how some of the urban and rural changes they are witnessing (and cheering) in southern Ecuador are the product of very unequal social relations, stemming from histories of exploitation and oppression. Moreover, as I discuss in chapter 3, North Americans negotiate new identities as racialized "gringos," as the visibility of their whiteness produces feelings of ambivalence and vulnerability, even as it is also a source of identification and social power.[7] As in other cases of lifestyle migration in postcolonial contexts, racialized whiteness calls for new types of identity and the negotiation of its reception and the privileges attached to it (Fechter 2005; Leonard 2008; Walsh 2010, 2012). It is a key source of identification for North American migrants in southern Ecuador, and a major source of preoccupation, even as research participants almost always disavowed any form of white superiority and stigmatized "obnoxious gringos" who failed to do so.

Just as migration of citizens of high-income, "developed" countries to lower-income, former European colonies has increased substantially over the last decade, so too has sociological literature intent on applying postcolonial frames to migration.[8] Existing studies have drawn attention to inequalities between privileged migrants and members of receiving communities focusing especially on the symbolic power of whiteness and the colonial privilege of British or French citizens in their former colonial territories. Much like mainstream migration approaches, this literature has been diverse in its use of concepts and in analytical approaches, but a key theme of this work in English has been a desire to integrate these migrations into a global framework of migration in a way that might reconceptualize contemporary migration and delve into existing global inequalities (Benson and O'Reilly 2018; Fechter and Walsh 2010; Kunz 2016; Lundström 2017). Although the experiences of North Americans in Ecuador may differ in some respects from the experiences of European migrants, an analysis of North–South migration is also in dialogue with this postcolonial turn in lifestyle migration research and shares its desire to expand and complicate mainstream migration research. Migration scholarship now more than ever requires a global frame (Castles 2010; Glick Schiller 2009), not merely because of the ongoing migrant crisis/crisis of global justice,[9] but also because of the way that new forms of transnational extraction and exploitation, increased environmental vulnerability, and the relative decline of the influence and power of a chronically divided United States are modifying global hierarchies. Part of this global frame means placing discussion of North–South migrants into greater dialogue with political economy and considering the spatial impacts of their relocations. This also means, therefore, that lifestyle migration must more closely consider issues of "planetary gentrification" (Lees, Shin, and López-Morales 2016; Slater 2017) as individuals from higher latitudes of the global division of labor seek out lower-cost living in previously colonized parts of the world. It is here where displacement of lower-income individuals and the symbolic and physical appropriation of space by higher incomes become a central focus of analysis. Such a focus further extends migration scholarship into larger questions about the normative contours of global society and into global sociological debate about coloniality and global injustice.

Links to political economy have never been entirely absent from lifestyle migration research, especially in Latin America, where several important articles draw out the uneven spatial impact of North American migrants (Bastos 2014; Benson 2013; Gascón 2016; Mollett 2016; Spalding 2013). By contrast, intra-European cases, where global-scale inequalities are relevant but less pronounced than in postcolonial contexts, have been the main sources of conceptual development and analysis in lifestyle migration scholarship.[10] Thus the analytical starting point of postcolonial approaches to lifestyle migration took up similar themes as the study of intra-European examples: individualism, identity, distinction, and imaginaries of travel and cross-cultural contact. Its most significant contribution has been to decenter racialized white identities and to bring "white migrants" into the frame of migration studies (Fechter 2005, 2007; Fechter and Walsh 2010; Knowles and Harper 2009; Korpela 2009a; Kunz 2016; Lehmann 2014; Leonard 2008; Lundström 2014, 2017; Walsh 2010). This has inevitably drawn postcolonial white migrations into dialogue with issues of power and inequality. French-language research has also developed similar themes, seeking to invert problematic French narratives about the supposed lack of "integration" of North African migrants in France and Belgium by highlighting the insularity and lack of contact between European migrants and members of receiving communities in North Africa and Senegal (Peraldi and Terrazzoni 2016; Quashie 2016b). This work is of great interest, especially in its attention to postcolonial "modes of presence" in non-Western social space, and it links with English-language concerns about "migrant skills" (Knowles and Harper 2009, 232–40) that highlight migrants' ability to live with difference and otherness. Yet scholars must remain critical of integration as a normative orientation toward transnationalism, as politicians and the public in Western Europe and North America often use it as a moral boundary to justify exclusion (Lamont 2000), thereby reproducing global hierarchies.

Expats or Migrants: Semantics and Inequality

One issue of contention across this literature is how to label North–South migrations, especially because most research participants in this field refer to themselves as expats and almost never as immigrants. The distinctions between categories of migrants appear to demonstrate the coloniality of power, which mainstream migration scholarship inscribes in its analytical focus on people in the Global South moving to higher-income countries. North American and Western European migrants, by contrast, rarely think of themselves as migrants at all, and migration scholarship rarely considers them as such, obscuring a fuller picture of global migrations (Lundström 2017).[11] Therefore particular attention must be paid to how to name North Americans in Ecuador, even though they most often call themselves "expats" or "gringos." As Kunz (2016) suggests, scholars should understand the term *expatriate* as a category of practice. It is constitutive of how migrants like the North Americans in Ecuador or the British in Hong Kong think about their emplacement in transnational contexts. It is thus entangled in global power relations that migration scholars working from a decolonial or postcolonial framework must help to clarify.

Likewise, the modifier "lifestyle" participates in conceptual distinctions that implicitly reference unequal latitudes of the global division of labor and are thus also entangled in asymmetrical global social relations. It is important to acknowledge the relatively privileged context in which Euro-American migrations have come to be termed *lifestyle migration*. At the same time, there are analytical advantages to using *lifestyle* as a soft modifier that can contribute to a more accurate categorical framing for global migration scholarship. As a soft modifier, *lifestyle* migration attends to the meanings that migrants make of their transnational movements, and it thus draws attention to different ways in which these meanings are socially organized. In this way, the term also references material and social inequalities that make harder distinctions between categories appear intuitive. The "adventure" that Diana and Rick undertake is materially different from the one that Ecuadorians might experience as labor migrants in the United States or the one that Colombian refugees endure in Quito or Cuenca—not least because of different mobility and citizenship rights in destination countries. These adventures are narrated and understood differently, from distinct social positions. As Benson and O'Reilly (2016) point out, the contribution of the modifier emphasizes how migrants narrate and understand lifestyle (rather than work opportunities or political rights) as a key part of migration, reinscribing apparently obvious differences back within the frame of "migration." This is distinct from a hard modifier, which would slice off so-called lifestyle migration from migration scholarship and focus on distinctive conceptual categories that detract from, rather than contribute to, an understanding of migration as a *common* human condition, marked by socially constructed and institutionalized forms of inequality.

Moreover, and as Knowles and Harper (2009, 11) explain, describing participants as lifestyle migrants highlights the way receiving nation-states administer North–South relocations. In the case of Ecuador, research participants obtained residency visas on the basis of an investment of at least $25,000 deposited in an Ecuadorian bank account ($25,500 for a couple) or on the basis of proof of perpetual income exceeding $800 per month ($850 for a couple)—attestations of material means that enable North Americans to live in Ecuador without working. Their right to remain in Ecuador is not tied to employment, nor does it require a work visa, though a few younger participants subsequently sought work visas. Often, references to lifestyle migrants are meant to highlight the greater agency and privilege they seem to possess (Croucher 2012; O'Reilly 2012). It is instructive, however, to see different categorizations of migrants as referents to social positions that exist in transnational relation (Weiß 2005) and that distinguish North American lifestyle migrations from other "service-class" migrations (Knowles and Harper 2009, 11–12). These positions are objectively evident through the border regimes of nation-states, which also discriminate between different types of migration. An analytical distinction helps to visualize the latitudes of the global division of labor in transnational perspective, as individuals from former colonies occupy positions of service for individuals who, in many cases, are citizens of states that those former colonies served.

Lifestyle migration, thus, is tied up with the coloniality of global regimes of mobility, drawing attention to the unequal regulation of bodies across borders and to the historical system of colonial labor that has persisted as capitalist production networks have helped to shrink space and facilitate transnational movement, especially in recent decades. The global coloniality to which privileged forms of migration draw attention is coupled with the internal colonialism that persists within the apparently postcolonial Ecuadorian state. It is to this latter that I now turn to set the scene of North American migration and emplacement in Gringolandia.

Cuenca, Ecuador: A Leisure City of Landowners

Since the 2008 financial crisis, perhaps as many as twelve thousand lifestyle migrants have relocated to Cuenca. There are no reliable figures on exactly how many have remained in the city, or how many have remained without obtaining a residency visa, but most estimates of the number of U.S. citizens in Cuenca at time of writing ran between eight thousand and ten thousand, plus a growing number of Canadians and Western Europeans, particularly from Britain, France, and Germany. Thousands more cycle through, trying the city out for a few weeks or a few months. Their relocation to Cuenca is not happenstance. Local elites and foreign real estate speculators have shaped the city into a destination for lifestyle migration, sometimes working in concert and sometimes separately. State-led processes aimed at increasing tourism revenue, particularly through the restoration of Cuenca's heritage architecture in its historic district, El Centro, have also been central to Cuenca's popularity with North Americans. The "touristification" of the city is the central dynamic transforming its space,[12] and it ties into other transnational processes that have long connected Cuenca and its residents with the core of the capitalist global economy. Lifestyle migrants like Rick and Diana are relocating to Cuenca as part of these processes, and while they most often think of their migration in terms of their own personal projects, they also participate in local relations of accumulation and domination.

Cuenca had a population of 330,000 according to the 2010 census and was named a UNESCO World Heritage Site in 1999 for its "colonial" El Centro neighborhood (Klaufus 2009; Mancero Acosta 2012; Scarpaci 2005). It is, in some respects, an unlikely location for North American migration. It sees considerably less annual average sunshine than traditional American retirement destinations in Florida and Arizona, and its altitude of twenty-five hundred meters gives it a consistently cool climate. International lifestyle marketers describe the climate as "eternal spring," while locals often refer to "all four seasons in one day." When the sun comes out, the temperature might top twenty degrees Celsius, or sixty-eight degrees Fahrenheit, but often it is cooler. It is ill advised to leave home at any time of the year without a sweater, and local people often wear their coats inside, befuddling North American visitors.

The city is located in a valley of the southern Ecuadorian Andes (see Figure 3), just to the east of the Cajas mountain range,

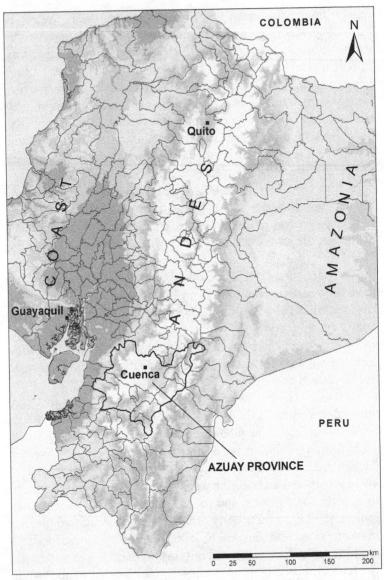

Map 1. Cuenca, Azuay, Ecuador. Courtesy of Joan Carles Membrado, Universidad de Valencia.

from which it gets its water. Its region is considerably more rugged than the Northern Andean volcanic lava fields. These latter spawned some of the largest haciendas, or plantation estates, in the Andean region. By contrast, the province of Azuay, of which Cuenca is the capital, as well as the province of Loja, farther to the south, comprise smaller, steeper valleys that have helped to shape politics and social life there. The more rugged geography, coupled with the relatively smaller number of indigenous peasant workers, contributed to smaller haciendas than those prevalent in the North. Historians and sociologists of southern Ecuador emphasize its relative depopulation in the aftermath of European colonial occupation, a historical process that began with the conflicts of the Inca period and the dynastic civil war (1529–1532 CE) in Tawantinsuyo, the Empire of the Four Regions (Cordero, Achig, and Carrasco 1989; Hurtado 2007; Pietri-Levy 1993). Citing primary sources from the early Spanish colonial period, Pribilsky (2007) noted how Atahualpa (who won the war against his brother Huáscar) massacred entire villages in what is now Azuay and Loja for their disloyalty. Coupled with European diseases, southern Ecuador was considerably depopulated relative to other parts of the Andes at the time of the Spanish conquest. European migrant-settlers became therefore an important part of southern Ecuador's labor force (Cordero, Achig, and Carrasco 1989; Hurtado 2007). Although there was a sizable European settler population, Cuenca, like other parts of the Andean region, was nonetheless built on a racialized class system, involving an elite of white and phenotypically lighter mestizo[13] landowners and a subordinate class of indigenous and phenotypically darker mestizo peasant laborers. The city's social relations are shaped by larger patterns of Spanish colonial occupation and settlement.

Shortly after the conquest in the 1530s, Spanish imperial authorities began granting *encomiendas,* or control of indigenous workers, to Spanish conquistadores, who were responsible for organizing their production and ensuring their indoctrination into the Catholic faith. This system evolved over the eighteenth century into the hacienda system of the nineteenth and twentieth centuries, characterized by tight control of landed estates by city-dwelling, Spanish-descended elites (Hurtado [1977] 2010). These haciendas were the basis of political and economic power in the country. Until the agrarian reforms of the 1960s and 1970s, the hacienda system embedded rural, often indigenous, labor power in a series of relations of obligation to the *hacendados*, or owners of the haciendas (Barsky 1988; Ibarra 2002a, 2002b, 2013). In most cases, peasant laborers, variously known as *huasipungeros, precaristas, peones,* or *arrimados,* received small lots on the hacienda for their own subsistence in exchange for their services to the *hacendados.* The hacienda form of indentured labor exploitation produced local inequalities, but it also manifested global relations of inequality, specifically what the Peruvian sociologist Aníbal Quijano (2000, 2007) calls the coloniality of power. This refers to a division of exploitation on the basis of phenotypical characteristics, which formed the basis of the colonial economic system centered in Europe from the sixteenth century onward. Nonwhite workers in non-European parts of the globe were submitted to regimes of labor, including *encomienda* (the main system the Spanish Crown used for extraction of wealth from its Andean colonies), *concertaje,* slavery, and indenture, which differed from labor regimes prevalent in Europe, and increasingly so during its economic liberalization in the nineteenth century (which consolidated a labor regime of white, male, supposedly free wage workers, a regime made possible by the establishment of a global economy premised on other forms of unfree and unremunerated labor, including the unpaid labor of women; see Mies [1986]).

This coloniality of power persists into the present, to the extent that the global economy continues to be divided between high-income activities concentrated in Europe or in areas settled by Europeans and their descendants (especially Canada and the United States) and lower-income activities performed by racialized nonwhite groups in the former European colonies. Colonial relations of exploitation enabled the accumulation of greater levels of wealth in certain global pockets and thus produced the artificial division between higher-cost and lower-cost regions—the distinct latitudes of the colonial economic system that is the foundation of contemporary economic globalization. Cuenca, as the seat of the landed elite of southern Ecuador, is itself a location where local accumulation took place and where elites expressed their wealth in forms that institutions like UNESCO now recognize as cultural heritage. Cities like Cuenca were established in the Spanish colonial period as sites for the supervision of the colonial *encomienda* and as market centers for supplying the rural labor force (Jamieson 2002; Mumford 2012). They were sites where value-added labor took place and where indigenous artisans could present themselves as mestizo, expressing a colonial "civilizing" ideal. Andean cities were the seat of European colonial governance, establishing a geography of inequality that, though modified slightly, persists in important ways to this day (Kingman 2006).

This geography is evident in the many town plazas and squares of Cuenca, which historically served as marketplaces bringing together social classes that were both racialized and spatially separated, reflecting a caste system of town and countryside, *hacendado* and *huasipunguero*. As many studies of race in the Andes have pointed out, racialized hierarchies shape urban–rural boundaries, whereby the city represents modernity and whiteness, while rural regions are coded as backward and indigenous (de la Cadena 2000; Ibarra 2013; Wade 2010). These symbolic boundaries are a relic of colonial exploitation. By moving to the city and adopting urban cultural practices, indigenous people from the countryside could pass as mestizo, although they were sometimes derogatively dismissed as *cholos,* a slur for indigenous people striving to acquire status beyond their social position (Ibarra 1992; Weismantel 2001). However, these forms of ethnic mobility belie the rigid racial caste system that assigns hegemony to the European-descended landowning and commercial elites. The haciendas of southern Ecuador produced important fortunes in the nineteenth century among a group of interrelated families, whose class unity distinguished them from other parts of Republican Ecuador (Palomeque 1990). And while the region is noted for the predominance of smallholder, *minifundista,* yeoman farmers in the eighteenth and nineteenth centuries (Cordero, Achig, and Carrasco 1989; Hurtado 2007; Kyle 2000; Palomeque 1990), this apparently more egalitarian access to land belies important concentration of ownership, especially in the sugarcane valleys of Paute and Yungilla, as well as in other valleys farther to the south of Cuenca, such as Nabón, Oña, and Susudel.

Though it is widely held that the fortunes of southern Ecuador were not as great as those of the larger haciendas of northern Ecuador, and that there was a sizable and industrious middle class of small landholders (Hurtado 2007; Jamieson 2002; Kyle 2000), Cuenca always has been and remains a very unequal place, in which concentrated ownership of land is a key factor. It was noted in the late twentieth century for having the highest level of wealth concentration in Ecuador, perhaps surpassing even that of Quito and Guayaquil (Fierro Carrión 1991, 408). By the late nineteenth century, yeoman farmers in Azuay lived on plots that were often too small to provide subsistence, forcing rural workers to search for other forms of sustenance, especially as weavers in the panama hat trade and as laborers collecting cascarilla bark for the production of quinine, an antimalarial drug (Cordero, Achig, and Carrasco 1989; Kyle 2000; Palomeque 1990). Forced to work long hours to maintain their precarious position as *minifundistas*, or small landholders, and to avoid falling into debt peonage and indenture on the large landed estates, rural workers helped build large commercial fortunes tied to the landed interests of hacienda elites. The concentrated wealth of "noble" families was almost entirely generated from exploitation of rural workforces, particularly in the sugarcane valleys of Paute and Yungilla and farther south in Vilcabamba, in Loja province, where relations of indenture were most pronounced and where landed families continue to own and profit from the most productive lands of the region. In Paute, flower plantations exporting to the United States now use some of the best-irrigated land, which generates important sources of foreign exchange for landowning families. In Yungilla, the powerful Eljuri family has moved from sugar production into alcohol distilling, small manufacturing, construction, and retail.

These fortunes coalesced into a city whose smaller size and relatively smaller fortunes (though highly concentrated) motivated Cuenca's establishment to emphasize their apparent modernity and cultural distinction. Labeling the city the "Athens of the Andes," they attempted to make Cuenca stand out nationally for its artistic production (Mancero Acosta 2012), particularly in the fields of literature and poetry, which are much loved locally. Moreover, the city's elite sent their children to Europe, particularly France and Belgium, to study medicine, law, and architecture (Espinoza and Achig 1989; Hirschkind 1980). The dominant classes of the city translated their incomplete monopoly of the land into a monopoly of the professions and municipal public offices. The economic elites of Cuenca were renowned for their transnational commercial connections and their ability to initiate and maintain these relations despite changes in politics and global trade patterns (Cordero, Achig, and Carrasco 1989; Hurtado 2007; Palomeque 1990). When the Panama hat industry closed down in the 1950s, these elites pursued new opportunities in transnational migration, especially to the United States (Kyle 2000; Miles 2004).

These transnational connections, and especially time spent outside of Ecuador, enabled local elites to import ideas, including architectural forms, from Europe and, later, North America (Klaufus 2009). As many authors on Ecuadorian culture have noted, the country is ethnically mestizo (de la Torre 1999; Hurtado [1977] 2010, 116–24; Mancero Acosta 2012; Roitman 2009; Wong Cruz 2013). However, they note that it remains culturally oriented toward Europe, producing ethnic and cultural ideals and identities that have sought to erase and subordinate indigenous traditions, while whitening or Europeanizing social tastes. Through their control of virtually all aspects of economic and political life, the dominant classes (composed of a small number of European-descendant families) have ensured almost total hegemony over the cultural and social life of the city. This hegemony is also evident in the municipality's project of making the city a heritage tourism and lifestyle migration hub. Heritage preservation in El Centro is the offspring of a social project of the landowning elites, who established a tradition of conferring social honor on architecture and built heritage, generally copying European styles (Mancero Acosta 2012).

This project of heritage preservation, however, also benefited from fortuitous circumstances. The city's main export industries, *paja toquilla* hats and cascarilla, went into terminal decline in the early 1950s, leaving the manufacturing establishment with few resources to reinvent the downtown neighborhoods they were rapidly abandoning for new, American-inspired, suburban-style housing in El Ejido, across the Tomebamba River, south of the old downtown (Klaufus 2009). By the mid-1970s, Ecuador had begun exporting oil, and its military government was anxious to invest in new urban infrastructure projects to demonstrate the country's modernity. These modern building projects, however, threatened the built heritage of old central districts of colonial cities, and there was little finance available to protect them. The urban growth and modernization of Quito in this period corresponded with UNESCO designating its historic core the world's first World Heritage City in 1978, a title designed to protect and preserve its heritage as a tourism site (Betancur 2014; Carrión Mena 2010). A similar process took place in Cuenca, where private interests began tearing down historic buildings in El Centro to make way for the modern office buildings of major banks, public enterprises, and other public institutions. A few wealthier professionals also built new, modernist buildings in a more commercial downtown, housing law or dentist's offices, and sometimes architecture firms. Yet Cuenca's community of architects had been schooled in the French tradition of the Beaux Arts and resisted the city's urban transformation, recoiling at the functionalism of American modernism in public buildings and fighting for the protection of the city's built heritage (Klaufus 2009).

Toward Cuenca Patrimonio

Taking their cue from events in Quito, including the Organization of American States's 1977 publication of the Quito Letter, which sought to preserve colonial, architectural heritage for the development of tourism industries (see Betancur 2014), Cuenca's professional elites began actively seeking recognition for their city's built heritage in the late 1970s. Cuenca gained special *patrimonio nacional* status from the national government in 1982 for its downtown neighborhoods. Soon after, local governments began searching for ways to leverage that status to en-

hance the value of the city's built heritage and to profit from
the cultural distinction the city supposedly had always had over
Quito and Guayaquil (Mancero Acosta 2012). Under the mayoralty of Fernando Cordero Cueva (1996–2004), Cuenca revitalized
its downtown core through tourism and heritage preservation,
"upgrading" and renovating its old squares and urban parks and
beautifying land along the four waterways that traverse the city
from west and north to east and onward to the Amazon basin.
The city paid particular attention to the walkways along the Rio
Tomebamba, which, along with El Barranco (the embankment
that rises above the northern side of the river), forms the southern wall of the colonial street grid.

The successful UNESCO World Heritage bid of 1999 gave new
impetus to Cuenca's attempts to turn itself into a tourist mecca,
trading on its "colonial," "Old World," and "European" style and
building on the success of previous Andean heritage sites, such
as Cusco in the Peruvian Andes. What stands as heritage is, of
course, socially constructed—the product of a process of selecting

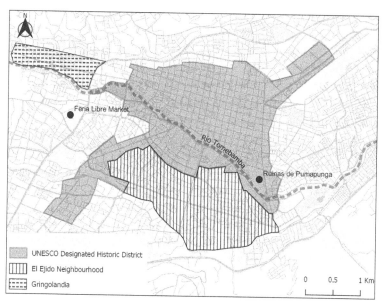

Map 2. Map of Cuenca, Gringolandia, and historic district. Map by Lola
Arteaga Revert.

objects that will symbolize a supposedly authentic past.[14] Alongside this process of identifying and preserving built heritage, the commodities boom of the late 2000s spurred a substantial construction and real estate boom. The central government supported this boom in part, but transnational sources provided increased demand, and the Inter-American Development Bank gave credit for urban "revitalization." The latter, along with UNESCO and other bilateral development agencies from high-income countries, have funded consultants and studies identifying new ways the city can enhance its heritage urbanism.

While there is some speculation that Ecuadorian workers have also invested part of their incomes earned abroad (Azuay province received almost one-third of Ecuador's total remittances in the 2000s), there is little evidence to prove that this has increased ground rents in El Centro. As Herrera (2005) points out, most remittances are used to support people living in or near poverty, and substantial amounts of the remittances she studied went to repay loans taken out to support the migrations—loans that members of higher social classes may have provided, to be repaid with interest. Ecuadorian migrants have invested some of their savings and remittance income in condos or houses in the Cuenca region, though it is important to note that the vast majority of Ecuadorians receiving remittances spend the money on daily expenses, with only a small portion going to real estate (Aguilar, Palacios, and Pozo 2007; Ponce, Olivié Aldasoro, and Onofa 2008; Universidad de Cuenca 2007).[15] Moreover, while studies note the important investments migrants make in self-built construction—investments often visible in the Ecuadorian countryside and in cities (see Klaufus 2009)—they have also shown that these remittances have little impact on development and only moderately effect poverty reduction (Acosta, Fajnzylber, and Lopez 2007; Ponce, Olivié Aldasoro, and Onofa 2008). The development of new condominium buildings in Gringolandia and other parts of Cuenca depends to a significant degree on foreign investment from sale or rental to the growing number of transnational lifestyle migrants. These latter have sometimes sold relatively expensive houses, cashing in on a lifetime of savings at high latitudes of the global division of labor, to buy (or rent) real estate and labor power at lower costs in Ecuador. As discussed in the next chapter, international lifestyle marketers actively promote transnational relocation on these terms, helping to foment new forms of lifestyle mobility, especially for North American retirees. In the process, however, they also push retirees who are often economically stressed into new relations of domination in a city whose history is marked by coloniality.

Outline of the Book

This ethnography of global inequality and coloniality in the local place transformation of an Andean heritage city proceeds in six chapters, with an appendix that outlines the methodology of the study. As I note there, this book is committed to greater global social justice, but at the same time, it is a product of the very thing it seeks to critique. My own position in this research is marked by overlapping social advantages, notably Canadian citizenship (which facilitated repeat visits to Ecuador); full-time academic employment (in a national academic system with resources to cultivate this type of research); and white, cis-gendered masculinity, which benefited me in most social encounters. These advantages shaped my approach to the topic of North–South migration as well as my findings, as I point out in the appendix and which I tried to bear in mind throughout.

The book's first three chapters focus primarily on lifestyle migrants from North America. I am interested in the stories and ideals of people like Diana, Lana, Joan, and Rick and the context within which they decided to come to Ecuador. Part of this context is cultural and refers to moral codes and cultural imaginaries of place. But part is also economic. About two-thirds of research participants mentioned economic reasons for relocating to Ecuador, and several identified as being "economic refugees"—an exaggeration to be sure, but one that speaks to a sense of being expelled or displaced. Their geographic relocations are thus a response to increased vulnerability and a decline in pension security. This vulnerability is also entwined with the inherited advantages of a global economy marked by coloniality. Chapter 1 looks at the utilitarian cultural codes that hone in on cost of living as a legitimate reason for initiating transnational relocation. Chapter 2 explores the imaginaries and desires of North American migrants, noting in particular their fantasy of a "colonial-style" Cuenca located outside the time of contemporary Western modernity. Chapter 3 explores the racialized identities that North Americans develop in Ecuador, noting in particular the ways in which they carry ideologies of race with them from North America. They often attempt to optimize the appearance of their whiteness so as to avoid discrimination, especially in the form of "gringo pricing," or the racialized price system to which they feel they are subjected.

The next three chapters are much more focused on the social history of southern Ecuador. Cuenca and nearby rural areas, such as Yungilla and Vilcabamba, where North Americans are also relocating, are experiencing processes of spatial transformation consistent with the gentrification that other studies have identified in Latin America (Betancur 2014; Janoschka and Sequera 2016; López-Morales 2010; Sigler and Wachsmuth 2016). These chapters draw gentrification studies together with lifestyle migration and develop a contextual reading of spatial exclusion and urban "upgrading" in a Latin American heritage city. Chapter 4 explores the displacement of informal vendors from the popular markets in Cuenca's El Centro, a practice of social cleansing that reproduces the experiences of municipal-led heritage gentrification in other Andean cities (Bromley 1998; Bromley and Mackie 2009; Durán 2015; Swanson 2007). Because the built heritage of Cuenca's El Centro is the product of the historical exploitation of a rural labor force, chapter 5 follows North American lifestyle migrants into the Ecuadorian countryside, where their individual projects of self-realization run headlong into processes of rural gentrification and "depeasantization" (Gascón 2016). These processes have enabled a new generation of landowners to benefit from historic land hoarding and evade a more just distribution of land that would favor rural workers, many of whom were indentured on hacienda estates into the 1970s, about the time many research participants were buying their first houses. Chapter 6 is a concluding chapter to the book and provides a theoretical reflection on urban "improvements" and the coloniality of Latin

American gentrification in an era of increased lifestyle-based transnationalism and heritage tourism. In the absence of significant structural reform on a global scale, the twenty-first century is poised to reproduce colonial forms of inequality and exploitation as a privileged caste of the globally mobile from high-income countries appropriate space and livelihoods in the lower-income countries of the Global South. I start, however, by exploring some of the underlying reasons for the sudden surge in North American migration to Cuenca.

1

Geoarbitrage and the Offshoring of Retirement

As I began drafting this chapter, news broke that eight hundred migrants from Africa had drowned in the Mediterranean off Lampedusa.

Colin was an affable man in his late sixties, one of the more outgoing North Americans I met in Cuenca. He is a practical, down-to-earth person who grew up in an immigrant family in Brooklyn. Diligent and with a varied career, one that saw him move across the country, Colin was proud of his work experience. He socialized easily with people from many different backgrounds, and although his Spanish was basic, he made use of what he knew and did so regularly. He did not hesitate to try to speak with people at restaurants or on the street, just as he probably would have done in his hometown. He disbursed humor with quick wit, peering out from under a baseball cap, which he wore any time he left the house. We met on the bus, which Colin said he enjoyed riding regularly. He had used the bus system to explore the city, sometimes riding the lines to the end just to see where they went.

In many respects, Colin and his wife were representative of an important subset of North American migrants in Ecuador. They moved to Cuenca from Oregon in 2011. When we sat down for an interview in 2013, I asked him if he had thought about moving abroad while he was working. "Never," he replied curtly. Like many participants, Colin and his wife were motivated to look for a lower-cost place to live to afford the retirement they wanted, and for them that meant living abroad. This prompted Colin to search online for low-cost places to live. Like many of his colleagues in Cuenca, Colin had come across the idea of retiring abroad on the internet. "I read what was essentially a reprint of an *International Living* article," he said, noting that he had read it online on MSNBC. Like a lot of other participants, Colin was skeptical. "I'm not naive. It sounded too good to be true," he said. Other participants less generously referred to the international lifestyle marketer as "International Lying," typically because it underestimates the cost of living in places like Cuenca in its attempt to appeal to retirees on tight budgets. Like other prospective lifestyle migrants who conducted varying degrees of internet research, Colin set out to look into things a little further and considered a few other places before making an exploratory visit to Cuenca. "I liked it better than my wife did," he said about his initial reaction to the city. Nonetheless, and despite her hesitancy to move farther away from their children, they made a move that allowed them to retire.

Colin considered himself an "economic refugee," someone who could not remain in the United States without continuing to work. The term is an exaggeration, but research participants frequently used it to speak to their sense of being expelled from their home country by forces beyond their control. Like many other respondents in their sixties and seventies, Colin had been looking for a way out of the labor market not only because of the physical effort of working but also because of the lack of stimulation. As he put it, "It's not that I'm afraid of hard work. My work wasn't even that physically hard, it was just mentally not challenging." He had had enough of the commuting from his home in the suburbs. In 2010, Colin turned sixty-five and started to think seriously about retiring:

> I had just come back from my fraternity reunion and, uh, was slightly envious of the majority of people who were already retired. And I realized that to sustain our quality of life, I'd have to work for another ten years.

He said he had a small teacher's pension from a short stint as a teacher, and aside from that, he and his wife only had their Social Security to live on. Like a lot of middle-class, suburban households in North America, they had hoped to use the equity in their home to downsize for retirement, but the economic crisis spoiled that idea. When they sold, they had no equity left and were only able to repay debts. "If we retired in Oregon, we couldn't afford to live a middle-class lifestyle on that income."

These apparent economic motivations are also wrapped up with other cultural ideals. Colin's sense that his retirement and aging process would turn out to be inadequate seems entwined in cultural notions of "successful aging" (Rowe and Kahn 1998) or "active aging" (Katz 2005) as well as a class-based "fear of falling" (Ehrenreich 1989). It was in comparison to other retired colleagues that Colin began to feel that he was missing out on something as he aged, and he then began searching for a retirement location abroad. His notion of successful aging reflects the cultural ideals of a generation that has defined itself through consumption and where added income may be needed to continue to live up to these ideals in the "third age," the life stage after retirement from the labor force but before physical decline and infirmity (Gilleard and Higgs 2011). Colin liked living in the city. He relished the walking culture of El Centro and enjoyed meeting up with friends on a regular basis for coffee or lunch. Moving to Ecuador enabled him and his wife to enjoy a much higher standard of living, which is what justified the move for him. He explained:

We have a larger house. In a beautiful area. We can afford a housecleaner twice a week. We can afford someone that picks up and does the laundry and folds the laundry. We can afford a gardener. We can afford, if we wanted to, we could eat out all the time, but I enjoy cooking, so. Um, and we can afford to travel.

As Colin mentioned to me in the interview, and in subsequent conversations when we met again in following years, he and his wife could not remain in the United States without continuing to work or without seriously compromising the "middle-class" lifestyle to which he was accustomed. By contrast, relocating to Ecuador had enabled him to afford services that would have been luxuries in the United States.

Many of Colin's compatriots shared his reasons for relocating to a country with which they had no familiarity prior to their internet research. Louise, age sixty-seven, was a former social worker from Hawai'i who had some travel experience prior to moving to Cuenca. She described herself as a progressive and an activist. Shortly after turning sixty, Louise said she realized she was not going to be able to retire in the United States. "They were sending you your Social Security statements," she said, "and I was a single parent, and I worked under the table a lot, so I don't have a lot of Social Security." Having divorced several decades ago, she spent much of her working life as a single mother, and while she was well educated and had had opportunities to travel, she did not have a lot of savings to enable her to retire securely. "I needed every dime I could get to raise the kids, because my ex-husband didn't help," she said. This had a serious impact on her retirement, as it did for other women I interviewed, many of whom had experience as single mothers. "So, you know, I was just looking around, trying to figure out what I could do," she said. While she spent time helping her children raise their own children, she also yearned for some space for herself. This became possible when she realized that she could move to South America. She began traveling to different locations after she turned sixty, scouting out where she could go. She mentioned that in Hawai'i, her small apartment cost her $1,200 per month. "Now I pay $200," she said of her spacious apartment with a terrace, which she colorfully decorated with local artisanal products. She was able to get what she considered a very good price because an Ecuadorian family had "adopted" her and helped her find housing.[1] Her Social Security, she said, was so low that she did not qualify for the Ecuadorian residency visa. Instead, what little savings she had were tied up in an Ecuadorian bank account so that she could live in Ecuador on an investor's visa, an option many participants said they used, because they only needed $25,000 of capital to obtain one.

This chapter explores the cultural and economic contexts of these cost-of-living narratives, which were so important to so many of the people with whom I spoke in Cuenca. They say a great deal about the transnationalization of space as well as how cultural frames justify migration for an increasing number of North

Americans who had never previously traveled to Latin America, let alone considered relocating there. These cost-of-living narratives connect economic changes occurring in the Global North to the coloniality of the global division of labor, particularly the unequal latitudes that structurally advantaged individuals inherit as part of the colonial legacy. It is an element of coloniality that is very important to the rise of lifestyle migration flows to places like Cuenca. This chapter draws out narratives that relate economic motivations fueling these migrations to a changing U.S. economy, to their cultural foundations, and to the international lifestyle marketers who encourage potential migrants to take advantage of global inequalities.

Utilitarian Individualism and Lifestyle Migration

The story North Americans typically tell others about their migration starts with how much money they can save by living in Ecuador and what luxuries they can buy (including domestic service work) for significantly less. This is perhaps most typified in U.S. news coverage about moving to Ecuador, which advertises its economic benefits.[2] When asked for the reasons for relocating abroad, about three-quarters of my research participants (sixty-two of eighty-three interviews in Cuenca) explained their decision with specific reference to economic circumstances. In a few cases, participants did not want to describe their migration in economic terms and avoided the issue. For example, Robert (age seventy-one, from Denver) initially said he had always wanted to live abroad, but toward the end of the interview, he admitted, "You could not retire in the U.S. on the amount of money that we make."

Colin and Louise, mentioned at the beginning of this chapter, were economic migrants like the majority of my research participants. Their economic reasoning may appear crass, especially as grounds for relocating to a lower-income country with a different language and culture. But it may also be a cultural proclivity typical of North Americans, albeit one that says quite a lot about their mobility at this moment in history, and about the state of global mobility regimes, which are also largely based on access to economic assets. Crucially, it is important to understand that these economic reasons do not signal that choices about retirement and migration follow some kind of rational action theory, where migrants calculate push-and-pull factors. Rather, calculations are always embedded in cultural codes, in this case the North American tradition of utilitarian individualism (Bellah et al. 1985).[3] Not only did research participants speak openly about economic reasons for their relocations but many, like Colin, had no inkling of moving abroad until they started thinking about their pocketbooks in contexts of financial constraint. While financial considerations have long been important to decisions about retirement migration within the United States (Fournier, Rasmussen, and Serow 1988a, 1988b; Longino 1995), their role in transnational North–South migration appears relatively new as a mass phenomenon.[4]

Moreover, this utilitarian individualism fits with cultural notions of aging that many participants expressed. The lifestyle ideal of "active" or "successful" aging (Ekerdt 1986; Katz 2000) is often associated with consumption activities, travel, and social agendas that are designed to maintain a busy-ethic associated with success in the third age but that in reality often also cost money and therefore, have to be factored into retirement financial planning (Gibson 2002; Gilleard and Higgs 2011; Hitchings, Venn, and Day 2016). Moreover, financial institutions, business interests that cater to the lifestyle interests of people in the third age (itself a culturally constructed "phase" of the life cycle), and public institutions all promote such utilitarianism in a bid to take advantage of the consumer practices of the large baby boomer demographic (Hitchings, Venn, and Day 2016; McHugh 2003; Rudman 2006). In the absence of adequate savings, the ideal of successful aging and of maintaining an active lifestyle may require lower-cost locations and may stimulate calculative utilitarianism with respect to certain forms of transnational relocation. Post–Great Recession, marketers present relocation to lower-income countries as a viable retirement option. An Investopedia article from 2015 suggested, "If you weren't able to save the massive amount of money the retirement experts say you need, rest assured there are plenty of places you can live a comfortable life on not much more than your Social Security benefits."[5]

I argue that this economic calculativeness, so important to North American culture, has begun to spawn new forms of transnationalism, which may not be specific to North American groups (cf. Dennie-Filion 2013; Ono 2015). Research participants in Ecuador often expressed the transnational ethos of geoarbitrage, or the lifestyle equivalent of corporate offshoring. Just like corporations seeking to reduce costs by relocating production offshore, individuals with information gleaned from the internet are deciding to relocate to places where their savings carry further than they would at home. The ethos of geoarbitrage—whereby income and savings accrued at high latitudes of the global division of labor are relocated to low-income countries where savings stretch further—is shaped by the cultural frame of utilitarian individualism. Just like in the corporate world, where profit, accumulation, and growth are the ultimate ends of productive activity, so too in our private worlds do accumulative strategies increasingly seem self-evident, natural, and desirable as ends in themselves. This is why Colin and Louise can justify their relocations by referencing economic reasons—it is part of their cultural tool kit (Swidler 2001). Transnational lifestyle migrants often mix utilitarian ideals with the expressive individualism of projects of personal growth, attained through the pursuit of as many challenging, intense, or personally enriching experiences as possible—experiences that leave inner feelings of success and that often are more difficult to pursue on limited retirement incomes.

In some cases, North American migrants are relocating well before traditional retirement years, and a few people with whom I spoke had relocated to start businesses in an environment where they perceived they would not have to work as hard, where they might have more control over their work than they would at home, or where they would not need as much capital to get started. These individuals are also geoarbitrageurs, relocating to lower-cost regions where the cost of labor power is significantly less than it is in high-income countries. The reasons for this disparity are grounded in the history and social structures that well-intentioned individuals inherit, and from which they benefit, despite often having little knowledge of these circumstances or little explicit attachment to the normative traditions of colonial domination. They too fuse economic circumstances with cultural ideals of freedom and independence, often escaping jobs and workplaces with complicated social relations they could not control. In some cases, the relocations of younger migrants were also tied to job loss or economic stagnation that prevented career advancement. For these migrants, Cuenca represented a kind of existential Shangri-La, where life projects could unfold according to cultural ideals of success, irrespective of local structural circumstances related to a sluggish economy.

The Changing Face of Retirement in North America

The economic motivations research participants expressed are not just ex post facto rationalizations of their relocations. The stories participants told also positioned their decisions against a backdrop of financial insecurity and economic crisis. Mary and Grant, a couple in their mid-sixties, help to illustrate some of the structural conditions that shape North American migration to Ecuador. Like Colin and his wife, they considered themselves "economic refugees." While they had once considered themselves well-off, they migrated to Cuenca in early 2012 after more than two years of being unemployed. Grant worked in the hotel industry, and Mary was a substance abuse therapist working in alternative medicine. Still in their early sixties, they lost their jobs within months of one another in 2009. Grant had held down a good management position for a number of years, but the couple had lost what savings they had. "I made a comfortable living, nothing extravagant, but, uh, when it came time to retire, and losing my job, and when you're sixty-plus, it's very difficult to find a job," Grant said. Mary had needed surgery for cancer. That, coupled with the job loss, meant they had to sell their house. Grant got a part-time job working on the census, but aside from that, he had been on unemployment for longer than a year. Running out of options, they began exploring lower-cost locations to which to retire so that they could get by on their early retirement pension from U.S. Social Security.[6] In all, they said they had between the two of them just less than $2,000 per month of income and no other savings. They could have remained in the United States, but they either would have had to continue searching for work or make other significant adjustments. They also said they could not afford ongoing health care, particularly for Mary. As Grant put it, "we're both economic and medical refugees, medical because of her cancer, and ongoing, uh, treatments for that. And just, being able to comfortably live here, uh, economically, with the cost of rent and food and everything [makes everything easier]," he continued.

Izzy and Sam moved to Cuenca from the Tampa area, and they also both lost their jobs within a year of one another in 2009 and 2010. They also were motivated by "survival," as they put it, to downsize their lifestyle and try to figure some way to get by in retirement. Izzy and Sam were a team, but Sam did most of the talking when I met them in 2011. He had a certain masculine certainty to him, and he clearly enjoyed telling his version of their story, interspersed with testimony from Izzy. Izzy was quiet, but sincere in her support of how her husband told their story. She sat comfortably across from me on the sofa in their condominium, which looked out onto the mountains. Their situation, which they narrated in terms just as urgent as Mary and Grant, involved downsizing from a high-income bracket, because they were not ready to retire. Sam had been a consulting engineer in the financial sector whose contract work dried up in 2009. Izzy had "earned good money" as an accountant but was let go on her birthday, just as she turned sixty-two. "We did not intend to retire at sixty-two," Sam said. "On Friday, everything was fine, and by Sunday, I was out," Izzy said. The surprise job losses put them in a financial bind, having to cut back what Sam described as a relatively lavish lifestyle "with all the toys." As he put it, "we were going to have to scale back. And we were fixing to go from what I consider living in the top 20 percent in the United States, to the bottom 20 percent." This was not going to work for him. "I'm sorry," he said, "but I'm spoiled." In Cuenca, he said, he could live in the "top 4 percent" of the population. By relocating, Izzy and

Sam had moved up the social status ladder. "Our quality of life right now is so much higher than it was in the sixty-two years we lived in the United States, it isn't even funny," Sam said. "We're living in the top 4 percent of a population and right now you can't live in the United States like we live, for less than ten times the money that we spend." This included the ability to throw very large, catered, black-tie parties for other "expats."

Ray and Simone were a third couple I met who had both lost jobs as a result of the financial crisis. They had lived more independent lives, working in publishing and moving from job to job, sometimes across states. They were in Las Vegas when the financial crisis hit. Neither was thinking of retirement yet—Ray wasn't even sixty. "We had no notion other than what most people, working people our age in the U.S., did, which was that we were going to work till we dropped," Simone explained. Suddenly faced without work, their financial situation deteriorated. "We were kind of pulling together our financial situation and, you know, doing pretty well paying off our debt load, all that kind of thing. And then the bottom fell out with the recession," Ray said. Finding new jobs was especially hard. They moved to San Francisco, where they had family and professional ties, hoping it might be a better job market, and were living off savings and unemployment benefits. "So we looked at our, our personal situation there in San Francisco, we had been living on our unemployment benefits. And . . . we were renting a small studio apartment, which our unemployment benefits basically covered as long as we were very very frugal," Ray continued. They knew when their benefits ran out, they would have even less income than before. Simone in particular was finding it harder to get paid work. She still wanted to work, but, as she put it philosophically, "My days of working for someone else were over." She felt that what jobs there were went to younger people and that she was being overlooked because she was in her early sixties at the time. For Simone, accepting that her working days were over "is kind of annoying . . . and a little depressing. Because it's like, I'm still working, in my head. . . . I still have things to offer. And even people want them, but they just don't want to buy them," she said, having explained that she had received numerous calls to do pro bono work. "They, they don't want to buy the talent for whatever their reasoning." This was painful for Simone, as it was for others I interviewed, people who found themselves running out of work at the end of their careers, without expecting it and without a fallback plan. While Simone said they might have been able to remain in the United States, "we would've had to have been living in essentially a rural or small-town place where the expenses were minimal but there wouldn't be any real attraction to be there other than, you know, the, the, the cheapness of it." They said they would rather remain in San Francisco, but with rents going sky high, they knew they could not afford it, and Cuenca made sense as an urban alternative.

For many research participants, Cuenca came up as a kind of social safety net in the event of an unexpected early exit from the labor market. While the employment situation for those over age fifty-five recovered somewhat in the mid-2010s in the United States, older workers—both men and women—who lost their jobs in the aftermath of the 2008 financial crisis faced historically high levels of unemployment for their demographic. The U.S. Bureau of Labor Statistics (BLS) reported a record high rate of unemployment of 7.2 percent among older workers in December 2009, and the level remained at or above 7 percent for most of the next two years (Bureau of Labor Statistics 2010, 2011). While this may seem low by some standards, unemployment for older workers in the United States had not gone above 6 percent since 1949. Moreover, it hides the real number of those affected by unemployment, because it doesn't count those who gave up looking for work or who are underemployed. One U.S. government estimate put the real unemployment rate for older workers at approximately double the official rate (U.S. Government Accountability Office 2012, 13). The length of unemployment older workers were experiencing also reached historic highs, biting into savings that otherwise may have provided more secure retirements. The BLS noted that the time older workers spent looking for jobs was considerably longer than the time workers of other age categories spent (Bureau of Labor Statistics 2010). During 2011, 36 percent of older unemployed workers (over fifty-five years of age) spent longer than a year looking for work, and the median had increased to thirty-five weeks, compared to twenty-six weeks for younger job seekers (U.S. Government Accountability Office 2012). Even workers with higher education levels, who generally have lower unemployment rates, saw rates double between 2007 and 2011, just as the rates did for workers without a high school diploma (U.S. Government Accountability Office 2012). Given these structural factors, many research participants seemed to have a harder time living up to cultural ideals of aging and retirement that often required middle-class incomes, which Social Security alone did not provide. To maintain their material quality of life, they opted for transnational relocation.

Several research participants mentioned job loss or the loss of income due to the so-called Great Recession as the "watershed moment" (Benson 2012, 1690) that led to their migration decision. Although it is important, following O'Reilly (2000, 28), to recognize that respondents provide "post hoc justifications" rather than outright explanations, their justifications also pointed to real events in their lives that shaped their migration decisions. In many cases, job loss or financial distress marked decisions to move to Latin America, and to Cuenca in particular. Evan (age sixty-nine, from Toronto) offers another example. He was an independent consultant living in a city whose rents were skyrocketing. In recent years, following a divorce, his expenses had outstripped his income and he began running down his retirement savings, even before being able to retire. "But then the work was drying up," he said. "Quite, quite a bit. So, um, and then you, you just begin to worry. I don't want to die poor, you know, it's, Canada's a great country, but being poor, eh, in Toronto [laughs]. So where's this going to end?" Referring to his depleting savings, he quipped, "Nobody likes to bleed to death."

Migrant Women: Between Vulnerability and Adventure

Research participants discussed these concerns about running out of money quite a bit, most often in reference to others whom they perceived as being worse off than themselves. Aside from the "economic refugees" who were a frequent topic of conversation during my research visits, women migrating on their own were another group that frequently came up, much like Diana from the introduction and Louise mentioned earlier in this chapter. The generation of women who helped expand labor market participation from the 1970s to the 1990s is now entering retirement, imbued with cultural ideals of successful and active aging, on one hand (Allain and Marshall 2017; Gilleard and Higgs 2011), but also carrying with them the financial burdens of work lives that were more precarious and less well paid than for their male counterparts.[7] Independent women like Louise and Diana often narrate their relocations to Ecuador in terms of adventure and risk taking. However, North American labor markets and gender roles structure these risks, as does the fact that relocating to a lower-cost location in the Global South seems less financially risky than remaining in the United States or Canada.

Women aging into poverty on their own at this moment in history face many gender-specific challenges, including cultural frames that influence how they evaluate relocation. As Gambold (2013) points out, gendered responses to aging may lead to new lifestyle strategies involving transnational relocation, strategies grounded in what she refers to as a "fear of the known." Women research participants who moved on their own mentioned the camaraderie and opportunities for socializing, particularly with other women at the same stage in life. Women without partners in Cuenca (eighteen of whom participated in this research) generally seem to have tight social connections built around mutual care. Several mentioned belonging to a "buddy system" that has them look in on one another and care for one another in the event of illness. In many respects, these women's ways of aging together indicate interesting new experiments in solidarity and mutual care. Yet what makes these experiments possible are the cost differences between their home countries and Cuenca. Moreover, they also often come into contact with and depend on other women, Ecuadorian domestic workers, whose economic and social precarity makes them more vulnerable to similar forms of gendered exploitation (cf. Masi de Casanova, Rodríguez, and Bueno Roldán 2017).

As Sheila Croucher (2014) points out, North American women who migrate alone are often seen as more adventurous, even when this adventurousness is premised on relative privilege with respect to the receiving community.[8] Research participants who were not single women, as well as others with whom I spoke in casual conversation, often mentioned this group, as though their particular relocation was invested with special characteristics that ennobled it and set it apart from others. Melanie (age fifty-five, from Wisconsin), who was recently widowed (she had moved to Cuenca with her husband), provides an example of this type of discourse:

> I think the kind of single women that come here are more adventurous, and they are risk takers too. And they're very brave. And they're willing to try new things. Meet new people. Have new adventures. Travel. . . . The single women community, here, we're always out and about. Always. We don't sit at home at all.

Women who moved to Cuenca on their own perceived their relocations as a release from North American gender relations in which they were often supposed to be dependent on a man. The way they narrated adventure cannot be separated from the gender order of North American culture, which regulates and tightly polices women's bodies and personal freedom. They saw migration to Ecuador as an opportunity to meet new people, stay feeling young and useful, contribute to the receiving community, and develop more independent lifestyles. These opportunities played out between the economic insecurity many of them left and the economic and social advantages they gained by being in Cuenca. Given the constraints that many seem to have faced with respect to their relocation, evaluations of braveness and adventure speak to the cultural markers that give meaning to relocations, which were often imbued with the utilitarian spirit of arbitrage. This is not to say that economic decision making cannot also be brave or that independent women undertaking these relocations are not in many respects adventurous. However, the ability to translate precarity into adventure is, I argue, the product of social structures that are often left unexamined by cultural modes of justification that present adventure and risk taking as moral ideals. These cultural modes of justification tend to highlight individual choice and responsibility, belying both the structural conditions of women's collective economic and social vulnerability in an individualistic, free market society and the factors conditioning their relative freedom (especially vis-à-vis Ecuadorian women workers), namely, an unequal global division of labor and the relative symbolic power of racialized whiteness in Ecuador.

Like other participants, Melanie thought of women living on their own in Cuenca as adventurous, but she was also well aware of their vulnerability. "There's many more single women here [than single men], because we tend to not have as much money," she said. "And we can't possibly live comfortably . . . in the United States and Canada, on the income from Social Security." This may be a generalization, but there are cases of extremely precarious women in Cuenca. Several research participants reported barely having enough pension income to qualify for an Ecuadorian residency visa, which requires that independent migrants be able to show $800 of continuous income. Though many on Social Security are able to do so, not all can. In fact, the Ecuadorian Ministerio de relaciones exteriores took a limited sample of migrants—men and women—arriving in Pichincha province in northern Ecuador in early 2013 and found that 54 percent of U.S. migrants seeking residency visas declared incomes between the minimum of $800 and $1,500 per month.[9] The numbers may be quite different for the situation in Cuenca, but they nonetheless point to the importance of Ecuador as a low-cost destination for North American retirees. To put the figures into perspective, the U.S. Census Bureau calculated its low-income cutoff (LICO) at just under $24,000 in 2017 for a single person. Slightly less than half of that income, or $11,511 (about $1,000 per month), would have classified the recipient as being in absolute poverty in 2016. A portion of North American migrants in Cuenca would fall under this poverty line. Yet, in Ecuador, the monthly minimum income is much smaller: $375 per month in 2017. Thus individuals who would be poor in the United States are by comparison much better off in Ecuador.

Jennie is one of those people. A former bookkeeper, she said she woke up the day she turned sixty-two and decided she wanted to retire. She was tired of working and wanted to spend her time doing something else, but she had no savings. "I just began to look at how I could retire," she recounted earnestly. "And, obviously, you can't do that in America if you are only going to have Social Security to live off of. So that's the reason I began looking overseas." Even if she had worked longer, it would not have made that much of a difference, she said. She had not amassed any savings, "for whatever reason." But these reasons surely included the fact that Jennie was divorced and had stopped working for several years to care for her children, a role typical of the gender order that women of her age faced during their reproductive years. The demands of that role had a real impact on her ability to retire. "There was no way to stay in Houston," she said. She was not interested in moving in with family. When she factored in medical insurance, "there's no way. I mean, it's impossible. So, it's why, . . . there's a lot of us here, for that very reason," she said, echoing what other research participants said about other "economic refugees," particularly independent women who had decided to retire to Ecuador.

Jennie found out about Cuenca the same way a lot of research participants did: through online advertising by *International Living*. She said it was a fluke that she happened across the idea of retiring abroad. She logged into her email, and there was a banner for the ten cheapest places to retire. That enticed her. At first, she said, she was interested in retiring to Panama, but she did not have enough income to meet the $1,000 per month minimum requirement. Consequently, Ecuador moved up her list. She began reading all the blogs and social media posts of people who had already made the move—easily accessible online material that has functioned as an important recruitment post for many. Online commentaries typically focus on how much it costs to live in Ecuador, which is one of the principal concerns North Americans on tight budgets express. As Jennie said:

the necessities, to live, are much, much cheaper than in America, food especially. And rent. Services are much, everything, here, is much, much cheaper than in America. That's why you can live here on, well, I guess it depends on your style. I was not one to eat out every day and, you know, big social go here, go there, travel, I didn't do any of that. So I don't really live any differently, here, than what I did in America.

Jennie had been concerned about whether she could live in a different cultural environment, particularly in terms of negotiating a different series of gender relations. However, the cost of living made it desirable for her to migrate, as did the large number of women who migrated in similar conditions and provided communities of support, which helped reshape how they collectively experienced gender relations in both the North American and Ecuadorian communities there. While she continued to refrain from overindulging on her small pension, Jennie still had much greater freedom in Cuenca than she would have had if she had remained in the United States. "I mean, you don't have to sit in your apartment and stare at four walls just because you're living on Social Security, not here," she said.

There are other North Americans in Cuenca who may not be doing as well. Shelley, whom I interviewed in 2012, expressed concern about the conditions of some of the women moving to Cuenca. She said she had met one woman who told her she was looking for an apartment. At the time, she was spending $100 on a room in a house and could not afford a place above $200. Shelley, who lived a middle-class life and rented a house with her husband, said she felt bad. "I was at a total loss to help her, because I don't know anything about apartments [*whispering*] *like that*, you know?" When the inequalities of Ecuadorian society itself are not enough to cause consternation among North Americans in Ecuador (they often do), the inequalities and poverty within the "expat" community itself often draws their attention.

Freedom from Work

Migration was an escape hatch for some research participants facing dire financial conditions, but for most others, it was just a way out of the labor market itself, used by workers who were tired of late capitalist work schedules or who found their work lives devoid of meaning at this later stage in life, when they would have preferred to develop other interests or socialize with like-minded fellow travelers. Thus, although Cuenca was a destination for some former workers, like Mary and Grant and Simone and Ray, who found themselves unemployed during the Great Recession, most participants were people who had been able to retire earlier as a result of cost differentials between the Global North and Global South. In this respect, their relocations run counter to labor market trends, which show older workers in the United States working longer, despite higher rates of unemployment (Bureau of Labor Statistics 2010; Mosisa and Hipple 2006; Toossi 2015; U.S. Government Accountability Office 2012). Labor force participation for workers over age fifty-five has hovered for several years around 40 percent, up from a low of 29 percent in the late 1980s, with projections for participation rates set to rise for workers older than sixty-five over the next decade. A number of factors have contributed to this, including the shift in the 1990s from defined benefit to defined contribution pension plans, which has encouraged older workers to remain in the labor force longer, beyond the traditional age of retirement (Bureau of Labor Statistics 2010; Tang, Choi, and Goode 2013). Another important factor, of course, has been the economic crisis and subsequent recession (Fichtner, Phillips, and Smith 2012; Munnell and Rutledge 2013).

Given that many research participants had low savings, depleted in some cases as a result of the financial crisis and housing collapse, Cuenca was the safety net that made retirement possible. North Americans approaching retirement are not as financially secure as previous generations, with one recent U.S. study suggesting that about 30 percent of households over the age of fifty-five lack retirement savings (U.S. Government Accountability 2015). High household debt levels for some,[10] coupled with the emergence and proliferation of welfare markets for elder care (Bode 2008), have also undermined retirement security. Moreover, in the risk society, which individualizes responsibility for retirement, older workers are increasingly exposed to the hazards of deregulated financial markets and the large and unpredictable fluctuations of neoliberal housing and stock markets (Blackburn 2011; Weller 2016). These factors have, in general, contributed to longer work lives and higher labor market participation for older workers. As Engemann and Wall (2010, 18) point out, "a dominant feature of the recession has been a significant collapse of stock prices and the resulting devaluation of many people's retirement savings. So, instead of retiring, large numbers of this age group have elected to remain employed, thereby suppressing the normal effect that the recession would have had." But not everyone is electing to remain employed well into their sixties or even seventies. The unequal structure of the global political economy enables those located at higher latitudes to recoup lost savings and spending power in the Global South.

Typically, research participants wanted to stop working and enjoy life while they still had relatively good health and were able to travel. In this context, marked by the individualization of risk, Cuenca and locations like it in the Global South operate as global safe havens for people caught out in the generational change of retirement financing, which, since the 1990s, has placed much more responsibility for saving on individuals than on employers or the state.[11] Colin, mentioned earlier, is a case in point. But so too is Clem, who said he "burned out" at age sixty-two and decided to leave his job with the U.S. military to live "overseas" with his second wife, Phyllis. Their intent, Clem said, "was to be able to go someplace, live a reasonable lifestyle, and be able to afford it on my early retirement [pension]." Similarly, Harry, age sixty-eight, was able to retire because he moved abroad. He had been working on commission in a hardware store prior to his re-location. "I would say that I left the U.S. because I wanted to be able to live on the means that I have, uh, and I could not do that, in the U.S., without continuing to work," he said.

While most research participants who retired in this way did so in their late fifties or early sixties, a few participants found themselves stuck in the labor market well beyond the traditional retirement age. Barry and Lynn, seventy-five and seventy-three, respectively, offer an especially salient example of those who were able to stop working through migration. They had worked well past the traditional retirement age, retiring two years prior to our interview after completing short-term contract work in a northern Canadian city. They had had to work longer in part because their earning years were marked by increasingly typical life events, including difficult and expensive divorces from previous spouses for both. They had also worked for themselves and said they had been unable to save sufficiently for their retirement. Relocating to Ecuador had enabled them to stop working. During our interview, they admitted wanting to return to Canada. But they could not afford to do so without finding new jobs. "If we were able to like their food and to, to learn the language, to speak the language well enough to get by on, we would probably look at our situation a little differently," Barry said. In their mid-seventies, Barry and Lynn needed to find work if they wanted to return home. The retirement lifestyles of these middle-class Canadians were unaffordable on their meager pension incomes.

Migrants' narratives may have expressed cultural ideals related to material lifestyles, but to treat these merely as post hoc justifications, or as rationalizations migrants use to give meaning to their transnational migrations, turns them into free-floating signifiers and underplays the structural contexts that shaped migrants' decisions. Part of these contexts were cultural and consisted of lifestyle ideals that migrants had internalized, as previous studies have suggested (Benson 2012; O'Reilly 2012). In this case, North American expectations around aging actively are an essential structuring feature. However, global economic differences were crucial to realizing these ideals. Many participants were not merely relocating for the lifestyle motivations typical of many North–South migrations. Rather, they are a type of economic migrant, expanding leisure and consumption options by relocating across the latitudes of the global division of labor, taking with them savings or pensions earned at high latitudes and buying labor power in lower-cost locations. Doing this enables both financially vulnerable retirees and prospective retirees to fulfill cultural ideals of aging focused on living as intensely and adventurously as possible.

The Rise of International Lifestyle Marketers

Financial instability and labor market insecurity have created potential markets for new types of transnational relocation. Just as homes in global cities have become safe deposit boxes for the

global superelite (Fernandez, Hofman, and Aalbers 2016), locations like Cuenca have become safe havens for people like Louise, Evan, and Jennie, who saw themselves aging into poverty.
However, while economic and cultural changes motivate North
American migration to Ecuador, there are also powerful media
actors who help to shape the process. Developers, real estate
speculators, and their financiers (both local and transnational)
have helped to promote North–South transnational relocation
for economic purposes, particularly online. They benefit from the
social media sharing of the mostly white North American communities in Latin America, who provide prospective "expats"
with information about receiving communities. As noted, prospective migrants often do research, much of it online, and often
also shop or compare between locations. Louise, for instance, visited several locations before deciding Cuenca was the best place
for her. Others, like Barry and Lynn, had limited means to do
these comparisons but were able to get a sense of where they
were going through the social media testimonies of those who
had preceded them.

Online advertisements, popular travel writing, and television
programs like *House Hunters International* increasingly present
North Americans with the idea of transnational relocation and
residential migration to lower-cost environments. In the case of
Cuenca, a key player has been the magazine *International Living,*
which has built a niche around promoting international lifestyles
to a demographic that sees travel as a symbol of successful aging. Moreover, the company, owned by the libertarian publishing
house Agora Inc., which specializes in financial disasterism (see
Hayes 2014), promotes the idea of transnational retirement as
a way to save money in a neoliberal, individualist environment.
True to its libertarian ideological commitments, it calls on its
English-language readership to take responsibility as individuals
for their well-being in retirement. As one of its daily mass email
"postcards" provocatively stated, "As the US economy dims, it's
turning out the lights on the comfortable retirement so many
people imagined and worked hard for. But you do have options. . . .
Because in havens beyond our borders, you can live comfortably
on less than $700 a month . . . or with a $2,500-a-month budget,

retire like royalty." For many of the research participants with whom I spoke, this idea of taking ownership of an insecure retirement (often caused by economic and political forces beyond their individual control) seemed appealing. *International Living* is run by former journalists who are well connected with mainstream media outlets looking for cheap media content and specializes in producing the now-popular top-ten lists of best places to retire, which have received wide media attention. But this attention should also be read against the backdrop of libertarian political currents in the United States, where powerful economic actors actively seek to reduce their tax burden by cutting working people off from entitlement programs into which employees and employers spend a lifetime paying. In global competition based on free trade, however, pensions are a net weight, a "legacy cost" that needs to be cut, as a growing number of workers who thought they had stable pensions are finding out. In this context, *International Living* is a vehicle of elite libertarian worldviews, intent on offshoring care work and postproductive workers to lower-cost regions.

Research participants in forty-nine of ninety-five interviews (in both Cuenca and Vilcabamba) mentioned *International Living* as a source they consulted. In an additional thirteen interviews, participants mentioned internet sources other than *International Living*. Others still had heard from friends, who initially learned about Cuenca through lifestyle marketers online. *International Living*'s website plays an outsized role in promoting the idea of transnational retirement and spreads this idea on internet banners and newsfeeds. The publication was clearly influential with participants, even if they did not always believe the specific claims that it made. Arguably, *International Living* teases financially vulnerable North Americans with the idea of a dream retirement and thereby lures prospective retirees into exploring the option of migration in ever-increasing depth, often by selling products such as "owner's manuals" that explain how to buy property in foreign countries. Its online content and daily postcards utilize cultural codes that portray those who can relocate "to another culture" as self-reliant, special people ("expatriation is not for everyone"), whose daring will be repaid if they are sufficiently "flexible."[12]

International lifestyle marketers also provide new ways of thinking about achieving financial security through transnational geographic mobility, borrowing concepts and ideas long applied to North American business networks and extending them into the day-to-day lives of individuals. In particular, firms like *International Living* promote an ideal of improving one's class position by relocating to a lower-cost area and "living big" on a budget income, a transnational lifestyle ideal that I refer to here as geoarbitrage. The idea of geoarbitrage first appeared in the libertarian business press. *Forbes* magazine published a couple of articles mentioning relocation to low-income countries as a way to maximize material well-being for a growing group of online workers (Karlgaard 2004, 2006). Online businesses and online contracting have created a growing class of workers who are no longer tied to a specific place and therefore are sufficiently flexible to relocate to lower-cost locations, often where they can live in greater luxury. This doesn't always take the form of transnational migration, but it is increasingly possible in the IT economy (cf. Bantman-Masum 2015b; Crispin 2017). Individuals whose jobs no longer require them to be geographically fixed can relocate to low-income countries, while they make their income in the core economies of the global division of labor. The best-selling book by Timothy Ferriss (2007), *The 4-Hour Work Week*, has popularized the concept of "geoarbitrage." Part of what Ferriss calls "lifestyle design" involves taking greater control of one's time by moving to a lower-cost location and outsourcing daily income-generating tasks via the internet to people living in India or the Philippines. *International Living* has applied this logic to a retirement demographic. Ostensibly libertarian, these publications advise taking advantage of an unequal global division of labor. They are, therefore, not really libertarian at all, because the freedom they promise to some is premised on the exploitation and marginalization of others, whose lives are valued less for reasons uncomfortably connected to colonial and racist forms of exploitation. Perhaps unsurprisingly, Karlgaard and Ferriss's notions of geographic arbitrage take the standpoint of the citizen of the wealthy Global North, whose mobility is lightly regulated and whose ability to work across borders is presented as unproblematic and legitimate. Yet the legacy of colonialism is the condition that makes such lifestyles possible.

Geoarbitrage and Global Inequality

Colin, Louise, Sam, Jennie, and other research participants illustrated variations of geoarbitrage. They enjoyed the enhanced material lifestyle afforded by transnational relocation through higher material consumption or by working less and spending more time doing more personally rewarding activities. Participants identified with these benefits—it was often the main reason they relocated, even if these material reasons were frequently also intertwined with other ideals related to discovering new landscapes and cultures (see chapter 2) or with the desire for cross-cultural integration (Hayes and Carlson 2018). As Ron, a retiree from Atlanta, mentioned, "the main reason [for the move to Cuenca] was you could live a lot better. You could maintain your standard of living without worrying about every little penny being spent." The use of cost-of-living narratives to justify and make sense of relocation demonstrates the cultural appeal of geoarbitrage. In an individualistic environment, in which everyone is responsible for his own life trajectory, geoarbitrage is the economically "smart" thing to do. Many research participants expressed pride in being able to save money by taking what they considered to be a bit of a risk. Sam, mentioned earlier, provides a case in point. He saw his relocation as a trade-off, but one well worth making. He remarked, "I said [to Izzy], 'We're going to have to give up a lot. We're going to have to change our lifestyle.' . . . But we can go live in Cuenca, Ecuador, from what they tell me, in the top 2, 3, 4, 5 percent of the population."

These cultural narratives of getting a better deal through transnational relocation are also tied up with global inequalities. The geoarbitrage strategy of class mobility and maximizing one's potential day-to-day spending power in a low-cost country is the correlate of corporate offshoring, whereby corporations take advantage of lower labor costs in developing countries and sell finished products to higher-earning laborers in high-cost geographic regions. Like the corporations in question, the lifestyle migrants

I interviewed deemed their transnationalism unproblematic and often even helpful to the local community. They felt entitled to the better deal they were getting and often mentioned the lighter regulatory environment as a good thing, feeling less oppressed by government-enforced rules and regulations. Instead, social order is voluntary, and individuals are responsible. These benefits are, of course, the legacy of a colonial global political economy. By shifting latitudes of the division of labor, lifestyle migrants are also able to take advantage of historically different regimes of labor and live in places where workers were superexploited (enslaved, tortured, indentured, and denied basic rights) for the benefit of the core regions of accumulation.

It is this colonial inheritance that makes geoarbitrage possible. Research participants could not have produced these global-scale inequalities, but they do benefit from them and identify with those benefits. There were instances when migrants seemed genuinely troubled by the apparently arbitrary benefits they obtained, but nonetheless, they mostly described Cuenca as a godsend. Geoarbitrage illustrates how market modes of rationality have penetrated the cultural lives of individuals. Cultural codes informing where to live, which may once have been considered sacred—dealing with obligations to community or to family (particularly gendered obligations of care) and with attachments to place and people—have shifted toward market rationalities, where individuals' decisions focus on maximizing material self-interests. Just as the commodification of care has shifted moral discourses about care work (Doucet et al. 2016; Hochschild 2013), the extension of market rationality into calculations about where and with whom to live seems to have deeply affected identification to place and attachment to others.

The scope for private calculations about geographic differences in the cost of living has expanded, as market-driven innovations have further compressed space and time (Harvey 1990, 240–59; Rosa 2013) and produced lifestyles that are less place attached. Research participants typically mentioned being able to spend as much time with family and friends on Skype as they would have if they had remained at home, thus making their physical location of little import. Others expressed hopes—sometimes disappointed—that family or friends who lived elsewhere would come visit more often if they were in a setting that seemed more exciting. They did not express obligations toward family in terms of a duty to live nearby but rather, most often, in terms of commitment to return if they were needed. In a few cases, however, participants had no family ties or were alienated from relatives.

The calculative individualism that North American migrants express is also related to other forms of financial and productive arbitrage. Practices of arbitrage became central to global finance in the late 1970s as investment banks began speculating on price fluctuations as a source of potential financial profits and, later, through derivatives trading and futures markets, as a mechanism to help spread risk across financial markets. This enabled private banks to increase their leverage and thereby accrue higher returns, especially post-1971, in an age of much more intense financial fluctuations owing to the end of the U.S. dollar–backed gold standard (Blackburn 2006; Gowan 2009). Arbitrage has now spilled out into everyday life, where it takes different forms and combines with cultural ideals of intense and adventurous living. Yet geoarbitrage and financial arbitrage are also connected in a material sense. Productive investment and offshoring from North America to lower-income countries with more flexible environmental and labor regimes and lower labor costs helped erode the geographically based social benefits that working-class individuals obtained from the postwar settlements in the Global North (Duménil and Lévy 2011; Harvey 2005, 2010, 1–39). In many respects, the emergence of a neoliberal or flexible regime of accumulation has helped to shape the current flow of North–South lifestyle migration to Ecuador just as much as scholars of transnational migration note it has reshaped South–North labor migration (Castles 2010; Faist 2008; Glick Schiller 2009; Horgan and Liinamaa 2017). The accentuation of capitalist competition from the last decades of the twentieth century has repositioned geographic regions and social classes within the stratified latitudes of the global division of labor, creating new linkages between distant social spaces. It has also produced new opportunities for profit by exploiting geographically mobile and cost-differentiated labor and opened opportunities for speculation through the transnationalization of local real estate markets. Thus, just as labor markets have been increasingly de-territorialized and unbounded, so too have the social spaces of postproductive or leisure life. These social spaces therefore increasingly become the object of calculative, utilitarian cultural frames, which orient transnational lifestyle strategies toward maintaining or enhancing quality of life in the third age, itself a culturally produced notion of a period of life marked by ideals of individual freedom, self-expression, and possibility.

As I point out in the second part of the book, the effects of geoarbitrage on local communities are asymmetrical and often reproduce unequal social relations. However, the way North Americans settle in Cuenca, and the ideals they develop about Ecuador and Ecuadorians, also perpetuate coloniality. The next two chapters take up some of the cultural ideals and identities that shape the relocations of these North American migrants and participate in global inequalities inherited from the period of European colonialism.

2

Migrant Imaginaries

A colonial jewel of Ecuador, spilling over with cobblestoned streets, well-preserved churches and attractive leafy plazas— all tucked into a verdant Andean valley traversed by four winding rivers—Cuenca wins out as the country's most idyllic urban locale.

—Elissa Richard, Cuenca High Life
e-newsletter, November 7, 2016

Paula was in her late fifties when I interviewed her. Having traveled a lot in her youth, she spent most of her life in Austin, Texas, where she had studied in the mid-1970s. We sat at a table in her spacious condo apartment, located west of El Centro, with a view of the Cajas Mountains to the west. Well dressed and outgoing, Paula had economic motivations for her decision to relocate to Ecuador's "powerful" mountains. "I don't have to watch my savings [*laughs*] . . . deteriorate while I'm working full-time in America, just trying to stay even," she said of her move. She had left "that party," as she ironically described it. Like Diana, she saw her life as coming to a head and wanted to live the rest of it on her terms. Relating a conversation she had with a friend in Texas, she said, "You know, we're almost sixty, we've got twenty really juicy years left, where we can travel and do stuff, and not have to worry. You know? How do you want to spend them?" Paula did not want to spend hers living in front of a computer screen. Instead, she yearned for a more "authentic" lifestyle, one deeply entwined with an image she had of Ecuador, Ecuadorians, and their relation to North American modernity.

During our discussions, Paula spoke openly about her spirituality, but she was not conspicuous about it. Paula mixed her Catholic upbringing with New Age mysticism she had encountered

< 63 >

during a break from her work life—a life spent doing various jobs while being married to a successful lawyer. She also had become familiar with Buddhism from travels to retreats in India. She was aware that to some, her spirituality might seem strange, or at the very least eclectic. But Paula was very serious about what made her tick. She combined an inward-looking self-reflection about her true self, intuiting what her inner spirit wanted out of life, with an outward attention to "energies" from the mountains or from angels and spirits, who helped to guide her inner search for authentic living in the external world around her. Coming to Cuenca was, in some respects, cathartic for Paula. "I stopped the crazymaker," she said with a laugh. "I stopped the rat wheel. I stopped and exhaled. I stopped and took a breath."

Paula found that Ecuador was a more authentic and conscious place than her hometown of Austin, and her understanding of Cuenca was also implicitly a critique of late capitalist work routines in North America. In our interview, she talked about "our culture" in North America, which, she said, was very hectic and focused on getting things done. "It's a very driven thing, it's a very weird thing. It's not a healthy thing at all," she said. "And so I wouldn't read in the middle of the day, I wouldn't take a nap. I wouldn't do things that were nurturing to me, you know? I would just be driven, working all the time. That's not the case here." Being in Ecuador, she said, had helped her gain a greater appreciation of how these external cultural forces—this "milieu" in which everyone was in a hurry—had shaped her previous life. "I think what's emerging here," she said, "is the thing that's inside of me, is dictating my life. Which is a much better way to live, and really a much more spiritual way to live." Paula seemed to be describing a situation in which individual authenticity could finally transcend the limitations of history and conjuncture, a situation made possible by her geoarbitrage.

The meaning Paula gave her migration was premised on an imaginary of Ecuador that reflected experiences and cultural codes that were broadly shared among North American migrants and that were transplanted to Latin America. The imaginaries of lifestyle migrants are the topic of this chapter, which, as Michaela Benson (2012) points out, are forged in the cultural environment of sending communities. They are collective representations, which, as Karen O'Reilly (2014) argues, participate in structuring social relations and in producing outcomes that may be asymmetrical or that reinforce inherited privileges or structural power. The social imaginaries of lifestyle migrants are produced in particular social contexts and reflect the shared experience of those who carry them. The imaginaries discussed here are produced in North America and reflect North American cultural codes and global social positions. They are carried with migrants as they cross borders, even as they privilege attempts to build entirely new lives or to leave their home countries and cultures behind as they leave their "comfort zones." The imaginaries of lifestyle migrants are oriented toward the ideals of the sending culture and reference a particular cultural response to North American modernity. As this chapter points out, such imaginaries are partly reliant on widely shared North American cultural codes. But they can also be manipulated by international lifestyle marketers like *International Living,* such that lifestyle migrants need not really reflect critically on the meaning of their advantages at lower latitudes of a global division of labor—advantages that signal the colonial continuities of their emplacement and enactment of self in the spaces of the Global South.

Paula described herself as a citizen of the world and had traveled broadly over her life, though not in Latin America, which she had never been to before starting the move to Cuenca. She had first heard of Cuenca through a friend, but like so many research participants, she said she had done a lot of online research. "Everybody, you know, starts with *International Living,*" she said, before noting her distrust in the company since they were "in it for profit." She said that the company had given "a lot of good information in the beginning, about visas and transitioning and starting businesses, and real estate." She said her first impression was that it was "a really sweet little city." Not wanting to live in a place that was too big, Cuenca seemed like the perfect antidote to the heat and urban sprawl of her hometown of Austin, Texas. "You know [Cuenca is] a UNESCO city, I really like the old-world stuff," she said. "It's easy to live here. It's simple. I mean, it's not a challenge," she added, referring to the layout of the city and its familiarity to an American public. Cuenca is laid out in a grid, and its streetscape often reminds North Americans of an idyllic North American town, with mom-and-pop shops dotting every corner. As Paula continued, "I like that I can just walk around and walk to things. And, you know, there's concerts, and the culture, there's culture here, which is different from other parts of Ecuador." The availability of cultural presentations, especially art shows, jazz nights, a publicly funded orchestra, and spaces for lifestyle migrants to unfurl their cultural creativity, was a major draw for Paula, who was an active participant in the cultural life of the North American community.

Ecuadorian people and culture were also an important part of Paula's imaginary of Cuenca and affected her sense of well-being there. While Cuenca's affordability was important for Paula, enabling her to live without having to generate significant income, it was her experience with Ecuadorians that helped to push Cuenca to the top as a place she wanted to live. "I mean, they're all wonderful," she said, when I asked her about her interactions with Ecuadorians:

That was one of the pulls for me, was the Ecuadorian people were incredible. I love them. Immediately liked them. They have heart, they're present to you. They're present in their bodies. You know, they're just, they're really nice people. And I like the culture because it was sort of an innocent culture, if that makes sense, like America in the '50s.

The likability of Ecuadorians, and their apparently "innocent" culture, circulates almost as broadly as the subjective sense that Cuenca is "like America in the '50s," which was so often repeated by participants and in casual conversations. For Paula, this meant that Cuenca was not overrun by many of the things that she felt plagued her own culture. "I don't see magazines with naked ladies on them in the newsstand," she said. Moreover, Ecuadorians had positive values that Paula much appreciated:

I love the fact that it's a Catholic culture and that, they're not repressed, by any measure, they're just very sovereign people.

You know, they're very proud, clean, they take pride in their city. They love their families. They're very family-based.

It was not just that Cuenca was "like America in the '50s" but that it was actually a better place, a truer place, a morally superior version of the North American present, which, for many participants, had degenerated and expelled them. Participants often seemed to find the institutional certainty symbolized by a nostalgic urbanism and apparently "traditional" families more meaningful and authentic than those of contemporary North America. Yet this subjective sense of meaning is also entangled in historical social relations that position Ecuador as a colonial space (as opposed to a modern one), different from and outside of North American modernity. It also conjures up an imaginary of Cuenca in relation to a romanticized European urbanism and culture, which is experienced by lifestyle migrants as more authentic and more meaningful and thus productive of new identities and subjective sensations of cultural difference, themselves also entangled in colonial relations of domination.

This chapter reflects on the imaginary that Paula and other North American lifestyle migrants developed in Ecuador, one in which a humble mountain city was transformed into a romanticized "colonial-style" nostalgia town, where an idealized people and place seemed to offer relief from the moral and material decay of North American society and potentially redeem the future. I argue that this subjective sensation of Cuenca relies on shared North American experiences of a stratified and shifting global social order, one in which the historically privileged middle classes of high-income countries like Canada and the United States are being globally repositioned after a generation of deindustrialization and neoliberal austerity. While often unfurled as praise of Ecuadorian places and people, it also misrecognizes them in ways that reproduce global social inequalities and complicates North American incorporation to the receiving community. The idealization of Cuenca as a nostalgia town is a product of a colonial imaginary, one that deprives Cuenca of its modernity and essentializes its people as "allochronic" (Fabian 1983), that is, as belonging to another time, outside North American modernity.

Idealized Ecuadorian particulars sometimes appear as decorative figures—especially indigenous people, who add authenticity to an idealized, UNESCO space. Yet their very modern struggles are located outside of modernity itself, in a previous phase of evolution, as though they were not tied up in the same global processes of accumulation that have made North American lives more casualized and more vulnerable. This exoticization of Ecuadorian struggles limits the development of bonds of solidarity in a common struggle for global justice (Kurasawa 2007).

At the same time, North American imaginaries of Cuenca reflect a shared—if sometimes contested—experience of socioeconomic transformation in North America, marked in particular by cultural pluralism and the provincialization of a formerly dominant, white working class. The nostalgic tones of their imaginaries and their critique of contemporary North America echo the political movements within Canadian and American political culture that seek to reclaim an idealized past (e.g., Make America Great Again) and that identify with global superiority rather than fundamentally transforming the trajectory of North American development and challenging social hierarchies at different geographic scales. North American migrants long for a past that is more authentic than the materialistic overaccumulation of contemporary U.S. and Canadian societies. In what follows, I attend to the ways that North American imaginaries participate in unequal social relations that are premised on hierarchically organized imaginings of place and people.

Staging the European Feel

Like Paula, many other North American participants mentioned Cuenca's "old-world" feel—a feel that says something about the shared cultural preferences of some North Americans as well as about their own identity in the "new" world of North American modernity. As Greg, a younger migrant in his late teens who came to Ecuador with his mother, told me, "It just feels very European. Like, this city is supposed to feel really European, and that's why a lot of people like it." Kelly, age forty-one, from Los Angeles, said she was told that it "looks like Portugal, but it's in South America," perhaps echoing the idea that Cuenca has a certain Southern European flavor to it, harkening back to a European mercantile nostalgia. Several research participants had either considered moving to Italy, Spain, or southern France before settling on Cuenca, often due to Ecuador being the most affordable.

Oftentimes, the idea that Cuenca has a European feel comes from things that North Americans have read online by international lifestyle marketers. Jennifer (age forty-six, from Hawai'i) described looking into different destinations, stating, "When you read about Cuenca, it's 'Little Europe.' There's people here from all over the world. There's seventeen universities. There's museums." This "cultural setting," as her friend Kate put it, was something that attracted them to Cuenca, even though it is also an exaggeration. For instance, there are not seventeen universities in the city. Scarlett (age sixty-two, from North Carolina) and her husband, Jeff, had also been doing a lot of online research, looking at blogs written by other lifestyle migrants and videos posted to YouTube. They said they also consulted a blog called *Gringos Abroad,* run by a Canadian family and featuring a great deal of advice on how to find real estate and what to see in Ecuador, particularly Cuenca, which it describes in these terms:

> Many people say that Cuenca looks a lot like a European city because of the Spanish colonial architecture. Many of the buildings in the center are beautifully decorated in colonial style with red-tiled roofs, and little flower filled wrought iron balconies.[1]

This and other websites help migrants like Scarlett and Jeff form a first opinion before arriving in Cuenca. Scarlett, who was still settling in to the city when I interviewed her and Jeff in 2011, had grown up in New Orleans, and she recognized a shared Spanish colonial influence. She remarked, "Cuenca looked kind of like that, to me, with the balconies and the colonial buildings. And, to me it just felt like it, I mean, Quito is more business, more government. Guayaquil is hot. But Cuenca had beauty and the churches, and all the festivals. And it just had more of a feeling quality, to me." Jeff agreed and asked me if I had been to Savannah, Georgia. This "old-world" feel, therefore, may be rooted in American architectural ideals of the typical colonial city, like New Orleans or Savannah, which evoke a historical character. The adjective describes a style that often provokes a subjective sensation of nostalgia or melancholia. Lance (age sixty-one, from Florida) had worked with *International Living* and had helped build interest in Cuenca. "Cuenca, as a city, kind of stood out," he said. "I mean, it's almost got a European feel to it. There's something that's, it's a city you could almost imagine in, in Spain or southern Italy, or something, you know?" While Lance had not invented this imaginary of Cuenca as a place that looks like Europe at a fraction of the cost, his writing about it—along with the blogging of many other lifestyle migrants—had helped to produce an ideal of the city as belonging to a colonial, European past. Cuenca's European feel is socially constructed, relying partly on cultural codes that circulate in North America and partly on the material interests of individual speculators, tourism operators, and international lifestyle marketing firms (cf. Bantman-Masum 2011; Salazar and Graburn 2014). It is reinforced by certain types of images and stories that are presented regularly on websites like Cuenca High Life or Gringo Tree, both of which are run by the same people who promoted Cuenca for *International Living*.

This staged European feel refers to a very specific type of European imaginary, associated with Southern European spaces, such as Spain and Italy, and not with the wealthier, Northern European centers of France, Britain, or Germany, despite the municipality's attempts to invoke French comparisons, as I discuss in chapter 4.[2] Cuenca's "old-world" feel is oriented toward the tourist gaze (Urry 1990) of the North American traveling classes and their taste for locations in France, Spain, and Italy, the most popular international tourism destinations alongside the United States and China (World Tourism Organization 2016, 6). Given the intense promotion of tourism in Southern Europe, a product of state-led industrial strategies and a postwar predilection for international travel to "old-world" countries (Apostolopoulos, Leontidou, and Loukissas 2001; Garcia 2014; Mantecón 2008), it is not surprising that associating Cuenca with the popular Mediterranean imaginary would be a successful branding for English-language lifestyle marketers. Yet the Andes are very different from the Mediterranean. The imaginary that produces Cuenca as a "European-style" space draws on the exoticization of an apparently more authentic culture and the idealization of certain types of close, familial social relations, which appear absent from North American modernity. It is fundamentally, thus, a melancholic longing for something that does not exist but that appears as absent from modern, postindustrial societies. This nostalgia circulates as critique of North American modernity and its mass consumer culture.

While lacking any apparently real foundation, the descriptions North Americans give to Cuenca's urbanism and architecture—a "colonial style" or "old-world feel"—participate in the hierarchical social relations and culture of Ecuador. The elite social classes of Ecuador have long harbored their own European imaginary and shaped their urban spaces and cultural life in relation to Europe and European cultural standards (Kingman 2006; Mancero Acosta 2012; Roitman 2009). As noted in the introduction, part of Cuenca's supposed old-world feel comes from an architectural tradition forged among the upper classes of the city, who sought to demonstrate their status by importing styles and ideas from Europe, mainly France (Klaufus 2009; Mancero Acosta 2012). Thus, elite classes' investment in European heritage and whiteness also helps reinforce North American imaginaries that would tend to culturally locate this Andean city in Southern Europe. Likewise, North American imaginaries of a European style reinforce the patrician representation of the city and its European origins, which Cuenca's elite social classes use to justify their claims to cultural and social superiority. In short, North American lifestyle migrants' attraction to the apparent European style of Cuenca was not merely an innocent description of subjective feelings. The emotional attachment to colonial styles is complicit with coloniality.

Cuenca can also be described in other ways. It was an important Cañarí city called Pumapunga before the arrival of the Inca, who refounded the city as Tomebamba. The northern capital of the Inca Empire under Huayna Capac, the city was destroyed in the early 1530s during the Inca civil war, which preceded the Spanish conquest, but some of its pre-Spanish geometry is said to remain. Ecuadorians often described it as a nice place to live and work, but, like a lot of Latin American cities, it is congested. Residents complained of air quality problems and traffic, and many from all classes found parts of it decidedly unsafe. Working Ecuadorians, most of whom work in Cuenca's expansive informal sector, often complained that it was expensive and found it difficult to afford housing, a problem exacerbated by the city's growing popularity.

While lifestyle migrants sometimes mentioned pollution, crime, and traffic, they drew on other impressions of place when justifying their relocation decisions. These justifications highlighted the city's colonial style but elided the colonial social relations they participated in reproducing—relations that often position indigenous people and traditions as decorative elements in European artistic traditions. The "feel" of the city, thus, is of some importance, because it allows North American migrants to romanticize their transnational relocations and ground them in cultural narratives of authenticity. These latter serve to disrupt meanings attached to migrations initiated by a change in financial circumstances. The expression of a colonial desire for "old-world" spaces, marked by certain architectural features and walkable downtown spaces—increasingly priced out of reach for many middle-class retirees in the United States and Canada—aestheticizes lifestyle decisions that are often made on utilitarian grounds, as discussed in chapter 1.

Like Kansas in the 1950s

Lifestyle migrants' widespread use of allochronic or asynchronous allusions to Cuenca are also a subtle critique of North American modernity. They frequently positioned Cuenca temporally in the past of a North American present by relating a narrative in which Cuenca was like "America in the 1950s." As Paula illustrated earlier, research participants viewed Cuenca not only as a "nifty old place" but as representative of a romanticized North American past—a denial of coevalness that might indicate emotional investments in unequal social relations (Fabian 1983), even though participants deployed it appreciatively. This notion that Cuenca is like America in the 1950s has also become one of the tropes that lifestyle marketers draw on to sell the city as a destination.[3] Younger research participants did not use this narrative to discuss their place impressions during interviews, but the narrative also circulates among younger migrants. It was most common, however, among participants who were retirees, who expressed a subjective, emotional reaction to the spaces of the city as well as a nostalgic critique of contemporary North American society. In other words, the allusion to America in the 1950s refers to an idealized American past that is redeemed or reclaimed in Ecuador. Moreover, such narratives are socially located within the racial and class formations of North America, such that imaginaries of cultural difference in Ecuador say more, perhaps, about perceptions of social structural transformations in the North than they do about realities in the South.

North American migrants frequently rendered their impressions of Cuenca in nostalgic tones. As Simone, the retired writer from San Francisco, stated, "one thing that kind of surprised me, and it was a pleasant surprise, was how much living in Ecuador reminded me of my childhood. That this was kind of the way people lived if you were working class, in the USA, back in the 1950s and early '60s." For Simone, this way of life was tied to practices of resourcefulness and fixing things when they are broken, something she said she saw a lot of in Ecuador. This impression also stemmed from a negative association of her home country with wastefulness. As she stated, "in the United States, we've gotten very spoiled, or people have gotten very spoiled, and they just throw stuff away and buy new." Ecuador's difference was mobilized to critique the present of the United States and in turn to idealize a lost past, to which Cuenca apparently still belonged.

Jackie, age sixty-four, a retired court reporter, provided another case in point from our interview in 2013. She and her husband, Benjamin, age seventy-three, were passionate conservative critics of what they saw happening to the United States. Jackie said they felt "an increasing discomfort" with the way things were going there, citing declining quality of life and the erosion of personal freedom. "Maybe you don't know all the details, and maybe you can't quite put your finger on it, but you know something's not right, and it's not going in a good direction," Jackie said, with Benjamin nodding his approbation. Ecuador, by contrast, belonged to an idealized past, one that was not just about physical spaces but also about idealized people. As Jackie put it, "people here are, by and large, in good shape, because they, they do a lot of physical work. They're not sitting around getting fat eating Twinkies and playing video games. They just don't do that, here." This idealization appears to reference a loss of connection with younger North American generations, whose childhood is unrecognizable from the one that Jackie and Benjamin knew. (It is also a lament that Ecuadorian research participants shared about their own children, who most definitely do eat Twinkies, drink pop, and play video games.) They described their country as lacking in work ethic and would share photos with friends and family in the United States that demonstrated the resourcefulness and creativity of Ecuadorians. "We've kind of lost that [in the United States]," Jackie opined. "You know, I think, I think we're back to, living down here is probably like the 1950s, maybe? Or maybe even before that; '40s, maybe even '30s, in some ways." Indeed, as Jackie admitted, this time stretched back to before her own birth.

Other research participants used similar narratives, which idealized Ecuadorian workers as a way to draw attention to an apparent decline of North American values. Krista, age sixty-four, a retiree from Phoenix (and originally from farther north) mentioned that Ecuadorians were "such loving, helpful people" and that the city was a "laid-back, stress-free environment." Ecuadorians sometimes described their lives in the city differently, but I was curious about what signaled this to Krista. What did she find laid back about it? Surprisingly, it was related to their work ethic, which was sensually present to her and which signaled physical effort and human pace. "They work really hard," she said. "You see them building a road, for instance, and they're using picks to take out the old concrete. You know? I mean, they do stuff by hand, still, like, '40s and '50s, in the United States." She saw this way of working, while perhaps less efficient by the standards of contemporary North America, as morally superior, and it gave some North Americans a sense of Ecuadorian work ethic, which they idealized, in this case as more "laid back," perhaps because of its perceived connection with antimodernity.

This idealization of the physically sensual pace of work says more about North American perceptions of modernized, deindustrialized, and automated work rhythms than it does about the real working conditions of Ecuadorians. Jackie's husband, Benjamin, similarly echoed this idealization of Ecuadorian labor. He noted, "I really respect how hard these people work, here. For such little reward, such little money. And they, and they really bust their butts." Jackie chimed in, "It is just amazing." Benjamin, a retired police officer, had strong views about how his country, of which he was fiercely proud (he was offended by the term *expatriate,* which he took to mean that he was no longer patriotic), had gone off the rails. Continuing, he said, "I respect that [hard work] a lot, because they're not back in a corner counting what kind of money they can make if they do this or if they do that, like the people in the United States are doing." He used this description further on in the interview to critique bureaucratic unions, which he saw as undermining the American work ethic, but he could just as easily have applied it to the managerialism of private corporations. For Benjamin, American work ethics were polluted by cold calculations about money, which he felt Ecuadorians did not express, though he was unable to communicate with them because of language barriers. For Jackie and Benjamin, then, this notion that Ecuador belonged to an idealized past referenced a lost work ethic, and their preference for Ecuador both justified their relocation and critiqued their homeland as morally lost.

As Ann Miles (2015) points out, this idealization of Ecuadorian work practices is not limited to blue-collar labor. Miles's concept of health care imaginaries taps the North American ideal of attentive doctors who care for their patients, in contrast to capitalistic, profit-focused medicine, which is perceived to have emerged in recent decades in the United States. As in Miles's interviews, I heard frequent allusions to the moral superiority of Ecuadorian doctors, who worked the way American doctors used to. Joel (age sixty-five, from Dallas) said, "These doctors here, are very similar in, before you were born, like doctors were back in the '50s, that I remember, and I was a kid, then, but I still remember. You know, they're just, they actually care [*laughs*]. I mean, the doctors here actually care." Joel's excitement is palpable in his use of run-on sentences and his emphasis: they *actually* care. This sense of authenticity ties into other aspects of North American impressions of Ecuador, which are deployed both to explain the superiority of Ecuadorian habits and to critique contemporary North America, where again professional ethics are polluted by the capitalist profit motive and a naked desire to make money. This latter is understood almost entirely in moral terms and individualized moral dispositions rather than locating it in the competitive forces unleashed by a deregulated, free market economy, increasingly dominated by large, rationalized corporate bureaucracies.

The Meanings of Lost Time

The nostalgic 1950s trope and its deployment in relation to cultural and material differences in Ecuador should also be understood in relation to the social positions of research participants. For instance, Colin (age sixty-eight, from Portland, Oregon) and Brett (age seventy-one, from Vancouver, British Columbia) were both middle-class, racialized white men from the West Coast, and both had been through a separation and divorce mid-career. While their imaginary of Cuenca partly reflects cultural codes that circulate broadly, it also partly reflects how male gender roles have changed over the course of their lives. Colin mentioned an intense emotional reaction to coming to Cuenca. "I fell in love in a week," he said of his first visit to the city. It took his second wife a bit longer to warm up to it, he said, but she also had developed an active social life in the city. When I asked him what exactly it was that he fell in love with, he said,

> Well, I can articulate it. It reminded me of the Brooklyn that I grew up in, of the 1950s. With the *tiendas*, the small neighborhoods, the small churches in the neighborhoods, and the friendliness of the people. And, except for the diesel buses, the cleanliness of the city.

My curiosity piqued, I asked what he meant by Brooklyn in the 1950s. Like Jackie and Benjamin, Colin saw Ecuador in terms of a lost past. "It was a, it was a time of innocence," he said. "Your mother let you out, and you went to the school, and the school-yard, and the neighborhood stores, and there wasn't a concern that you were going to get grabbed or mugged." As I fumbled for a question to try to better understand the sense of lost inno-cence that Colin experienced, he offered to help with an illustra-tion. "I'm recognized by the local shopkeepers. Even the guy on the *esquina* (corner), the one that sells the little candies, recog-nizes me and greets me." Colin enjoyed going through the ritual greeting, *"como le va,"* which Colin used frequently. "It's a local economy," he said, something that he apparently missed in the suburban environment he left in the United States. Perhaps the added opportunity for interaction also shaped his sense of com-munity and the feeling of openness he felt—he knew he would not be treated as just another stranger. Clearly part of this nos-talgia is related to anxieties produced, perhaps, by his changing position in North American society, a position marked by aging and declining income. His alterity in Ecuador allows his aging as well as his lower income to be coded differently. In Cuenca, North Americans frequently remark that older people are better appreciated and respected, but this is not universally the case. Their subjective experiences of this respect can be explained partly in relation to how migrants' alterity (gringoness) is coded positively—as distinct from migrants from Peru, Colombia, Haiti, or Cuba, who have also arrived in Cuenca in recent years. In Colin's case, this subjective sense of being more respected also appears to tap gendered and ethnically situated imaginaries of how North American society has changed and to select aspects of the 1950s for nostalgic remembrance. American cities, with their small neighborhood shops, were hollowed out in the 1960s as a result of a segregated pattern of suburbanization, which impov-erished downtown cores and spawned new concerns about safety and criminality that were spatially organized along racial lines (Avila and Rose 2009; Freund 2006, 2010; Sugrue 2014). A nos-talgic longing for 1950s urbanism reflects the experience of sub-urbanization from Colin's social position in North America and seems to be visible in the way social groups who were not victims of racist oppression in the United States talk about urban transformation: insensitive to the social injustices of exclusion but attuned to "lost innocence" and criminality. This socially situated, North American reality has been projected onto Cuenca, where place imaginaries help shape the meanings that migrants give to relocations most often undertaken for economic purposes.

The social position of nostalgic longings in transnational social space can also be visualized in the ways that Colin and other participants spoke about Ecuadorian families. "I see mothers picking up their sons, their nine-, ten-, eleven-year-old sons, from schools, when they're holding hands. I mean, they'd get beat up if it was in the United States," Colin remarked. The apparent closeness of Ecuadorian families, the respect Ecuadorians showed to the elderly, and the time spent together in activities reminiscent of an ideal past were frequently brought up. These ideals of family are sacred to North American migrants, but they also seem absent from their own backgrounds, perhaps most clearly evident in their own transnational migration away from family and friends. Typically, lifestyle migrants mention Ecuadorian families in nostalgic tones reminiscent, no doubt, of difficult and divisive debates from the 1980s and 1990s about the changing status of North American families (cf. Beck and Beck-Gernsheim 2004; Hochschild 2012; Stacey 1990, 1993).

Brett seemed to share Colin's idealization of family life in Ecuador, noting of his impressions of Cuenca, "You see families strolling in the park, the entire family, you know? And including grown kids and, so, the family structure is a lot stronger, here." In Canada, he said, grown kids move away, as his own had, and they were more individualistic. Given that Brett himself had moved a long way from his family and friends, one is tempted to read this as either a cultural code that idealizes family connection or as a melancholic projection of an idealized family that history or fortune had not favored for Brett, Colin, and men like them—men who lived through a period where the male dividend of marriage, family, and relationships was challenged in ways that they may not have anticipated or been fully prepared for (both men are remarried). As Brett put it, "there is an innocence to it [life in

Cuenca] that we don't have anymore [in North America]." This innocence may be more projection than reality and should be understood from Brett's racialized and gendered social position. "[Ecuadorians] are not as guarded, you know? In North America, we tend to get a little jaded," he added, referring to the apparent facility of interactions between people. Colin's and Brett's idealizations of Ecuadorian families, moreover, crossed ethnocultural differences and thus may also implicitly reference North American racial formations, where distrust and racism are often directed toward nonwhite, racialized groups. The North Americans Brett appeared to be talking about were other white North Americans like him, who were jaded as a result of social injustices and transformations that are rarely articulated in terms of inequalities of caste and class. Cuenca's "old-world" feel and its "innocent people" echo North American preoccupations about race and reference a time of racist subordination, before large-scale nonwhite migration and the efforts to build cultural pluralism that have provincialized dominant social positions. Cultural pluralism and diversity are, however, different in Ecuador, where whiteness continues to reap important symbolic dividends and racialized mestizo and indigenous people's manual labor occurs in the context of colonial caste relations that often benefit phenotypically lighter, higher-income groups.

But this is largely not how North American lifestyle migrants subjectively experience their presence in Ecuador. They normally do not see how experiences from their home countries shape their imaginaries of Cuenca and its people. Instead, they describe their experiences by reference to a lost past that is retrieved and redeemed in Cuenca. As Brett put it, "when researching about Cuenca, I encountered a phrase, that living in Ecuador was like living in Kansas in the '50s. And it is like that." Evidently, for Brett, that content helped shape the way he organized his emotional reaction to the cultural and spatial differences between Cuenca and his hometown of Vancouver. "Life here is not as complicated," he said. It was, he said, like "Middle America when life was simple," a time "before the '60s." People didn't lock their front doors, for instance, he said, noting, on my prompting, that in Ecuador, people very much locked their front doors, which were often behind gated fences. "Go sit in any park here and compare it with any park in America. It is more tranquil and less complicated here," he said. There were, he said, not as many anxieties.

These narratives were a source of meaning for Colin, Brett, and many others, but they are implicated in global social inequalities. They misrecognize the social relations of their new home, where important cultural changes have taken place under a process of rapid urbanization and South–North migration, which have deeply affected idealized family units (Donoso Correa 2016; Escobar García 2008; Herrera 2012; Pedone 2008; Pribilsky 2007). Ecuadorians spoke about the city in very different terms and without reference to a nostalgic past like the 1950s, when a majority of the population continued to live in rural areas, in rigid patriarchal families, and often under the yoke of a racialized system of indentured labor. Ecuadorians who remember the 1970s talk about how fast the city has grown, how traffic and pollution have gotten much worse, and how violence and insecurity have increased. The idealized picture that North Americans have is based partly on their lack of language skills, but it is also produced by subjective feelings that are implicit critiques of where they have come from, critiques that are socially organized around key themes that circulate in North American culture and that are shaped by their ethnic, gender, and class positions as they come into contact with new situations in transnational space.

This calls for greater attention to what North Americans mean when they refer to Cuenca as being "like the 1950s." References to the 1950s constitute a narrative trope, similar to Eleanor Townsley's (2001) discussion of how "the Sixties" are deployed to make sense of changes in North American culture. As Townsley suggests, reference to this type of trope belies and obscures deeper political meanings as well as political cleavages that cannot easily be resolved. Different political ideologies read the 1960s differently, but the use of the trope marks a kind of watershed. Unlike the "Sixties" trope, reference to Cuenca being like "Kansas in the 1950s" is deployed in transnational space and references a time prior to the cultural and political upheavals that are frequently understood in American culture as leading to some sort of decline—one upon which cultural liberals and conservatives usually do not agree. This decline is unfurled in the meanings associated with America in the 1950s, which were widely shared by racialized white participants, whether they identified as conservative or liberal. It is a time before the decline or the loss of sacred values associated with the family, with work, or with community and local belonging.

Brett helped to put the 1950s trope into perspective and into dialogue with the culturally divisive 1960s. "Prior to the '60s," he said, "you followed a path that was largely predetermined." He mentioned his family, and how his father worked in the logging business—a normatively male industry that carried certain expectations with it. His father had worked hard and had been able to buy a Buick Roadmaster, which was just down from a Cadillac as the best car on the road. For Brett, these memories were assuring; they gave the sense of a time of safety and security, perhaps underestimating how buying a Buick Roadmaster and expressing success through material things might have been a new cultural experience for his father, one with its own joys to be sure, but perhaps also with its own letdowns and disappointments. "Then the '60s came along," Brett said, and evidently it changed everything. It was, he said, "a 'me' generation, and instead of following that [established] path, people started to realize that they didn't have to follow what their parents did. Your parents' values were not necessarily the same as your values," and things began to change. People became more "selfish," as he put it. Given that he himself had participated in these individualistic changes—illustrated in part by his own transnational mobility and adventurousness—the nostalgic idealization seems contradictory. Brett mentioned that he too had gone through this process, but he seemed to see it as an inevitable process, one over which he had had little control. He thought of Cuenca as a place that was not as "selfish" and therefore as an idealized place that was potentially morally superior to North America. "That shift," he said, "hasn't happened here. But it will," he concluded, pessimistically. Brett felt this moral decline was inevitable. "This is the age of the internet," he said, perhaps fatalistically explaining his own transformation (and transnationalism), under social forces that seemed to him to be opaque. These changes and perceptions of selfishness, however, might also be understood differently from diverse social positions.

Not all research participants bought into the ideal of Cuenca being like North America in the 1950s. Andrea, age sixty-seven, who lived in Chicago before expatriating first to Mexico and later to Ecuador, said that she was amused at some of the "newcomers," whom she felt were going through a phase that she had already passed through years prior. "I enjoy seeing their reaction and the opinions they form about how, sort of, 1950s Ecuador is,"[4] she remarked. Though she did not identify with the trope, Andrea nonetheless reproduced the meaning that it had for others. She continued,

> [The 1950s], to me, harkens back to a good time when things were more personalized and we saw small businessmen prospering rather than big-box stores. . . . And some people are delighted by going back to a time when you actually know your merchant and get called by name in the store and things are more personalized.

This imaginary of a nostalgic 1950s recalls a time before mass-produced suburbs and "white flight" from the supposed dangers of racialized poverty and crime.

Likewise, Daphney, age sixty-three, thought that Cuenca was a nice place to learn Spanish for a few weeks but was surprised to have settled there. Daphney was a retired civil servant, highly educated, well traveled, and of Afro-Caribbean heritage. She was a self-described "immigrant" to the United States and spoke about how she could not really understand what it was that her white husband saw in Cuenca. "He always liked Cuenca. I mean, for me, being from [X],[5] and because I traveled to so many countries while I was [working], I like it, but, you know, I had other plans," she said. She said she would have been happy remaining in the United States but relocated because she was convinced her husband was happier in Cuenca. The romantic ideal of nostalgic past was not something she harbored about Cuenca. As an African American, the 1950s symbolized racist oppression and segregation—not a condition to harken back to. The 1950s trope is a nostalgia specific to social groups unfamiliar with these in-justices—or at least, unfamiliar with how their own lives and memories are wrapped up in coloniality and racist exploitation. It demonstrates a cultural longing—easily perceptible in parts of North American society—for a past where gender roles were more static, where women selflessly served their families, and where nonwhite workers showed respect and knew their place. It was a time when the cultural particularities of racialized white men were not picked apart by feminist and antiracist analyses. They remained hegemonic rather than particularistic. Research participants did not often openly express investment in mid-twentieth-century patriarchy and white supremacy, but their nostalgia for the social dividends these systems avail seemed at times to suggest otherwise.

A "Constant Rub"

North American nostalgia narratives say more about North Americans than about the actual social relations of Cuenca. Moreover, they used similar narratives to allude to cultural and material differences in ways that justified social hierarchies and undermined the agency of Ecuadorians. For instance, while Ecuadorians' work ethic is frequently idealized, it is even more often associated with laziness. Prevalent in these narratives was a critique of what Lance called "the *mañana* complex," that is, the tendency of workers to be less precise than North Americans about their use of time. Sometimes, as with Lance, getting used to this different pace of life was one of the challenges that you had to accept about being in a different culture.[6] While different perceptions of time are a concern sometimes shared by Ecuadorians (upper-class Cuencanos I spoke with mentioned it, for instance), workers' practices were also often ethnicized in relation to time, such that the social and cultural roots of different ways of perceiving and organizing time were misunderstood. Paula, for instance, discussed her own frustrations with and attempts at acceptance of this different notion of time. "It's not that they're being rude, it's just in the culture," she opined. Yet this notion of culture was influenced by perceptions of race. "Maybe it has something to do with the indigenous roots," she went on to ponder, "and, just that sort of spontaneity. . . . So, the upside of that is, you could say there's less stress, but there is the stress of that, you know [*laughing*], of that, that rub, you know that constant rub." The rub Paula was referring to was the irritation of continuously having to adapt to workers being inaccurate about when they would get work done, inaccuracies that repeat the labor process of the racialized hacienda system, where, as I discuss in chapter 5, landowners inaccurately kept time to extract more labor time from indentured workers.

Moreover, even while Ecuadorian workers are idealized as hard workers, they are just as often critiqued for doing shoddy work. Esther, a retiree from Alaska, said, "Generally when workers come their work is sloppy. Take forever. Also, I mean, you get a, somebody coming to fix a certain thing, or to install, or whatever, they never bring tools. And they expect you to provide tools." Likewise, while North Americans also frequently talked about how nice and welcoming Ecuadorians are, they are also critiqued for lacking decorum. Fred, age sixty-four, from North Carolina, said, "As a general rule, they're rude. They don't know what a queue is. Don't exist," he complained, noting that Ecuadorians were continuously trying to cut him off in line. And while nostalgic gazes are often turned toward apparently "tight" Ecuadorian families, these latter are also sometimes perceived in racist ways. As one female participant from Texas related, "I've heard others say it. . . . Ecuadorians will do just about anything to get money. They will betray their grandmother or their best friend or a family member if it's about money." Thus Ecuadorian families are not to be trusted. Fred, again, claimed, "They are not friendly people, and they're not friendly to their own immediate family."

These ethnocentric narratives demonstrate the problematic imaginary that locates Cuenca in a lost American past. These tropes classify Ecuadorian workmanship, notions of time, and family as belonging to the past or as being irrational or backward. Thus they participate in rank ordering different cultural traits—traits that are often ethnicized or seen to be essential elements of an ethnically or racially defined group. This complicates North American incorporation and has real and immedi-

ate material consequences for working Ecuadorians. In addition
to reproducing elite representations of nonwhite labor power,
North Americans in Cuenca have a tendency to seek out English-
speaking help—from health care to gardening—that will abide
by their cultural perceptions of time commitments and diligence,
potentially excluding working-class Ecuadorians unaccustomed
to these cultural perceptions of time and whose time management may reflect their social position, which often requires them
to hold more than one job to make ends meet. Moreover, because
there are so many Cuencanos who have been to the United States
and have internalized colonial attitudes toward their home country, North Americans hear some of their ethnocentric criticisms
echoed by Ecuadorians. This plays into deep historical inequalities of caste and class in southern Ecuador, which often overlook
the social conditions—the hacienda and land reform—which are
quite central to Ecuadorian cultures of work, just as the factory
and industrial mass production are central to much North American and West European work culture (Braverman 1974; Thompson [1967] 1993). Because North Americans so often idealize
Ecuador and Ecuadorians as belonging to an idealized past, their
critiques often also reproduce the notion that Ecuador is in the
past, backward and out of date, and lacking in modernity.

Coloniality and the Denial of Coevalness

The temporal location of Cuenca in a past of North America's
present illustrates an evolutionary notion of history character-
istic of what Aníbal Quijano (2000, 2007) calls "Eurocentrism."
Key to Eurocentrism, for Quijano, is a culturally specific notion
of time and history, which are experienced from an ethnocentric,
European perspective as a series of evolutionary and teleologi-
cal developments leading up to European modernity, the highest
stage of historical evolution. As Johannes Fabian (1983) points
out, this notion of an apparently natural, evolutionary time is actually historically produced and served to rationalize hierarchical
social relations between European centers of accumulation (more
evolved) and their colonies (which belong to a "primitive" past),
beginning in the nineteenth century. For Quijano, this culturally

< 86 >

specific notion of time relegates non-Western groups to an irrational (or less rational) past, marked by proximity to nature,
innocence, and simplicity, as opposed to modern European ra-
tionalism, precision, and technical mastery. It is complicit, therefore, with epistemological forms of colonialism, which have been
central to the decolonial critique in Latin American sociology.
Latin American decolonial scholars argue that our worldview or
picture of social reality remains deeply invested in colonial patterns of domination, providing a rationale and justification for
the superiority of European political and cultural domination,
from the conquest to the project of "development" (Escobar 1995;
Mignolo 2000; Santos 2014). The sense of an evolutionary time
circulates broadly among lifestyle migrants and shapes their understanding of contemporary global inequalities.

The subjective experience of Ecuador as belonging to the past
illustrates the persistence of a colonial imaginary that exoticizes
and idealizes cultural difference, much as in earlier colonialist
narratives of the "noble savage," while at the same time denying
ethnocultural Others their full modernity and equal standing as
agents of social transformation. In this respect, it negates Ecuadorian modernity, placing it at a lesser stage of a development
that has been fully realized elsewhere. These white North Americans, thus, recognize themselves and their own lives as being
more evolved, a type of superiority that research participants
seemed to underappreciate in a context in which other forms of
superiority were shunned and seen as illegitimate.

Clearly the denial of coevalness is partly a product of cultural
codes founded in Eurocentric understandings of cultural difference. But it is also the product of material differences, which are
culturalized through Eurocentric and evolutionary notions of
time and history. Lifestyle migrants experience these differences
from within the trajectory of their own modernity, transported
from North America. The sensation that Cuenca belongs to an
idealized past is partly the reflection of a nostalgic sense of loss,
but it is also the product of a material process of surplus accumulation that transforms social space more rapidly in some places
than it has in others. Thus the apparent modernity of certain
spaces in the United States—airports come to mind—represents

the expression of globally accumulated capital in fixed places. This gives certain spaces the appearance and feeling of belonging to the future, of being futuristic or "modern," and is often the product of public investment, as in the case of large infrastructure projects that facilitate private forms of accumulation. The appearance of temporal dissociations is an important subjective element of the capitalist process of modernization—certain places take on a character quite different than others as they express the accumulated and pooled surpluses (cultural as well as economic) of a global market economy, organized by powerful state institutions. These surpluses permit continuous investment in ever newer, apparently more efficient or more modern productive processes, which facilitate even more accumulation.

This leaves an objective mark on place that shapes the emotional grammar of North American perceptions, often translated as a feeling of being in a "European-style" or "colonial-style" space that belongs to an idealized past—a nostalgic past with which migrants often say they fell in love. This "old-world" feel, as Paula described it, is the subjective feeling generated by asymmetrical, global accumulation, which sucks capital away from places like Cuenca, preventing the city from experimenting in social forms that might be considered more modern, and overconcentrates it in places where it is expressed in ways that are subjectively experienced as "more advanced," "more modern," or "more developed." Of course, the "colonial-style" heritage buildings of Cuenca's El Centro also reflect the pooled surpluses expressed at earlier historical moments, the products of distinct forms of peripheral accumulation, at a scale and in styles that reflect its location in the global division of labor. The potential for more value-added activity has been progressively siphoned off to core regions of the global economy. For instance, the industrialization of the textile industry, centered on Great Britain at the start of the nineteenth century, destroyed the local Azuay industry, which had supplied textiles to Peru throughout the Spanish colonial period, leading to a period of economic uncertainty and crisis in the nineteenth century (Cordero, Achig, and Carrasco 1989). At the same time, in Cuenca and in similar cities in Latin America (see Croucher 2016; Sigler and Wachsmuth 2016), the lag in new investment potential has left an urban environment that symbolizes, for the higher latitudes of the global division of labor, a nostalgic past which has become rare, destroyed by the process of modernization itself. Cuenca's "old-world" feel represents a certain authenticity, which is an inner, emotional response from the vantage point of the Global North to the diachronic cultural perception of time in the spaces of the Global South. This diachronism (or simultaneous experience of time as both past and present) understands objective cultural differences in Eurocentric terms that assign "underdevelopment" to a temporal field of sociohistorical stages and thus racializes, ethnicizes, or culturalizes sociospatial differences in wealth, facilitating colonial racism. From this vantage point, Cuenca appears to be in the past of a North American present, either trying to catch up or doomed to repeat a disenchanting process of modernization. The alternative would be to see these differences as the result of an arbitrary and unequal history of accumulation, initiated through colonial exploitation and now carried on through competition in a globally integrated market economy. This historical process of accumulation through production and trade has allowed surplus capital to pool in certain global centers, transforming them in the process (cf. Sassen 2001) and producing the sensation of temporal distinction between latitudes of production and accumulation.

The subjective experience of diachronic time is germane to the social transformations that have enabled the growth of North American lifestyle migration. A group that is culturally attracted to personal growth through intense encounters with difference and authenticity creates new opportunities for investment and accumulation through the restoration of old rental stock, as I point out in later chapters. The recovery of an aesthetic of early industrial America in contemporary hipster culture in North America also illustrates the asymmetrical accumulation cycles of late capitalist real estate markets, where rent gaps determine what neighborhoods will be upgraded for investment (Slater 2017; Smith 1996). As local real estate markets have globalized, international lifestyle marketers like *International Living* play a crucial role in "staging" cities for new types of investment, a process that is very deliberate and that permits even higher profits

(Bantman-Masum 2011; Sigler and Wachsmuth 2016; Slater 2017; van Noorloos and Steel 2016). The fetishization of certain early modern spaces is a reflection of an ideal of cultural authenticity, projected onto spaces that seem to belong to an idealized past, and perhaps all the more intensely felt given the contemporary alienation from mass-produced urban and suburban spaces in North America. Access to less alienating and apparently more authentic places has become prohibitively expensive at the higher latitudes of the global division of labor, increasing the opportunities for arbitrage in the real estate markets of cities in Latin America.

Perhaps there are also other meanings that North Americans associate with the notion that Cuenca is like "Kansas in the 1950s," a "simple" and "innocent" time before the social conflicts of the civil rights movement, Johnson's Great Society, Trudeaumania, and the Vietnam War. But this narrative seems deeply embedded in how racialized white North Americans describe the historical development of their countries, both on the liberal left and the conservative right. As one blog mentions, "those who grew up in the very early '60s or before have actually experienced two VERY different worlds in one lifetime. What used to be the standards of society for many, many decades has been virtually obliterated since then."[7] The melancholic longing for a return to that imaginary time has important implications for the possibility of building egalitarian social relations with members of receiving communities in Latin America. The energies of exoticized peoples and places may have helped Paula to find a peace in which she can express her own inner essence in a postproductive lifestyle. Yet it seems contradictory that a project of constructing a truer, more authentic self would unfold in a place that doesn't exist anymore and, indeed, may perhaps never have existed at all. No doubt, there is something about Paula's search for a more authentic way of life with which many contemporary North Americans can identify. However, their melancholic lament for a lost past elides other possible moral critiques of North American society that might stem from a deeper understanding of the roots of the crises of the 1960s and 1970s in the institutional and cultural architecture of the immediate postwar period. Such an understanding may draw attention not to a simplified moral rupture but rather to sociohistoric continuities based on exploitation and dispossession on a global scale. A deeper understanding of this as an alternative to the 1950s trope might give access to different moral critiques, perhaps ones with greater possibility of building bridges with Ecuadorians and grounded less in individualism and more in collective solidarity.

3

Gringo Identities

Stan, originally from Florida, cared deeply about Cuenca, and given his knowledge of the historical inequalities between his home country and Latin American countries, many of his conversations centered on how important it was for his compatriots to make efforts to fit in and behave as good guests in a foreign culture. Stan was seventy-two when we sat down in a Peruvian restaurant nestled in a growing entertainment area in El Centro. We had met in this area before and spoken several times about the North American community, which he had seen grow substantially during his time in the city. He was a long-timer, having moved to Cuenca several years before the financial crisis. Stan had worked in higher education and spoke Spanish fluently. He also knew Ecuador well from his days as a Peace Corps volunteer and had traveled to the country going back decades. He was knowledgeable about the history of racist oppression in Latin American societies and was also well informed about the imperial meddling that North American governments and corporations had inflicted on various Latin American countries, Ecuador among them.

One of Stan's chief concerns was the growing number of his co-nationals who were relocating to the city in retirement—a migration that changed his own position relative to the Ecuadorian society and which, he felt, potentially threatened the harmony he saw between Ecuadorians and North Americans. The large number of recent arrivals had not yet become accustomed to Ecuadorian culture and showed little interest in "integrating" or taking on the customs of their adopted city. They were coming for the wrong reasons, he said. They had no preparation and were uninterested in learning Spanish. This irked Stan, who felt, from his days in the Peace Corps, that when you were abroad, you represented your country. As he said, "I've been here a lot of years, speak the language, and, frankly, I try to present a positive image of who we are. I really am conscious of that." By "we," he specified "gringos," the identity category that most research participants seemed to use to describe their group.

North Americans see themselves as *gringos* in Ecuador, a term used there to describe phenotypically white foreigners but that can also refer to nonwhite North Americans or Europeans (*gringo negro,* for instance), such that its reference to phenotypical markers is not entirely strict. It is a racial descriptor in Ecuador and is not intended as a slur. Migrants in my research used this term to describe themselves and their community even more than "expat," and certainly more so than "migrant," which they almost never used. While the term also carries connotations to Anglo-American and European ethnicities, its reliance on physical markers and the way North American participants described being a "gringo" also underscore its racial contours. Through migration, North Americans experience their somatic difference in new ways and describe themselves in racialized terms, that is, in terms that illustrate a process of racial "subjectification" (Miles and Brown 2003). Miles and Brown refer to racialization as a process of defining racial subjects who come to see themselves and others according to racial categories that lack the stable biological or natural foundations that are often ascribed to them. In the Andean context, North Americans refer to their somatic difference in terms borrowed from North American racial formations, even as their new gringo identities demonstrate the social and contextual aspects of their apparent whiteness.

In this chapter, I attend to white racial identity formation among North American migrants in Cuenca, identities that drew heavily on North American ideologies of race. The gringoness of North American participants and their attempts to optimize it—and therefore to benefit from it materially and symbolically—were tied up with the changing signification and social position of whiteness in North America. At the same time, gringo identities participated and continue to participate in the racial formation of Ecuador, where whiteness has entirely different meanings and histories. In Ecuador, the term *los blancos* refers to the descendants of Europeans, especially of Spanish landowners from the time of the conquest in the sixteenth century. North Americans, on the other hand, are gringos in this racial formation. Given the coloniality of power and the racial system that originated with European colonialism, the somatic markers of European descent have, for centuries in the Americas, been a symbol of power, modernity, and privilege. Thus, while gringo identity formation may seem benign, I argue that these identities warrant deeper reflection.

North American migrants to Ecuador, almost all of whom are racialized as white,[1] conceived of their differences from Ecuadorians in a variety of ways, but their racialized whiteness stood out in the stories they told themselves and others about their emplacement in Cuenca. They negotiated their white privilege by policing and disciplining the behavior of the group and by excluding or marking distance from forms of whiteness that they perceived as ethnocentric, impolite, or obnoxious. In short, North American gringos were supposed to behave as good guests to facilitate their incorporation into Cuenca. Yet, in the process, they participated in material practices that surreptitiously (and sometimes consciously) reproduced white supremacy, conceiving of themselves as benign migrants whose presence could help Ecuadorians achieve a higher standard of living. Most importantly, they identified with their whiteness and with the symbolic and material privileges it represented—privileges in their home country that growing cultural diversity has changed and that social movements such as Black Lives Matter and Idle No More have challenged.

As the meaning of whiteness shifts in the United States and Canada, geoarbitrage also enables the reclamation of hegemonic and privileged forms of whiteness through participation in white racial projects (Winant 2001) within Ecuador, which reproduce colonial forms of white supremacy and exploit nonwhite groups in a city and country where those kinds of oppression might otherwise be increasingly resisted and transformed. As we will see in later chapters of this book, North Americans' migrations to Cuenca had material effects that reproduced the coloniality of power through the use and valuation of space.

Mobility and Racialized Whiteness

Participating in white racial projects in a different country was not what most participants had in mind when they relocated to Cuenca. They spoke primarily of moving to a new culture and discovering a foreign country. But Cuenca was also a place where they discovered different social meanings of their whiteness and where they developed new identities and new practices on the basis thereof. No doubt, part of "leaving one's comfort zone," so important to the way North Americans made sense of their decision to migrate (as we saw in the introduction), was also about leaving the comforts of a space where their whiteness may have been invisible. In Cuenca, whiteness is highly visible and plays an important role in social status hierarchies. Regimes of racialization and representation of racialized difference have mostly been under the control of racialized white Ecuadorian elites and their political institutions (Guerrero 2003; Mancero Acosta 2012; Roitman 2009). The migration of a significant number of North Americans brings together two ostensibly white groups, but where their whiteness is not wholly commensurable. North Americans cannot generally assume airs as landowning elites or be perceived as belonging to the same group as nonelite *blancos*, of whom there are many in Cuenca. While they may share somatic features with phenotypically lighter Ecuadorians, their whiteness is socially coded as foreign, demonstrating the contextuality and social construction of identities that are often conceived as having phenotypical and biological foundations. Participants often said they could not pass as Ecuadorian. In the racial hierarchy of Cuenca, the gringoness or white alterity of North Americans has historically enjoyed significant symbolic prestige. Moreover, North Americans identify with the category "gringo" and often describe their community in these terms, as evinced by online forums like Gringo Tree and Gringo Post, or Gringos Abroad, the Facebook group for North Americans in Cuenca. The migration of a significant number of racialized white North Americans has also affected the racialized social order of the city in ways that are uneven and often congruent with the colonial racial formation of Ecuador, as we will see in the following two chapters.

North Americans relocating to Cuenca are moving to a place where the visibility of their somatic whiteness contrasts with its invisibility in North America, as classical studies of whiteness as racial normativity have pointed out (Bush 2004; Lewis 2004). Like European lifestyle migrants moving to former European colonies (Benson and O'Reilly 2018; Fechter 2005, 2007; Fechter and Walsh 2010; Knowles and Harper 2009; Leonard 2008; Maher and Lafferty 2014; Quashie 2016b), racialized white North American migrants in Ecuador spoke about standing out, something that took getting used to. The subjective experience of being racialized as a "white foreigner"—or a gringo—created for most a new awareness of their whiteness and its symbolic association with economic and other privileges. Participants relied on racial categories or language to describe their feelings of difference, and while such categories are not the only form of conceiving this difference, they were an important way they came to understand and experience it. As Elise (age sixty-six, from Seattle) stated, "you feel like you stick out like a gringa, you know, like a white person."[2] Being a gringo or gringa gave rise to new narratives and practices, which migrants used to mediate their bodily difference and influence the character of their incorporation into Cuenca. Often, participants expressed ambivalence about their visible difference, yet at the same time, they most often identified with the privileges of being gringos. Moreover, they recognized themselves as belonging to a racialized group and repeated historical practices in North American white racial formation that imposed homogeneity based on discipline and civility and on behaving as good guests, not as "obnoxious gringos" (Hayes and Carlson 2018).

Because so-called white migrations are marginal to mainstream migration scholarship, few studies exist on how circumstances of transnational mobility modify and contextualize whiteness and white privilege (Lundström 2017). The present study draws on previous literature that historicizes, contextualizes, and destabilizes notions of whiteness (cf. Frankenburg 1997; Jacobson 1999; Painter 2010; Roediger 1991, 2005), demonstrating how racialized white identities are contextual and how they are transformed by geographic relocation and immersion in distinct racial formations (Fechter 2005; Lundström 2014). It also explores how these identities are bound up with social inequalities in countries with complex histories of class and caste, such as Ecuador. As scholars of whiteness in postcolonial contexts have pointed out, the privileges associated with whiteness are sometimes experienced ambivalently, have to be negotiated in different settings and contexts, and produce new identities that both modify and reproduce colonial patterns of white supremacy (cf. Appleby 2013; Benson 2013, 2015; Debnár 2016; Dos Santos 2016; Fechter 2005; Green 2017; Hayes 2015b; Knowles 2006; Lan 2011; Leonard 2008; Lundström 2014, 2017; Maher and Lafferty 2014; Quashie 2016a, 2016b; Walsh 2010). Much of this literature deals with the ambivalent feeling of being visibly different in ways that grant access to important social and material advantages. As Lundström (2014) points out, "moving and re-installing whiteness in different national racial systems may well improve one's opportunities in life, but may also result in the sense of being deprived of a normative and structurally invisible position" (5–6). In this respect, studies of lifestyle migration to non-European spaces demonstrate how notions of whiteness and white privilege depend upon the presence of, and interaction with, nonwhite Others—interactions that were historically key to the formation of white racial identities in the colonial period (see especially Allan 1994; Stoler 1995). Studies of whiteness in tourism attend, justifiably, to the advantages—economic and otherwise—of racialized white tourists in contexts of mobility and transnationalism (Echtner and Prasad 2004; Hill 2008; Meisch 1995). Literature on mobility has discussed whiteness and white identity formation (Lundström and Twine 2011), and scholars of lifestyle migration to Latin America, in particular, have touched on white privilege (Benson 2013, 2015; Croucher 2012, 2014, 2016). These studies often treat lifestyle migrants as bodies "out of place" and pay closer attention to racialized interactions and white privilege than to how migrants construct and negotiate new white identities. Issues of white privilege in tourism and postcolonial settings are, of course, of interest, but here I want to focus on how racialized white people in nonwhite social spaces come to recognize and grapple with their somatic difference.

Many North American research participants espoused egalitarian, antiracist beliefs that recognized arbitrary racial inequalities in Ecuador. They could potentially contest a social order highly marked by racialized hierarchies (Kyle 2000, 45–72; Roitman 2009; Wade 2010; Weismantel 2001). However, they lacked reflexivity about the power and meanings associated with their gringoness in Ecuador and, as discussed in the last chapter, about the ways their subjective experiences and feelings (of acceptance or respect, for instance) were sometimes tied to socially produced racial formations. Moreover, they generally lacked knowledge of the social movements and struggles that have shaped modern Ecuador and that contested coloniality and racist exclusion (cf. Becker 2010; Bretón Solo de Zaldívar 2008; Guerrero 2003). There were real material consequences to this lack of reflexivity that impacted North Americans' incorporation in Cuenca and their relations with Ecuadorians. North Americans in Ecuador most often positioned themselves as patrons of poor Ecuadorians (rather than as equals and allies)[3] and appeared more likely to socialize with their landlords and service providers from the upper social classes, who were phenotypically lighter. In these ways, they may reproduce the racialized caste system of Ecuador rather than seriously challenging it.

As more and more white North Americans relocate to the city, investing their own economic and life projects into the "colonial-style" spaces of El Centro and nearby neighborhoods, the social and natural spaces of the city and its surroundings are phenotypically whitened—that is, they come to be planned and developed for an economy composed mostly of those from the lighter side of the global division of labor. The economic benefits of this process of transformation accrue mostly to phenotypically white groups, as chapters 4 and 5 discuss. This constitutes an important backdrop to the development of new racialized white identities among North Americans in Cuenca and is likely to continue to play a significant role as the lifestyle migrant community matures and "finds its place" on the racialized social field of Ecuador.[4] As the next section points out, North Americans see themselves as gringos and recognize their somatic difference as an important marker of cultural and class position. The importation of racial ideologies from the United States deeply affects the way North

Americans see themselves in Ecuador and potentially reinforces the existing racialized social order.

Discovering Whiteness

North Americans discovered their alterity—of being Other in a foreign culture—in an ongoing process that took up several regimes of differentiation. One of these was the somatic difference that North Americans expressed in terms of being gringos, a racialization of their identities as white foreigners. As one woman said in a group discussion, "we stand out here like Christmas tree lightbulbs." Likewise, Joe (age sixty-six), who was tall at more than six feet, joked about how he felt he stood out physically. "What are you going to do? I'm going to stick out. I got blond hair and theirs is not." Another male retiree with whom I spoke informally mentioned that kids tended to stare at him, something that did not happen at home. Or John (age sixty-nine, from Florida), who had lived for five years in Cuenca when I interviewed him, mentioned, "[I] stand out because of my complexion, my skin, my hair, my overall 'look.' You can't hide here and you can't meld into the population. So just by virtue of that, you, you represent your, you see yourself as different from the population." For many participants, this experience was part of being in Ecuador. As Jim (age seventy, originally from St. Louis) mentioned, "one of the interesting things that happens so often, is, hey, we're foreigners, they can tell us because we're white, we're tall, whatever." He mentioned this in terms of how other North Americans felt intimidated about moving around town—something to which many participants mentioned having to adjust. As Elise's husband, Sandy, age seventy-one, mentioned, "it feels like you're suddenly isolated. I mean, it's a little bit like 'us' and 'them,'" a feeling he felt you had to try to "break through." This feeling of always being visibly Other is one of the main sources of what Paula described in chapter 2 as "that constant rub" that led many North Americans to abandon their attempts to move abroad.

Participants often described standing out as being uncomfortable or as being a challenge that could be difficult to overcome, especially since they often lacked Spanish-language skills. As one woman stated in conversation, "it is just hard being the different one all the time." She was referring to being constantly noticed as physically different and therefore not anonymous—singled out for different types of treatment that she found tiring. "One of the hardest things is sticking out," Marilyn, a Canadian woman in her fifties, told me. Here the "shoe is on the other foot" in terms of being a "minority," she added. Or as Steve, a man from Chicago in his sixties, said, "Caucasians are visible, you can identify an *extranjero* (foreigner) easily" in Cuenca. Referring to racialized white migrants from northern countries, including himself, he commented, "They are very visible. . . . You can tell when you see them, they also dress differently." According to Cynthia, a Canadian who had lived before in a country where whiteness was visible and racialized, part of the adjustment process was getting used to being viewed as different. Although it is a given that migrants would have to make certain adjustments to how their somatic features might be coded in different cultures and social traditions, some of these comments also demonstrate a racial consciousness, especially when cultural markers like dress are themselves racialized as "Caucasian," as Steve put it. While participants may have also understood themselves and their differences in more than just racial terms (for instance, they recognized ethnocultural and language differences), it is clear that their use of terms like *white* and *Caucasian* and references to physical features to describe how they stand out drew on historical traditions that have coded human diversity in terms of somatically defined races. North Americans rely on these colonially derived identities as commonsense signifiers of difference, though they are a product of diverse social projects of racial formation.

North Americans in Ecuador typically developed an awareness about what their gringoness meant in their Latin American surroundings, though this perhaps drew on their own imaginaries as much as on how they were treated by Ecuadorians. Typically, the meaning of their gringoness was, in their view, tied to perceptions of wealth and economic privilege. As one woman who lived in Vilcabamba proclaimed, "they [Ecuadorians] think we are cash cows." This was a recurring theme. As John, mentioned earlier, put it, Ecuadorians think "you're rich and affluent, and you can do what you want to do." Or as Steve put it, "the general perception has seen that Americans are more affluent, they have more resources." Stan mentioned that "gringos are perceived as rich." He paused briefly but with candor added, "Well, by [Ecuadorian] standards we are." While this is true in a material sense (the basic monthly salary for an individual in Ecuador in 2017 was $375, and many workers have more than one job to meet their basic needs), the subjective experience of being physically identified as wealthy was uncomfortable for many research participants, even though they also identified with the privileges of being wealthier.

The apparent meanings North Americans assigned to their gringoness were not only a source of discomfort but also an intense source of distrust toward Ecuadorians.[5] Migrants often complained of "gringo prices," the perceived racialized price system—one of their chief frustrations with living in Ecuador. As Michael (age sixty, a retired contractor) mentioned, "if they [Cuencanos] see that white face across the table, it is like, boom! Double [the price]. Because you can afford it, you are a rich American. You get that action quite a bit down here." Or as Clem, age sixty-three, put it colorfully, "all gringos have ATM stamped across their forehead." He felt this led to a "double standard" between gringos and Ecuadorians. Guy, a Canadian in his late fifties, mentioned, "Being a gringo is mainly about being charged more. You are going to get gringoed, because you are considered rich." Thus the meaning of gringoness extended to certain material relations, which were shaped by real and perceived inequalities and informed practices aimed at compensating for the relative material affluence of migrants. Lola, a younger migrant in her thirties, originally from Kansas, had a similar comment: "North Americans . . . are always, always also looked at to be taken advantage of, because people know they have money." She was referring specifically to retirees but acknowledged that higher prices also affected her, despite being on a lower income. While never explicitly mentioned, concern about "gringo pricing" was also obviously a preoccupation with the appearance of whiteness and differentiated treatment, which North American migrants sought to avoid. As Dan mentioned, "I know so many people, you know, who are so resentful over, over *precio gringo*

[gringo prices]. They go, 'Oh, why should, why should we have to pay more than the other people?'" There was a debate over this within the North American community, where some felt that paying higher prices led to a negative impact for others, a concern that was not unfounded given widespread perceptions among Cuencanos that the migration had led to price increases in real estate and other services (García Alvarez, Osorio-Guerrero, and Pastor Herrera 2017). However, this seemed to be due mostly to the increase in higher-income demand rather than a racialized price system per se. Still, there was a perception that overpaying affected the prices for Americans on low incomes and Cuencanos alike. John mentioned that a local woman yelled at him and a taxi driver when she saw him pay what she believed to be an unreasonable fare.[6] Not everyone, however, felt that North Americans should be treated the same as everyone else—because, of course, they are not. Dan, for instance, felt that it was morally wrong for him to haggle over, as he put it, fifty cents, stating, "I would much rather be considered a dumb gringo for overpaying than a dumb gringo for expecting to be treated like an Ecuadorian, right? I would rather line up on the overpaying side, and just circulate a little bit more currency." The concerns over gringo pricing seem to be one of the main ways that racialized white North Americans confronted perceptions of their white alterity, their gringoness, and from which they drew ideas about its meaning.

As Pauline Leonard (2008) argues, awareness of racialized whiteness in the context of expatriation is implicitly also a reaction to perceptions of white privilege. Participants in Cuenca resented these perceptions, even though in general North Americans did have access to higher incomes and more economic resources than Ecuadorians—to say nothing about the symbolic benefits of whiteness, such that Ecuadorians perceived North Americans as *tranquilo* and as good migrants, unlike others (Colombians and Peruvians), whom locals often subjected to discriminatory treatment. Although there were certainly many exceptions, the racial ideologies of most research participants differed from the unabashed white supremacy of the colonial past, as evinced in the partial rejection of racial superiority and the feelings of ambivalence and discomfort about being perceived as more trustworthy, superior, and rich. Migrants' life experiences have often brought them into contact with progressive, egalitarian, and antiracist ethics, even when these were incomplete. They often demonstrated reflexivity about being treated as superior and sought to avoid it.[7] Colin, for instance, told me during a conversation in 2013 that some of the "rural people" he had met in the market called him *patrón*, or boss, which made him feel very uncomfortable. "They see me as belonging to a completely different class," he said.

Lola, the younger migrant mentioned earlier, was in Cuenca with her partner, Jesse, where they were raising a family and working as missionaries. They also acknowledged discomfort about being treated better because they were white. As Jesse put it, "to have somebody always treating you like, like, almost like you're royalty is just—I still don't like it. It's still very uncomfortable." Lola continued, "We actually try to work against it. I mean, that's one of our goals, is to help people see that everyone is equal." But they also acknowledged that if they were Peruvian, they would not be able to do the work that they are doing. "For our type of work it was a great blessing to be white [*laughs*], North American, gringo, speak English, people don't fear you," Jesse said. While acknowledging that this respect was undeserved, the couple also recognized that they were able to gain the trust of others and work with them because of the ideas associated with their whiteness, ideas they also tried to combat. As Lola put it, "we are pretty equal with how we treat everybody." This egalitarianism included practices that middle-class Ecuadorian friends deprecated, such as inviting Peruvian migrants into their home for dinner.

At least some white North Americans, then, have developed or inherited antiracist ideals that potentially challenge Ecuadorian racial formations and caste hierarchies. But because they are also a product of North American racial formations—marked by racialized identities and color lines—these antiracist ideals exhibit deep-seated beliefs about the meanings of somatic differences that might also reinforce caste hierarchies (as with the white antiracists in Hughey 2010). The racial awareness that North

Americans developed in Ecuador had a significant impact on their incorporation and how they saw their place in their adopted city. Their physical differences brought their relative wealth into sharper focus. For some, this appeared to make them feel vulnerable and produced a series of reactions, including social isolation in gated communities or securitized condos. Yet most of those with whom I spoke engaged in another series of practices that exhibited anxiety about their racialized position in Ecuador, practices that aimed to optimize the appearance and importance of racialized difference.

Gringos Behaving Badly

While North Americans felt vulnerable to being racialized as wealthy by Ecuadorians, the effects of this realization seemed to be much broader, influencing how they negotiated whiteness as a group. As Lewis (2004) points out, white North Americans often do not see themselves as belonging to a racialized group. In postcolonial contexts, however, they do. North Americans racialized as white in Ecuador were often intensely aware of how other members of their group might also reflect on them. They worried that poor behavior and bad manners might change the generally positive reception they expected from the receiving community and negatively affect their ability to negotiate this reception individually. Stan's concern about what he called "obnoxious gringos" offers an entryway into how North Americans conceived of themselves and their alterity in Ecuador and how they made sense of the inequalities that their whiteness symbolized as they moved across latitudes of the global division of labor. I had several conversations with Stan during my fieldwork, and most of those were about his concern for people who left a bad impression on Ecuadorians. Stan described a "minority of jerks" who were coming to Ecuador with inappropriate expectations about how they should be treated. In short, they were "obnoxious gringos," a term several research participants used to distinguish between good migrants, whom they described as "guests in a foreign culture," and the bad ones, who were "wrecking it for everyone else." Stan was hesitant to use more colorful language to describe his intense emotions, but this "minority of jerks" was certainly causing him some measure of stress:

> They're so goddamn loud, and they are so visible, they make themselves visible, they scream and yell in banks. They scream. A guy goes up to the window, banging on the window, "Do you people speak English? Do you people speak English?" You know? "You need to speak English!" In a bank! Banging on the window while somebody else is at the window. I mean, just rude, obnoxious behavior. No class! No class! Probably had no class in their own country.

Stan was intensely insistent that this type of behavior must stop, because it posed a danger to the gringos as a group. This concern was shared fairly widely as the number of North Americans began to increase substantially in the early 2010s. Yet, an obnoxious gringo could potentially be any white North American. Experiences of frustration with life in Ecuador were not rare, especially in instances where migrants did not understand the language and where their more powerful social position allowed them to get away with public scenes that Latin American migrants in the United States probably would not even think to incite. In general, I did not observe specific instances of shouting or yelling— events that might be exceptional in any case. What I did observe was North Americans from different backgrounds and regions, and with different ideological beliefs—both disaffected Democrats and disaffected Republicans—who roughly echoed Stan's concerns about "obnoxious gringos," focusing especially on migrants acting out, being loud, or inappropriately shouting at service workers. They also shared his concern about the potential harm they might do.

As a Canadian, I had heard plenty about "ugly Americans" (a term sometimes also used by participants) and am familiar with some of my compatriots' desire to mark distance from Americans while abroad by doing things like putting a maple leaf on their backpacks. Because Anglo-Canadians and Americans generally sound and look alike, this is often a source of concern for the former, who do not want to be misrecognized, perhaps unaware of their own country's imperial rent seeking in Latin America and the Caribbean (Deneault and Sacher 2012; Drost and Stewart 2006; Gordon and Webber 2016), which certainly affects their reception there. Just as Canadians worry about being mistaken for Americans, perhaps Stan was concerned about how the increasing number of these obnoxious gringos, visible to everyone, might change the meaning of his own gringoness, stifling his attempts to negotiate his difference on more individualistic terms. The presence of large numbers of other North Americans might transform his gringoness from something unique and interesting into something humdrum and even somewhat of a hassle. As more and more white North Americans relocated to Cuenca, they sensed their whiteness taking on new meanings and felt that they were physically different not only from Ecuadorians but also in ways that made them representative of a defined racial group. What aroused so much of Stan's passion was not merely that obnoxious gringos were mistreating Ecuadorians but also that they were perhaps contributing to how Ecuadorians in general would see gringos as a group—a group to which Stan belonged. Thus their bad behavior potentially affected him and how he might be received. This sense of loss of individuality, and a desire to mitigate or recover it, seemed important to Stan and, indeed, to others with whom I spoke. After our interview, having finished up our meal, I walked with Stan across a cobblestoned street in Cuenca's El Centro. Amid the din of traffic, I asked him if he was concerned about obnoxious gringos because he felt that other Ecuadorians would also see his whiteness as negative. "Yes," he said. "I think that is part of it."

Policing Gringoness

The fear that Ecuadorians might develop racial stereotypes about gringos and discriminate against them was, I soon discovered, quite widespread. It led to practices of surveilling and policing other gringos on the basis of "civility" and appropriate behavior, reproducing white racial formations that have historically sought to marginalize deviant forms of whiteness (e.g., "rednecks" or "white trash") to solidify "white civility" (Coleman 2006) and white privilege (Sullivan 2014). In April 2013, a well-known, longtime North American expatriate in Cuenca sent an email to a large number of his friends, who shared it and discussed it broadly at social occasions and over social media. This email drew attention to the "obnoxious gringo," a term different research participants had mentioned several times in earlier fieldwork in 2011 and 2012, but which became much more important in 2013, as the population of North Americans reportedly continued to grow.[8] North Americans in Cuenca used the term to describe rude behavior and sometimes to denote cultural ignorance and ethnocentric notions of American superiority. Stan was part of that conversation. He and others felt some North Americans had inappropriate expectations about service in English in public places, for instance. In 2013, I heard several versions of a story about a North American acting out and causing a scene at a local bank. The story may have been real, but its wide circulation and the many variations it took on indicated to me that it functioned something like a cautionary tale, or a folk legend, whose moral message was more important than its reality. Many participants thought that loud, obnoxious behavior would potentially pollute their own presence in Ecuador, because Ecuadorians would come to think that all North American gringos behaved in this way. Prompted by the deleterious effect such behavior might have on the overall reception of gringos in Cuenca, the email asked people to take responsibility and intervene in situations where an obnoxious gringo may be illegitimately mistreating an Ecuadorian or otherwise behaving inappropriately. As Brett, age seventy-one, opined, if other Ecuadorians saw his intervention, it might allow them to realize that not all North Americans were like this, thus combating racialized stereotypes. Migrants framed these interventions as key to leaving a better impression and preserving the privileged, friendly reception that North Americans received from Cuencanos. While ostensibly based on a desire to undermine ethnocentrism and to recognize themselves as guests who had to adjust to the norms of Ecuadorian space, identifications with gringoness and the desire to optimize its meaning were contiguous with historic attempts to discipline racialized white groups so as to enforce forms of hegemonic whiteness and preserve racial dominance.

In light of the racialized subjectification of research participants, the concern about obnoxious gringos and ugly Americans was part of a broader, implicit strategy of managing Ecuadorian perceptions of lifestyle migrants. The desire to police the behavior of other gringos said more about the internalized racial ideologies of North Americans than it did about the meanings Ecuadorians formed about their gringoness. Implicitly, concern about "obnoxious gringos" assumed that the audience watching the performance of gringoness (a performance that relied on phenotypical features in the cultural imaginary of the North Americans) read individual performances through the frame of racial belonging. This appeared to be a key preoccupation of lifestyle migrants in Cuenca. Ernie (age sixty-six, from western Pennsylvania) shared Stan's concern. When I asked him about what it was like for him to be a gringo in Ecuador, he said he felt it was changing. He noticed some people who were giving him more "attitude." "I see more and more of that occurring," he said. "They're generalizing from the hopefully few, although growing number, of obnoxious idiots, to all gringos. And if they had a couple of particularly bad experiences, you can't really blame them." For him, as for others, this called for greater vigilance on the part of the North American community. There were some people, he felt, who should not be coming to Ecuador or who should be put in their place.

Similarly, Michael (age sixty, from San Francisco) mentioned how positive interactions that he used to enjoy had changed and that he now had more negative interactions in public places. "If you keep butting up to rude gringos, then pretty much you're going to consider gringos, as a whole, as being obnoxious," he remarked. This potential harm called for special forms of surveillance and control. Marion (age fifty-seven, from western Canada) was also concerned about ugly Americans:

Some people are here because it gives them a sense of superiority that they never had in their own country. And so they get here and they feel that they're finally better, and unfortunately

that comes out in the way they treat people in the service
industry, here, in banks, you know, just people, random Ecuadorians that you meet along the way, sort of thing.

Research participants consistently positioned those who felt
they were superior as illegitimate migrants who did not belong in
Ecuador and said they had an effect on Ecuadorians' perceptions
of all North Americans. "They've never met me," as John, mentioned above, put it. "They don't know if I'm an asshole or not,"
he said. "But they do know some Americans or North Americans,
that are assholes, so 'he [speaking of himself] might be one, too.'"
It is easy to identify this as a real problem insofar as many Ecuadorians see North Americans as a racialized/ethnicized group,
albeit more often in ways that view North Americans positively,
as friendly, trustworthy, and *tranquilo*, receptions that differ
from the experiences of Latin American migrants in the Global
North. Yet the obnoxious gringo controversy was also somewhat self-centered, because the concern was usually not for the
potential harm that may be inflicted on Ecuadorians, who may
be embarrassed, harassed, or confronted by a North American.
More often (but not always), lifestyle migrants were concerned
about the damage that may be done to the reputation of the
group of gringos and their opportunity to live out a project of
self-fulfillment through immersion in a different culture. Moreover, they experienced a sense of a loss of individuality, of being
treated merely as a member of a group, and attempted to mitigate this experience by maintaining its reputation. In doing so,
they also surreptitiously support investment in white privilege.
    Policing practices, based on civility and behavior that poten-
tially stratified a culturally, ideologically, and economically diverse population, provided symbolic cohesion to the group. These
practices performed group belonging and appeared to reproduce
a North American frame of "race relations," which has been challenged for constructing the very categories that structure racist
discourses (Miles 1993). North Americans' attempts to elicit good
race relations in Ecuador paralleled their experience of a color
line that predominates in North American racial formation (Omi
and Winant 1994; Winant 1999). North Americans who sought

to police the behavior of other white North Americans explicitly did so to maintain good race relations and thus sought to protect the interests of the group as a whole (which they perceived as being threatened by obnoxious gringos) or to protect the sanctity of an individualistic self-project, which was potentially polluted by the presence of culturally inappropriate members of the same identifiable ethnic group.

Maintaining good relations would enable the North American community to continue to benefit from a welcoming reception from the local Cuencano community, a reception that included access to special relocation services subsidized by the municipality and chamber of commerce and to other public funds, such as public health insurance for permanent residents and a 50 percent travel discount for residents over sixty-five years of age, legislated by the Ley de Ancianos (Law for the Elderly) and paid for with public funds. Thus lifestyle migrants policed the bad behavior of gringos in part to preserve gringoness as benign, constructive, and respectful of Ecuadorian culture. Ideas about policing other gringos to ensure good relations are congruent with the dominant racial formation of the United States, one marked by the idea that nonwhite Others in the United States should police the behavior of members of their own group to maintain interethnic harmony with other (notably white) ethnic groups. But it is also contiguous with a history of marginalizing deviant forms of whiteness so as to preserve a hegemonic whiteness that can live up to the justifications of white supremacy (Coleman 2006, 2008; Sullivan 2014). The preoccupation with ugly Americans and how they reflect on all racialized white gringos appeared to mirror North Americans' own racializing gaze toward different groups of Ecuadorians, especially those perceived as belonging to indigenous groups, of whom lifestyle migrants often spoke in essentializing terms, as though all indigenous Ecuadorians held the same beliefs or shared access to the same experiences on the basis of their ethnicity.

While North Americans imported these essentialized views of racialized groups from their own racial formations in the United States and Canada, Ecuadorians did not always share them and thus parried the notion that the actions of a few obnoxious gringos would ruin the reception of North Americans as a whole. While many Ecuadorians did tend to refer to North American gringos as a homogeneous ethno-racial group, at least some also recognized the heterogeneity of the category. "*Hay de todo* [there is a bit of everything]," I was often told when the topic came up, both in informal conversation and in interviews with Ecuadorian research participants (a group that included female service workers, male taxi drivers, and members of the professional classes of all genders). Ecuadorians appeared much less concerned about *el gringo malo*, though acknowledged that there were individuals who behaved badly. Most importantly, they did not share the view that ugly Americans might pose a threat to North American incorporation in Cuenca. Rather, the idea that obnoxious gringos were a threat was largely constructed and shared within the North American community itself, where it was intended to discipline and optimize the appearance of racialized white alterity.

The fact that North American participants feared being seen as obnoxious gringos illustrated the success of this narrative. For instance, when I spoke about the issue with Colin, he demonstrated real moral aversion to being identified as an ugly American. "I don't want to be like that," he said. "I want cultural exposure," he continued. Elise, mentioned earlier, provided another example. One day while paying her water bill in the community where she lives, near Cuenca, she said she "lost it" with people cutting in front of her in line. When she was finally served, there were others in the line who accused her of cutting in, and much shouting ensued, for which Elise felt quite badly. She lamented, "It took me two days to get over it, because I kept thinking, 'How could I have dealt with this differently?'" Her visibility as a foreigner enhanced her sense that others in her adopted community would see her as selfish and treat her accordingly, and her lack of Spanish skills left her feeling all the more ambivalent about her whiteness. Yet this discomfort was also a challenge that she and her husband, Sandy, sought to "break through." They did this, Elise said, by "pushing beyond our own little limitations," seeking out an instance that was uncomfortable and then "learning from it."

Thus, to some extent, it appears that the obnoxious gringo is also a moral boundary that distinguishes those migrants who

are "doing it right" from those who are "doing it wrong." This
moral boundary, however, refers to their own projects of self-
exploration rather than the building of antiracist solidarity and
shared projects for social justice with nonwhite people. The obnoxious gringo threatened to make cross-cultural contact more
difficult in a world shaped by North American imaginaries of the
color line. Although, no doubt, many North Americans in Cuenca
did not ascribe to white identities in this way, and were not anxious about obnoxious gringos devouring their opportunities for
"cultural exposure," this was an important line of thinking within
the North American community, one that painted the obnoxious
gringo as a threat to the group as a whole. As Michael pointed
out, "that [bad behavior] affects me, you know, and my relation to
the [*tienda*] operators, the bar people, the servers, the everything
else, because they're looking at me from their past experiences
with gringos and being incredibly obnoxious. Which makes me
angry." Amanda (age sixty, from Oregon) mentioned that there
were many ugly Americans and that it was upsetting to her. "I
mean, I'd really like to see some reason that they could just be
booted out of the country, because . . . they give everybody a bad
name," she remarked. Likewise, two men in a café that participants identified as an "obnoxious gringo hangout" were passion-
ately discussing the issue. One of them said, "It is very important
that the gringos behave," because it would have negative reper-
cussions for them and everyone else who looked like a gringo.
Thus the fear of being considered an obnoxious gringo also potentially disrupted the experience of transnationalism, leading to
emotional responses of anger, disgust, and aversion.

Identity and Racial Practice

While not all white North Americans identified with their whiteness in the same way, and while ideals of cultural openness may
well be commendable, hidden behind narratives of the obnoxious
gringo and gringo pricing was a shared identification with the
privileges of being white, which call for greater reflexivity and
critical interrogation.[9] North American identities in Ecuador,
and the practices they developed to police and discipline other

members of their own community, are informed by racial thinking, which assumes the social realism of what are in fact socially
constructed categories (Keita and Kittles 1997). Practices based
on this racial thinking and oriented toward policing gringoness
were key to North American racial formation in the context of
lifestyle migration to Cuenca. These practices were not egalitarian and demonstrated how North Americans identified with the
advantages of somatic whiteness, advantages they wanted to
retain. Policing the behavior of other migrants and circulating
a moral disdain for the obnoxious gringo operated to discipline
group members and optimize the meaning of their shared somatic whiteness.

Because of the privileged position of whiteness in contemporary global society (a position forged in the cauldron of European colonialism), identification with whiteness poses particular
problems, because it also means, to varying degrees, identification with the privileges that are attached to whiteness—in the
present case, with the open reception and friendliness that North
Americans hoped to continue receiving in Cuenca, among other
material and symbolic advantages. This renders white identity
formation, or gringoness in this case, particularly fraught. While
blackness and indigeneity are racialized categories often defined
in relation to shared histories of discrimination and oppression,
the same cannot be said of whiteness or gringoness. North Americans participated in constructing and reinforcing racial thinking
through discourses of the obnoxious gringo and through practices intended to invigilate and police the activity and behavior
of other members of a diverse North American community who
also had different experiences of being white in their home countries. These practices helped North Americans develop a sense of
being gringos and of having a shared responsibility toward other
supposed gringos. By learning to become "good guests" rather
than "obnoxious gringos," they participated in reproducing the
coherence of their group as worthy of special attention and privileged reception.

Finally, policing practices also illustrated important continuities with colonialist notions of whiteness, which produced white
supremacy by disciplining white bodies to abide by behavioral

standards that would be deserving of better treatment and consideration. In this respect, most of all, North American imaginaries of their gringoness participated in elite Cuencano racial formations that hierarchically rank bodies on the basis of proximity to European origin. In contemporary Cuenca, an English or German last name carries symbolic prestige, while students at the Universidad de Azuay and the Universidad de Cuenca informed me that students from elite or Spanish family backgrounds regularly belittle peers with indigenous-sounding last names. For Ecuadorians as well, the performance of white supremacy involves observing proper etiquette, which is oriented toward preserving the purity of European descent.

The obnoxious gringo controversy is fraught with coloniality, but it is important to recognize that it also illustrates ways in which North American racial formation is undergoing important transformations at present. These transformations include a more virulent and visible white supremacy that coexists with and is also a reaction against ever-greater cultural pluralism and ethnic diversity. While there are variations in how individual North Americans seek to elide or mitigate white privilege and white supremacy, there are limitations evident in their practices that seek to invigilate and optimize whiteness. Moreover, such practices do not address the severe imbalances of material wealth, status, and opportunity that continue to accrue primarily to groups that were invested with whiteness in the European colonial project, and from which North Americans of European descent in Cuenca continue to benefit. Rather than arresting the dispossession of formerly colonized groups, policing practices help legitimize and justify privileged settlement in a lower-income, primarily "nonwhite" location. The identification with whiteness and white civility map onto elite representations of Cuenca as the "Athens of the Andes" (Mancero Acosta 2012) and enable North Americans to participate in their project of transforming the landscapes of southern Ecuador, starting with the city's historic El Centro neighborhood.

4

Transforming the City

*There are fabulous possibilities here. . . . If traffic is reduced
and if more areas are converted for pedestrian use, I believe
Cuenca's historic district would become a world-class tourist
destination. More important, it would be a great destination
for residents of Cuenca.*

> —Pierre LeBlanc, urban planner and
> UNESCO consultant[1]

It is going to be good if they don't throw me out of El Centro.

> —autonomous street vendor,
> El Centro, Cuenca, June 2016

Around the corner from the plaza Cívica and Mercado 9 de
Octubre, in the northeast reaches of Cuenca's El Centro, is
a nondescript building, three stories tall. Its broad entrance leads
to a series of small stalls that are grouped together, almost like a
miniature shopping mall. It doesn't have any of the flashiness of a
suburban mall. Its stalls are fixed and organized into narrow rows,
packed in one with the other. A popular market for lower-income
Ecuadorians, it is a place foreigners usually do not visit, but that
does not mean that their presence in Cuenca has no influence on
what is happening here. The first two floors are mostly dedicated to
off-brand clothing and some footwear, especially imported sneakers. The items are cheap, and some may be considered fashionable
for moderate budgets. Several stalls sell jeans decorated with fake
diamond studs or tie-dye along the legs. At the back of the second
floor is a small food court serving dishes typically found in popular Andean markets and which caters to the working-class stall
workers, most of whom are women. Some tend to small children
as they work. On the third floor, most stalls are closed or empty.

< 115 >

A woman tells me that since no one comes up here, most of the people who have been assigned space on the third floor end up in the street as informal, mobile vendors. The floor houses childcare facilities. When I visited, it appeared that the older children were taking care of younger ones, much as they would in neighborhood streets. The children were playful and curious about why this foreigner had suddenly come into their space. They looked at one another, smiled, shouted "gringoooo," and ran away.

The vendors housed in this facility used to be on plaza Cívica, in front of Mercado 9 de Octubre. The city cleared the plaza and it is now an open square, or *plaza seca* (dry square), as Cuencanos call it, an allusion to urban cleanliness with a deep history in the racial and class hierarchies of Ecuadorian cities (Kingman 2006). While food merchants were given space in the basement of a remodeled market building, these textile merchants have been removed not only from public sight but apparently also from public mind. One of the women who organized vendors and resisted their displacement said that the move had not been all that bad. It was safer, she said, a message echoed by vendors in the basement of the market. She and others with whom I spoke said they appreciated the space for their kids, which they also noted was much safer. But in terms of sales, it was a disaster. "It depends on the position of your place," she said. She occupied a corner position at the front of the second floor. Other stallholders said that they had seen sales drop by about a third since they had moved into the building, and the local press had also reported that the new center needed visitors to stay open.[2]

The drop in sales had led vendors to abandon the building, built with money obtained through an Inter-American Development Bank (IADB) loan in 2006. Loans such as this, as well as other municipal interventions to "improve" or "upgrade" public places in El Centro, have sought to valorize the city's heritage by drawing tourists, lifestyle migrants, and second home investors from higher latitudes of the global division of labor. The 2006 loan was intended to "improve" the neighborhood and raise real estate values. However, ten years later, in 2016, it had yet to dispel the popular belief that plaza Cívica was dangerous. Perhaps it will eventually. But for vendors, most of whom were women on low incomes with children to support, displacement from the plaza reduced their income and their quality of life along with it. A few months after my visit to the square, violent confrontations took place there between male vendors and members of the police who moved in with riot gear to remove those who were selling in contravention of municipal by-laws.[3] Driven into the streets, the area around the northeast corner of plaza Cívica and along Gaspar Sagurima to plaza Rotary has become a small class battlefield for informal vendors, many of whom cannot continue to survive working inside or who have been displaced from other parts of the city where they used to be able to sell. These skirmishes pit opposing visions of the future of the "colonial-style" city against one another. On one hand, the business community and municipal officials see El Centro as a commodity, to be sold at the highest price in an increasingly global real estate market, shaped by the tastes of foreign tourists and lifestyle migrants. On the other, the informal vendors demand inclusion and the democratization of the city's spaces for the future of the city. This chapter explores this opposition and lifestyle migrants' role in it.

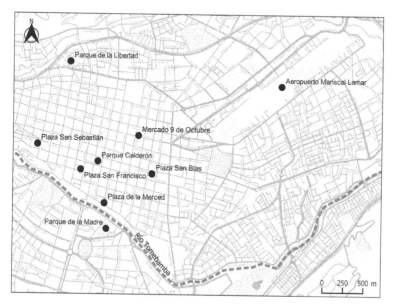

Map 3. Cuenca, main historic squares. Map by Lola Arteaga Revert.

Even if the "rehabilitation" project at Mercado 9 de Octubre and plaza Cívica is an "improvement," some have paid a heavy price for it. Aesthetically, the market building is pleasing and tourists now wander its aisles, occasionally having breakfast or lunch there. Yet it has not been good for everyone, as the situation with informal vendors can attest. Moreover, the biggest benefactors of the rehabilitation and revitalization of the neighborhood are property owners and those in positions to acquire property that is expected to rise in value in the coming years, especially as more foreigners come to the city. This is where North American migration most directly confronts the unequal social relations of Ecuador's third largest city and where the presence of a growing number of North Americans, who were financially vulnerable in their own countries, also unintentionally wreaks havoc on the lives of working Ecuadorians who have their own long history of struggles for social justice. North American lifestyle migrants have the illusion of control over their lives and emplacement in Ecuador, but this "control" is in fact a reflection of their positions at higher latitudes of the global division of labor. They experience their relocation as a sort of freedom, since their presence in Cuenca as high-income members of society entitles them to low regulation and higher spending power. Meanwhile, the projects of urban "revitalization" and patrimonialization—or the process of selecting and preserving the city's heritage (cf. Boltanski and Esquerre 2014; Franquesa 2013; Greffe 2011; Kingman 2004)—recast the lives of individuals living in very different global social positions. Working-class Ecuadorians find themselves having to move around the city as El Centro neighborhoods gentrify under pressure from the transnational tastes of North Americans and the cosmopolitan aspirations of local upper and middle classes.

Just as for workers in the Global North, neoliberal restructuring has led to increased social vulnerability for working Ecuadorians, many of them first- or second-generation residents of the urban center of Cuenca. Though many saw their livelihood improve in the resource boom of 2009–14, the collapse of oil prices increased economic insecurity again. Unlike North American migrants, who can move to lower latitudes of a neoliberal global division of labor, these workers have nowhere further to fall, and they are vulnerable to economic fluctuations beyond their government's control or ability to remediate. Moreover, they are often part of racialized groups who face discrimination in Cuenca. Many have Kichwa names and identify as mestizo or as having indigenous heritage (Kichwa being the language spoken by indigenous people). Vendors like the women in Centro Comercial 9 de Octubre may not be at the lowest rung of Ecuadorian society, but they are often not far from it. Moreover, their own aging processes occur in conditions of vulnerability. Because there is no retirement, they age into poverty if family members are unable to support them or if they are no longer able to work. The growth of tourism in downtown locations presents new opportunities but also new challenges related to real estate speculation and land hoarding.

This chapter explores how the city's manufacturing and landowning elites have mobilized heritage and the impact heritage preservation and tourism have had on popular vendors in El Centro, with special focus on plaza San Francisco, a square undergoing a similar transformation as plaza Cívica, in the heart of Cuenca's historic district. I pay attention here primarily to how some in the city have pursued heritage preservation as a distinction project grounded in European traditions, of which the landed and manufacturing elites are the chief carriers. Their project of heritage tourism has had uneven effects on other social positions, notably those of less mobile, lower-income Ecuadorians, who often work informally in low-paid, low-skilled and precarious jobs. It is easy, in a book like this, to conceive of elites as an evil monolith and as informal vendors as the downtrodden masses, but the truth is more complex. Landowners in El Centro are also a varied group with different economic agency, and often, their objectives in the neighborhood are tied up with family businesses and projects of generational social mobility in an already stratified and elitist social field.[4] Vendors, likewise, operate in a highly stratified environment, dominated by *mama luchas*—powerful market women who are charged with distributing available stall spaces—and other clientelistic networks that are not always easy to document as an outsider (but see Weismantel 2001). The growing presence of North American lifestyle migrants and the expansion of the tourist sector are the primary forces transforming business plans, family positions, and the popular uses of public space in contemporary Cuenca. A study of how these projects intersect is an ethnography of globalization, rooted in local place.

Cuenca Patrimonio

While international lifestyle marketers from the Global North have played a key role in putting Cuenca on the map for those seeking to relocate abroad, the real stagers of the Andean city are its traditional elites, the commercial and landowning classes of Cuenca and Azuay province, who now see an opportunity to valorize their property and heritage by appealing to lifestyle migrants and tourists from the Global North. The streetscapes, plazas, and architecture, which feature so prominently in this city of the four rivers, are the product of its economic expansion in the nineteenth and first half of the twentieth centuries, when small landholders were forced to supplement their subsistence through paid labor benefiting the dominant classes (Cordero, Achig, and Carrasco 1989; Kyle 2000; Mancero Acosta 2012; Palomeque 1990; Pribilsky 2007). Large fortunes also came from the haciendas of the "nobles" who dominated the land of the most productive valleys, especially Yungilla and Paute, which were important centers of sugar production and refining. There, hacienda landlords exploited an indentured workforce.

El Centro is a product of this exploitation of a rural and indigenous–mestizo labor force. It represents unevenly accumulated wealth, and those who own most of the land continue to use it to serve their interests. Cuenca's urban past also reflects the tastes and interests of an elite that practiced its own privileged transnationalism in the nineteenth and twentieth centuries, spending time especially in France, where they developed an idea of the city quite distinct from its humble adobe origins. The hard materiality of Cuenca's El Centro is a product of social relations. But so too were the distinction practices that created the built environment of the city, where claims to prestige and heritage status were molded on a hierarchically ordered field of cultural symbols (cf. Durán 2015). Cuenca's elite sought to create spaces that reflected the ideal of a more European, more modern, and more advanced urbanity than those of other Andean centers (Mancero Acosta 2012). Mónica Mancero Acosta argues that these cultural distinction practices emerged out the historic decline in economic and political importance of the city of Cuenca relative to Guayaquil and Quito in the nineteenth century. In the absence of real power, Cuenca's elites could nonetheless signal their cultural influence, and did so consistently in literature and architecture, forms of cultural capital that held significant symbolic power on the Ecuadorian cultural field, preoccupied with aping European styles and tastes (Mancero Acosta 2012; Roitman 2009). Cuenca's patrician artists and poets promoted their city as the "Athens of the Andes," a reference to its European origins but also to its literary and artistic traditions, which the city's elites celebrated as evidence of the city's vanguardist position in the early twentieth century (Martínez 2013). The exclusion of non-Europeans from the formation of Cuencano cultural fields is echoed in a civic culture where explicitly racist narratives are never far from the surface.

From the period of political independence in 1830 to World War II, Cuenca's self-proclaimed "nobles" would spend several years living and studying in Paris, absorbing the cultural tastes of nineteenth-century Europe, which they then displayed in Cuenca, in particular by building large houses in El Centro that copied nineteenth-century French neoclassicism (Klaufus 2009; Mancero Acosta 2012; van Noorloos and Steel 2016). Moreover, as Klaufus (2009) points out, these buildings copied the façades of French neoclassicism but in no way maintained their architectural techniques, which often were based on creole, colonial building forms—creating their own hybrid style whose outward expression represented European modernity in the southern Ecuadorian Andes. These styles are also a reflection of Ecuador's colonial social relations, but this is not necessarily how Cuenca's heritage urbanism is understood. As Kingman (2004) points out, heritage is political. The process by which objects are "patrimonialized" or produced as heritage is the result of social relations that often express the desires and tastes of powerful social classes. In Cuenca, patrimonialization of the "colonial-style" city was founded on the selection of built objects that reflected the transnational tastes of a landed elite, and it continues to both reproduce and mask the colonial domination of a rural and non-white labor force. As the city's 1998 application document for UNESCO heritage status argues (cited in Mancero Acosta 2012, 71),

> La arquitectura cuencana puede ser entendida como una simbiosis de fuerzas culturales, sintetizada en una misma estructura: columnas, pilastras, arquitrabes, frisos, cornisas, enmarcamientos, alfices se suman al aporte local de materiales y mano de obra indígena.

> Cuencano architecture can be understood as the symbiosis of cultural forces, synthesized in one structure: columns, pillars, architraves, friezes, cornices, and framings are joined with local materials and indigenous labor.

This apparently innocuous sentence reflects a colonial order that prioritized European architectural traditions and concepts over indigenous ones. As Mancero Acosta notes, the place of indigeneity is limited to the subordinate construction worker. European intellect is presented as the agent of cultural tradition, whereas Andean labor power is merely its instrument. Mancero Acosta further states that patrimonialization should be read as a struggle over the representation of the past and the objects that come to constitute "heritage." Thus, in many respects, the patrimonialization process—and its fixation on certain objects, places, and traditions—reflects the traditions of Ecuador's colonial haciendas, where a European-descended elite exploited non-white workers and held them in bonds of servitude.

Patrimonialization is not only an ideological process of identifying and ordering the past but also a material process of intervening in public and private spaces to regulate the way that the past appears in the present and how it is projected into the future. In Cuenca, it has involved large sums of public investment aimed at specific interventions designed to increase the heritage value of certain sites, not only by beautifying them but also by placing them into a collection of heritage objects (Boltanski and

Esquerre 2014) that can be appreciated from new, transnational standpoints. The value the municipal government, or Municipio de Cuenca, seeks to enhance is not the use value of the citizens who live in the city. Rather, UNESCO has turned heritage into a unique form of exchange value, where the city supposedly belongs to humanity as a whole and should be enjoyed by all and where the Municipio puts traditions on display to increase rents in the tourist sector. Indeed, the production and enhancement of heritage can only be profitable if there is a segment of the global market willing to consume it. In the case of Cuenca, as I pointed out in chapters 1 and 2, that segment is a growing number of North Americans looking for the advantages of a less expensive version of a European-style city. It also includes an increasing number of tourists from high-income countries in the Global North. But what fits the tastes and interests of elite social positions does not necessarily benefit everyone in Cuenca equally.

While some Ecuadorian social classes clearly either benefit from lifestyle migrants or see their arrival as a boon for the city, others are less certain of how to engage with these changes, have fewer opportunities to interact with North Americans, and are oftentimes displaced as prices and rents increase or urban landscapes take on new uses and meanings. Displacement not only means that activities and residences are relocated. It may also take place through a form of "displacement-in-place" (Mollett 2014), under the pressure of neoliberal market forces. Lower-income classes in many places experience symbolic displacement as a sense of alienation from habitual urban spaces that have been transformed to suit new tastes and new social positions, breaking popular notions of community as higher-income positions transform local neighborhoods (Atkinson 2015; Janoschka, Sequera, and Salinas 2014). Symbolic displacement occurs when the meaning and uses of neighborhoods in which lower-income people live are changed in the presence of higher-income groups. This process is now occurring in Cuenca, in ways that further complicate the incorporation of North American lifestyle migrants. To be clear, the displacement of local Ecuadorian residents is not the deliberate intent of any North Americans in Cuenca. Some see their effect as positive. As Colin, whom I introduced in chapter 1, stated, "the restaurants, for sure, are benefiting from the Americans." And Krista (age sixty-four, from Phoenix) noted, "It's helping the children," referencing charity work Canadian and American retirees perform. Other participants cataloged similar benefits. But others were more cautious and seemed aware of the potential to raise prices for the local population, a problem they sought to avoid. As Nicholas, a younger "retiree" in his forties, stated, "it has an impact on the locals that we try to be very aware of, in that it raises prices." Nicholas and others said they tried to make sure they paid local prices to minimize their impact. Daphney pointed out, "A lot of gringos, since they are not home, they want to have the type of place they'd like. They are willing to pay what people are asking for, and that really spoiled the market, not only for Cuencanos, but also for the gringos who cannot afford that." Likewise, Nicholas noted, "There are landlords, here in Cuenca, who won't rent to Ecuadorians anymore, because they know they'll get more money from the Americans." These perceptions varied within the North American community; however, lifestyle migrants were having an outsized influence on property in certain neighborhoods. Local newspaper and Airbnb listings demonstrated that an increasingly important stock of rental housing in El Centro—to say nothing of ongoing real estate developments and heritage restorations—were targeting a transnational class of renters and buyers from higher latitudes of the global division of labor.

The potential negative impacts of neighborhood "upgrading" on lower-income residents is high in Cuenca, given the great levels of inequality between rich and poor residents and the large pool of informal laborers working in precarious conditions. Yet this has not led to vocal opposition to heritage preservation and neighborhood upgrading—at least not yet. In some cases, Ecuadorian residents have also shared in the benefits of new investment in certain public spaces, such as at Parque de la Madre and Parque Paraíso, where the refurbishment of public parks has increased their use by a broad spectrum of the public from many social classes. There appears to be broad support for the transformation of an old youth prison into an open square, ironically called Parque de la Libertad, near El Centro.[5] In addition, the land along the río Tomebamba, in the heart of the city, has been cleaned up and aesthetically upgraded, such that it has spawned a significant local jogging scene that did not exist when I began my research.

According to the reports of the Fundación El Barranco, which is responsible for planning and undertaking patrimonial revitalization initiatives, the most common form of upgrading is aimed at public squares or plazas, and especially small squares or *plazoletas* (Unidad Técnica 2009, 2015). The designation of Cuenca's El Centro as a UNESCO World Heritage site led the municipality to undertake a series of interventions aimed at "revitalizing" these squares. The struggle of Cuenca's vendors in plaza San Francisco between 2012 and 2017 is emblematic of the type of displacement that UNESCO World Heritage status has helped to bring about. Other studies have extensively documented heritage-related displacement in Latin America (Bromley and Mackie 2009; Cócola Gant, Durán Saavedra, and Janoschka 2016; Crossa 2012; Durán 2015; Manrique Gómez 2013; Janoschka and Sequera 2016; Kingman 2012; López-Morales, Shin, and Lees 2016; Scarpaci 2005). As tourist spaces proliferate, lower-income residents and the vendors who cater to them are increasingly displaced toward more marginal areas of the city, which are built specifically with the intention of housing them or which have not yet been improved for tourism purposes (Arce Abarca 2016). As in other cities, municipal managers have taken a lead role in promoting the "decentralization," or removal, of informal vendors from the city's center, a policy of social cleansing that municipal governments often see as necessary to the task of promoting tourism (cf. Bromley 1998; Bromley and Mackie 2009; Carrión Mena and Dammert Guardia 2011; Crossa 2012; Mackie, Bromley, and Brown 2014; Middleton 2003; Swanson 2007). In similar fashion, over the course of my research in Cuenca, the Municipio consistently relocated the activities of informal vendors away from El Centro's main tourist areas, concentrating them in popular neighborhoods around the Feria Libre market in the city's southwest or around new popular shopping centers in poorer suburbs.[6] Working-class vendors perceive this decentralization as ruinous to their businesses and present a vision of the city and its heritage different from that of the upper classes. In the next section, I describe the projects to rehabilitate plaza San Francisco, and in the following section, I outline the meaning that vendors give to the spaces in which they work. As previous studies have pointed out, the plaza has been central to tourism development and, as a result, to processes of gentrification and displacement, which have done damage to pre-existing communities (Angelcos and Méndez 2017; Crossa 2012; Inzulza-Contardo 2016).

Plaza San Francisco

Heritage preservation in El Centro demonstrates the coloniality of contemporary urban processes in Latin America. In other words, the remainders of colonial forms of domination compromise urban "revitalization," perhaps nowhere more forcefully than in plaza San Francisco, just a block from Cuenca's New Cathedral. The cathedral is one of the city's most recognizable landmarks. Its blue domes are recognized by lifestyle migrants as a symbol of their new city, and featured prominently in *International Living*'s representation of the city as a retirement hot spot in 2009. These blue domes are often hard to see from El Centro, because the cathedral itself is crowded into city blocks that do not provide good lines of sight. But from plaza San Francisco, the domes are clearly visible, always standing out against the sky, especially when it is covered over by the dark clouds that usually come down off the Cajas Mountains in the afternoon.

For years, the plaza was laid out for uses quite different from admiring the cathedral (see Figure 3). In a city that grew significantly in size and population from the 1950s to the 2000s, the El Centro neighborhood has undergone significant changes to its built environment, its uses, and its meaning. The city's upper classes began leaving El Centro in the 1950s for new, American-influenced houses in the El Ejido neighborhood, just opposite the Tomebamba (Klaufus 2009). Later, new suburban-style developments on the urban periphery would attract wealthier social classes along Ordoñez-Lasso and in nearby Challuabamba, which would eventually be added to the city. In the meantime, it was the popular classes who moved into El Centro and who were chiefly

Figure 3. Plaza San Francisco, Cuenca, 2016, looking toward the New Cathedral's blue domes. Photograph by the author.

responsible for elements of its preservation and identity (Mancero Acosta 2012). El Centro in the 1960s and 1970s sported neon signs (now prohibited) and commercial outlets catering to the tastes of the popular classes. The result of these urban tectonics was a decreasing interest in El Centro's architecture and infrastructure until the late 1970s. When interest returned, it was not as a result of changing middle-class urban tastes but rather as the result of processes aimed at commodifying built heritage, especially subsequent to the publication of the Quito Letter by the Organization of American States in 1977 (see Lees, Shin, and López-Morales 2016, 100–103), which promised public funding for heritage preservation in historic central neighborhoods where there were apparently new opportunities for tourism development. This new context led the city of Cuenca to become more actively engaged in heritage preservation, gaining national heritage status in the early 1980s. In 1998, under the leadership of then-mayor Fernando Cordero (1996–2005), the city applied for UNESCO World Heritage designation, which it received the following year, against a backdrop of growing interest in Latin American heritage urbanism on the part of international financial institutions, especially the World Bank Group (see Rojas 1999).

Over this period, the market at plaza San Francisco had

changed, reflecting Ecuador's own urbanization and modernization processes. Although the plaza was initially dedicated to
rural agricultural products, which were sold by vendors who
would leave the plaza in the evening, the sale of manufactured
goods, especially textiles, shoes, and kitchen implements, gradually came to dominate the square, as in the 1990s the city moved
food vending to Mercado 10 de Agosto, a municipally built market nearby. The sale of manufactured goods meant new business models and uses of the space, including the construction
of permanent stalls from the late 1970s. Since the late 1970s, the
market aimed to service the needs of El Centro's popular classes
and rural workers who would come into the city to shop. Over
time, the plaza developed into a large, permanent outdoor market, where vendors often grew up and where market stalls were
handed down from generation to generation. During fieldwork,
I spoke with one woman in her late thirties who was the third
generation to work as a vendor on the square. Testimonials about
the plaza in the local media also focus on the family orientation
of the square and how children used to play there while their parents worked.[7] Until its "renovation" in summer 2017, it remained
a mix of different popular uses, bringing together not only small
vendors in informal stalls but also a parking lot, a taxi stand, informal food vendors, and an under-utilized tourist kiosk set up
in the mid-2000s. The kiosk had been primarily used as an outdoor urinal for the men who sit in the square throughout the day,
sometimes chatting, sometimes drinking, but mostly passing the
time. The public men's room, located in the center of the square,
cost fifteen cents and was maintained by a woman for whom it
was the primary source of income. The day laborers (all are men)
were especially present on Monday mornings, when the east side
of the plaza served as an informal labor market where potential
employers—offering employment in everything from large construction projects to small moving jobs—stopped by in trucks
and asked for workers. The men sometimes lined up in the parking lot and often out onto calle Padre Aguirre, where there were
frequent fights to determine who would get jobs. There always
seemed to be more workers than work. During my fieldwork, I
saw large lineups of men remain well into the early afternoon on

Mondays, having started the line at six in the morning. Workers who did not find work sometimes spent parts of the day sitting on concrete slabs in the market's parking area, chatting, hanging out, and playing cards.

Along the northern face of the plaza, porticoes provided some cover for Otavalo vendors, who have removable stalls selling Andean textiles. The Otavalos rent space along this portico from the owners of the buildings there, which were renovated in 2015–16 in preparation for the remodeling of the square. The courtyards of the old houses are now market spaces filled with traditional Otavalo craft products. The colorful fabrics draw many tourists but also a large number of local buyers looking for sweaters, shawls, and blankets made with alpaca wool. Tourists usually stroll up and down this north side of the plaza, along the portico or in the street, which is used mostly by taxis and for pick up and drop off of textiles and other products. While tourists mostly ignored the maze of vendors' stalls, occasionally a few would wander in, perhaps to get a better sense of a unique, popular urban market.

The market's colors and sites were attention grabbing, but so too were its sounds and smells. Calle Presidente Cordoba passes on the south side of the plaza, ferrying traffic away from El Centro

Figure 4. The market at plaza San Francisco as seen from above, before it was destroyed. Copyright Proyecto de investigación vlirCPM, 2015.

in a westward direction. Some of El Centro's busiest bus routes pass by here. It was always bustling with traffic during the day, and owing to its upward slope, the city's large blue buses were forced to gear up, causing plumes of black smoke to waft through the streets and sometimes into the stalls. The sounds of traffic passing over cobblestones mixed with the din of bus engines and the occasional emergency vehicle using neighboring streets for access to El Centro. It is the busiest part of the city, and when I first visited, only its informally constructed, corrugated metal walls—lined with clothing and other goods—provided a sense of intimacy and shelter from the bustle of the city all around.

There were also several aisles of stalls organized at odd angles, creating inner sanctuaries from the noise outside. Yet this sense of shelter also provided opportunities in the evenings for men to use the plaza as an open-air urinal, which the vendors tried to stop with limited success. Sometimes I noticed while walking through the market during the day that the smells remained quite intense. In the run-up to renovations, the city provided only minimal policing, so the vendors were largely responsible for the safety and cleanliness of the square, which they paid for out of their own pockets through vendor's associations' fees. The City of Cuenca provided vendors with a night watchman only as renovation work was about to begin. But this did not dispel the plaza's reputation as dirty and dangerous, a reputation that helped legitimize renovation projects, and which vendors with whom I spoke noted was a direct result of deliberate municipal neglect. This reputation posed serious challenges to the vendors, who were increasingly perceived as out of place in an area with high traffic and lots of tourism potential. Cuencano residents generally said they believed the renovation of the plaza would clean it up.

Renovating the Plaza

Plaza San Francisco is a product of recent historical shifts in the demography and business models of popular markets in El Centro, but its importance in the center of the city's historic district has also put it at the forefront of several "revitalization" efforts involving new public building projects. Some of these preceded the UNESCO World Heritage designation,[8] but an agreement between the city and the IADB to fund a site-specific revitalization project accelerated planning for municipal intervention in the plaza beginning in 2006 (Inter-American Development Bank 2006). Between 2006 and 2016, architects submitted four plans for urban revitalization of plaza San Francisco, all of which faced significant opposition from different quarters and for different reasons—most notably from members of the architectural community, from UNESCO, and especially from the plaza's vendors. Although the details of the plans changed slightly between drafts, all called for more green space in the plaza and the removal of parking, taxi stands, and the permanent vending posts. Vendors consistently opposed these plans, arguing that they had a right to work and drawing attention to the negative effect a move off the square would have on their business. This opposition blocked an initial plan put forward by the mayor, Marcelo Cabrera (2005–9, 2014–19), and then again when mayor Paul Granda (2009–14) offered a similar and widely criticized plan in 2012 (Páez Barrera 2014, 107–19), which would have created underground parking and vending spaces.

In 2014, a new planning process for the plaza began under the second mayoralty of Marcelo Cabrera. This time, architects drew up "preplans," on which they would consult with the public before submitting a final plan. The public, the architectural community, and the mayor rejected the first phase of the plan, released in 2015, for aesthetic reasons. Vendors, who were not included in the design of the open plaza, also opposed it. The second phase of the plan, released in 2016, was also criticized, but in light of a tight funding deadline from the Banco del Estado, which agreed to provide $6.8 million for the revitalization, there was greater willingness to accept a compromise plan that met key demands from resistant vendors, who threatened to hold up construction. This was a key advantage for vendors, who nonetheless did not want to alienate public support by appearing to be opposed to any form of "improvement." Moreover, city councilors pushed for concessions in favor of recognizing the "intangible" heritage of popular uses of the square. In this context, a compromise was reached in June 2016 that would reduce the overall amount of space vendors used in the plaza but would leave them with fixed stalls on its outer rim. However, the city would be able to remove these "fixed" stalls for large public events, festivals, and concerts. The ultimate design of the stalls thus clearly prioritized the municipal government's desire to make them more ephemeral.[9]

Despite the compromise to recognize popular uses of the square, the city's revitalization initiative is steeped in the developmentalist discourses of improving the square from the standpoint of higher-income groups, especially lifestyle migrants. Moreover, it largely neglects the unique popular identity that the plaza and El Centro have developed over the last sixty years. Rather than improving business conditions for the small vendors who occupied the plaza, the city is instead attempting to produce a neighborhood that would better cater to the tastes and business opportunities of the tourism industry. The loan agreement between the Municipio and the IADB for the renovation of the San Francisco and 9 de Octubre sectors clearly illustrated the marginalization of popular activities in El Centro. It explicitly justified intervention to remove vendors on the expectation that "improvements" to the neighborhood would help appreciate 680,000 square meters of prime El Centro real estate by $23.2 million. According to surveys the IADB conducted as part of the loan proposal, local real estate agents expected real estate increases of 20 to 30 percent in the area, and the bank estimated that 15 to 22 percent increases would ensure the profitability of the loan (Inter-American Development Bank 2006, 29). While there were provisions for childcare space and bodegas to store goods offsite, it is not yet clear that the renovation of the square will be beneficial for vendors if their businesses are not able to survive the disruption, which includes their temporary removal to an adjacent street while the changes are made. As Hector, a food vendor, mentioned, his costs will remain the same during construction, even if he expected that his sales would suffer. During fieldwork at the market in its temporary location along calle Padre Aguirre, vendors spoke about having to make do with less. Just as Gago (2018) suggests, neoliberal urbanism challenges informal vendors to improvise new forms of calculation. When I asked Dolores,[10] a woman in her early sixties, how she was doing with the drop in business as a result of the "renovations," she said, "You eat less, and you don't waste anything." She and her husband, neither of whom had pensions, had stopped eating dinners. Another man in his seventies, who said he had no desire to retire from his work as a vendor, asked, "Where do we eat if we don't work?"

Fighting for the Right to Work

When I first began doing fieldwork on plaza San Francisco in April 2015, the vendors were facing imminent eviction for a municipally contracted construction and architecture firm to begin work on a *plaza seca,* which vendors called a *plaza muerta,* or "dead square." Vendors at this point said they had not been consulted about any changes and were going to be removed to adjacent buildings, or perhaps away from El Centro altogether. Yet not all vendors were treated equally in the initial phases of this process. Mayor Marcelo Cabrera's administration at first tried to divide workers, especially along ethnic lines.

The Otavalo vendors along the arched portico of the north side of the plaza have businesses that cater especially to tourists. Their traditional textiles and artisan products represented the tourism industry's "authentic" presentation of an indigenous Andean space.[11] During fieldwork in 2015, Otavalo vendors said that they had been consulted about moving into an adjoining building to allow for the renovation of the square. By contrast, vendors in the center of the market, who catered primarily to working Ecuadorians and who identified as mestizo, said they had not been consulted. "[The city] just tells us what they are planning," said Deyci, a woman who sold sneakers and shoes at a busy stall. She said she had heard about the plans in the media, but no one from the Municipio had ever stopped by to ask her about the changes. Just across the aisle was Mauricio, helping his wife, Patty, at her stall. Mauricio wore a red jumper and looked to be in his forties. "Remodeling is unjust," he told me. "They say the city wants something better," Patty said. In the absence of consultation, the vendors formed a central committee to help ensure unity and, with limited means, took up the task of saving their jobs and their workspace from the wrecking ball.

Their resistance to unpopular renovation plans proved some-what successful. They took advantage of a $6.8 million funding deadline from the Banco del Estado and forced the city to make compromises that would protect their right to remain in place and to continue to work in the square. However, those com-promises may prove to be temporary. Initially, the city wanted to retain a right to remove vendors' stalls for mega events, but ultimately vendor opposition made the city back down so that they could begin intervention work in fall 2016 and stay on schedule. (The bulk of the work did not begin until July 2017.) The vendors were also under intense pressure to reach a com-promise, because public support was crucial to their remaining in place, and the public supported improvements for the area. *El Mercurio*, one of the local newspapers, echoed the argument of some members of the city's architectural community, writing that vendors had an obligation to respect the "specifications of a technical character that the project contemplates"—that is, the installation of smaller, removable, mobile stalls, a nonstarter for the vendors who participated in this research. As the editorial in *El Mercurio* argued, "all citizens" had an interest in maintaining the "proper heritage characteristics of a historic center like Cuen-ca's. A UNESCO World Heritage designation requires maintain-ing spaces in accordance with these heritage characteristics."[12] Fitting the vendors of a popular market into the "authentic" colonial-style city that the Municipio has prioritized over several administrations has proven a challenge.

Vendors used UNESCO's technical rules strategically to sup-port their own interests, as in 2012–13, when they opposed the construction of an underground shopping facility. However, key to the vendors' campaign has been to fight for their right to work. They acknowledged early on what public opinion and the media had already decided: that the plaza was in need of improvements. But at the same time, they refused responsibility for the poor state of affairs. Research participants from San Francisco's mar-ket mentioned that responsibility for security and cleanliness had been loaded onto them, as the city gave up administering the plaza and even stopped charging rent in the early 2000s in prepa-ration for a campaign aimed at convincing the public that vendors had no right to the square. As Edison put it, "everything was passed on to us." Therefore municipal administration and regulation of plaza San Francisco were largely absent. This created space for the development of forms of self-organization and workplace hierarchy that differed from those of the traditional economic and municipal establishment of El Centro. The project to "revitalize" the plaza clashed with the interests of informal vendors who had self-organized to produce some level of order over the last four decades. And while vendors wanted to maintain autonomy, they seemed willing to allow the state to reenter their space and provide greater regulation to improve security and cleanliness if it would help improve their lives and their businesses.

The Municipio's approach, by contrast, was most often to try to marginalize vendors and define heritage in ways that excluded popular social classes. Ultimately, the city reneged on its commitment to make stalls permanent in early 2017, unveiling a design for semipermanent vendor stalls, consisting of fixed posts with retractable shelving. Retractable shelving will allow the city to make alternative uses of the square and make informal vendors' livelihoods more precarious than ever. Shops that sell traditional Andean clothing, such as women's *pollera* or dresses, and other accessories traditional to indigenous and mestizo groups are also threatened with relocation as gentrification along the plaza has the effect of removing workers who buy these products and replacing them with North American and European tourists. The Municipio has not fully accounted for the potential long-term impact of revitalization on the identities and cultural practices of indigenous–mestizo Cuencanos. Cuenca Patrimonio remains primarily a distinction strategy, one aimed at receiving recognition for European architectural traditions from higher latitudes of global society.

The Meanings of the Market

For the city, the market at plaza San Francisco was an eyesore. But the plaza itself has potential to become a major tourist hub, as urban planners and real estate speculators like those associated with UNESCO, *International Living,* and Cuenca High Life frequently point out. The city and the Ecuadorian government are keen to increase tourism revenues and are spending public money on projects that enhance tourism infrastructure. Ecuador, like many lower-income countries, is dependent on extraction of natural resources for much of its wealth, and tourism is seen as an opportunity to diversify local economies, even though in many respects tourism also consists of packaging and exporting a certain image of the country that services foreign needs. Ecuador has invested significant funds into its expanding tourism industry in recent years, with the central government aiming to double tourism revenues between 2015 and 2020 and to make the tourism industry the most important economic sector behind oil extraction as soon as 2018.[13]

Cuenca's El Centro is an important piece of the national tourism puzzle, as evinced by the national government's investment in new light-rail infrastructure designed to improve traffic flow but also to further deepen the "old-world" feel of a city that looks to European centers for its aesthetic inspiration.[14] The national government and bilateral development agencies have also played important roles through investment in a number of other heritage preservation projects and through leveraging municipal loan agreements, mostly with the intention of boosting the value of heritage properties in El Centro.[15] Cuenca Patrimonio represents the values of Cuenca's elites, but it also represents the developmentalist agenda of international financial institutions, who have extended loans for the plaza San Francisco reconstruction through the national government's Banco del Estado and have been actively involved in other urban "rehabilitation" projects. From the standpoint of financial institutions in the Global North, the tourism trades, and UNESCO, renewal of plaza San Francisco offers a "fabulous opportunity" primarily to increase business activity and rents along the plaza, putting it to work for the country's current account and financial needs, which were strained after 2014 by the decline of international oil prices. In this way, too, the mobilization and valorization of heritage in Cuenca serve to integrate its land and labor force more fully into regimes of accumulation that serve financial interests in the Global North. From the vantage point of international finance,

Cuenca's heritage is a resource that can be monetized, drawing it further into the tourist gaze of *International Living* and the tastes of transnational lifestyle migrants.

In this respect, the renovation of plaza San Francisco demonstrates fluid lines of continuity with a colonial past that marginalized popular classes, such as independent vendors. The city's attempts to persuade vendors to accept the redevelopment of plaza San Francisco in 2015–16 took the form of small concessions, such as allowing vendors to have display stands along the edges of a renovated plaza. Yet, as clashes in December 2016 at plaza Cívica suggested, there is always the possibility that the state will use violence to enforce the touristification of the city, as it has in Quito, for instance (Middleton 2003; Swanson 2007). At the root of popular marginalization in the remodeling of plaza San Francisco is the unspoken developmentalist goal of increasing the relative exchange value of the plaza, which is explicit in the loan proposal between the IADB and the municipal government. Their goal is to increase real estate values, which will make El Centro less affordable and less useful for popular classes, whose wages are not intended to increase proportionately. Creating spaces more attractive to higher-income individuals can sustain higher-income activity and generate higher rents and real estate values. A similar square that was renovated in 2010–11, plaza de la Merced, now boasts a café and terrace, kept dry with a generous awning. It is among the most popular foreign resident hangout spots in El Centro at time of writing and is at the center of much of El Centro's nightlife, along calle Larga and calle Honorato Vázquez. The city regularly makes use of the small open area in front of a church there for musical concerts and other cultural performances aimed at tourists and foreign residents. One can see the potential for similar types of businesses in plaza San Francisco, given its perspective on the cathedral. Indeed, the city's proposal for removable stalls for vendors stems from its explicit desire to use the square for cultural events and concerts.

The developmentalist needs of the state perfectly align with those of private business in Cuenca in this case. Ecuador's tourism ministry works to increase the value of the tourist sector, which is one of the main motivations for the remodeling of plaza

San Francisco as well as other projects all around Cuenca. This has knock-on effects on other industries, particularly initiatives aimed at making Cuenca a conference and events destination capable of leveraging its heritage status to bring in new businesses, including a proposed Sheraton Hotel and conference center.[16] Although there are private economic interests behind these proposals, the public necessity of generating foreign exchange revenue is also an unspoken logic in the redevelopment plans. Foreign spending in Ecuador enables the government to import products from abroad, helps service foreign loans, and participates in developing the country through large infrastructure projects, which were the hallmark of Rafael Correa's Revolución ciudadana (Houtart 2015). Even in a dollarized economy, Ecuador remains dependent on being able to bring in enough dollars to be able to maintain its monetary mass and keep its economy running. In light of large current account deficits in the 2010s, the Correa government was obliged to borrow dollars, primarily from China, which asked for mining concessions and large infrastructure projects aimed at extractive industries in return. Urban "place making" fits within a developmentalist vision of space, wherein the meaning of a location like plaza San Francisco is bounded by the possibility of increasing its exchange value as a tourist destination.

Yet the meaning that the vendors give to plaza San Francisco is quite different.[17] When asked directly what the plaza meant for them ("¿Qué significa la Plaza para usted?"), research participants who were vendors in the plaza responded immediately, linking the square to feelings of home. Vendors talked about spending their whole day at the square and raising their kids there. "They did their homework here," Edison said of his own kids, sitting across a small table in a stall that sold sunglasses and schoolbags. Another man who sold leather belts, Julio, perhaps in his late fifties or early sixties, said the plaza "represents a whole life of work and sacrifice." Raúl, a clothing salesman who occupied a leadership position among the vendors, said, "All our life is here; our businesses are our daily sustenance." Another clothing salesman, Jorge, forty-seven, said, "We have our families to maintain." This was never a "plaza seca," he said; there has always been commerce there. Gloria, who sold shoes, said that for her, the plaza was a second home, and despite its appearance—which she thought could be improved—she did not want to leave. Her business, she said, would not be viable if the Municipio forced them into smaller stalls. "Plaza San Francisco, for me, it means the place where I, practically, I live, I spend twelve hours a day working here," she said. Yet another woman, Ana, who sold children's dresses and baby blankets, said that she had grown up on the square and been there since she was two. While some may think of a public plaza as a poor place to grow up—some of my middle-class contacts in Cuenca seemed to think so—Ana was a shrewd businesswoman who learned her trade from being around the market as a kid. With great sincerity, she said, "Plaza San Francisco is my whole life, it is the place where I work, I spend almost all the time here, from six in the morning to ten at night. It is more like my home than anything else." Faced with the possibility of displacement, these vendors quite naturally sought to defend their right to work, as though they were also defending their own dwellings.

Many other research participants identified strongly with their work on the square and saw it as being a principal part of their lives. Jorge admitted to spending so much time working at his stall that he wasn't sure what to do with his time when he wasn't there. "A break is a break without pay," he intoned. Gloria echoed this, saying that the vendors liked to work. While this might be an exaggeration for some, it certainly seemed true for Gloria, who had a lot of social contact on the square and who said that work gave her an opportunity to interact with the public. Most of the vendors on the square were heavily in debt. Their merchandise was provided on consignment, so they had to repay debt on a monthly basis. However, they maintained greater control of the labor process than many other workers, particularly those in retail chains. Workers largely decided for themselves the organization of their space, their work schedule, and its pace. The meaning they gave to the space was thus imbued with notions of community and home, lacking the sharp distinction between work and home typical of capitalist wage workers.

For Julio, the people who wanted to make "radical" change were the *gente de dinero* (people with money), who weren't coming to the mercado in plaza San Francisco anymore. According to him, *gente de dinero* did not recognize the plaza as a community for the vendors, nor did they seem to appreciate the importance it had to the lives of the people who lived there. For many research participants who grew up on the square, the market held fond memories. Mauricio, interviewed in 2015, said, "This is our way of life. We educate our kids here," echoing a theme many others stated. Children who were too young to go to school played together among the stalls or the parked cars. Often, working parents looked after them from their stalls and were able to supervise them in a community where all members knew one another—not terribly different from the conditions in which children were supervised at the facility near plaza Cívica. For the vendors, plaza San Francisco was more than just a place where they plied their trades. It was also a community where everyone knew one another and with which they identified. Vendors initially gained public support for their right to work through these community networks and thus were able to lay claim to a right to stay put.

At time of writing, the city had moved vendors off the square and destroyed their stalls to make way for renovation.[18] The plan for new stalls dramatically reduces their presence on the plaza and the potential for retractable shelving units facilitates alternative commercial uses of the square (see Figures 5 and 6). These changes stand to be detrimental to the business interests of informal vendors, whose desires were largely marginalized or ignored during the run-up to renovations. Gloria mentioned that a smaller stall would deeply affect her business selling footwear. She did not feel that she would be able to have enough merchandise on hand to service clients, a concern others echoed. Vendors felt the changes would diminish the character of the popular mercado that had developed there. "It is better than a mall," Julio said. "You can bargain for prices here. . . . People will always need an affordable market." It also threatened to change and reduce popular uses of the square, including foot traffic through the area. Municipal planners and local architects undervalue this "social heritage," which may potentially affect the neighborhood in ways not easily tangible in dollars and cents. Despite the intrinsic value this space has for lower-income people, they lack symbolic power within important state institutions, which are organized to support the developmentalist goals of generating higher rents. Higher rents threaten to marginalize the large number of informal workers in Cuenca's El Centro as space is appropriated for uses by higher latitudes of the global division of labor.

Moreover, the vendors of plaza San Francisco face new challenges relating to how Andean markets have changed in recent years. In an age of globalization and the global circulation of inexpensive imports from China or knock-offs produced in other small manufacturing centers, the relative affordability of goods sold in popular markets like the one in San Francisco has declined. Spending, even for lower-income groups, has shifted from small vendors to larger retailers, like the Ecuadorian big box chain Coral, a situation abetted by the suburbanization of the city since the 1980s and the tremendous growth in personal automobiles associated with it (Hermida et al. 2015). Both the expansion of suburbs and the development of new retail businesses are controlled by firms owned by elite landowning families, the "nobles" of Cuenca, whose wealth came from exploiting rural workers, as

Figure 5. Plaza San Francisco, Cuenca, July 2017. Photograph by Israel Idrovo.

we will see in the next chapter. The middle classes tend not to go to popular mercados anymore. Instead, they shop in the city's suburban malls, particularly Mall del Río in the city's south.[19] They do their grocery shopping at Supermaxi, the supermarket that has several outlets in different middle-class neighborhoods to the west and south of El Centro. Supermaxi also sells inexpensive household implements that were available at plaza San Francisco, including pots, pans, kitchen utensils, and clothing. Moreover, El Centro has been progressively hollowed out of its population, especially those on lower incomes, who seek cheaper rents at the city's outskirts, in rural areas like Tarquí and Chilcapamba in the city's south, or north in Hermano Miguel and along the río Machangara. The population of El Centro is now about sixty thousand,[20] considerably less than it was in the 1960s and 1970s. This has exacerbated the challenges informal vendors face as they try to remain in place.

The vendors of plaza San Francisco were not alone in their struggle with the city for a permanent space to do their work. Crackdowns on "itinerant" vendors and peddlers, who refer to themselves as autonomous vendors (comerciantes autónomas), have occurred off and on for years. These autonomous vendors, lacking a fixed stall or position, usually circulate through the city, selling in the street. Owing to remodeling of small squares all over El Centro as part of the urban renewal process led by Fundación El Barranco, autonomous vendors who were mainstays on the streets of Cuenca have been increasingly marginalized in an economy that does not provide sufficient opportunities outside informal and precarious work. Displaced from these plazoletas, they have been moved to streets or other parts of the city where their itinerancy is more visible and where they are more vulnerable to police harassment. Many of the autonomous vendors with whom I spoke were from rural areas around Cuenca and depended on selling produce from their small farms to meet their needs. They carried on the traditions of rural workers, who sought to supplement meager incomes by selling to the townspeople, usually at low prices, reflecting the value of their position at the lowest rungs of the global division of labor. Urban "revitalization" for tourism purposes, however, increasingly mar-

Figure 6. Plan submitted by Boris Albernoz Arquitectura for plaza San Francisco. http://www.borisalbornoz.com/proyectos/plaza-san-francisco/. Copyright Boris Albornoz Arquitectura.

ginalizes and oppresses these vendors, whose traditions are not included within the frame of "heritage." Their place within the city as informal salespeople is now increasingly criminalized and excluded. A man with whom I spoke who led one of the associations representing autonomous vendors said they wanted to be given fixed stalls somewhere in El Centro. "But the city has to take us seriously." He said he wanted to have a location in the center that would be good for business. He did not want to be moved to the outskirts of town where there was less traffic, a relocation the city nevertheless proposes as the ideal location for street vending.[21]

Displacement in Global Perspective

Plaza San Francisco illustrates that not everyone has an equal place in the vision of Cuenca Patrimonio. As elsewhere in El Centro, the meaning of space is being recoded to cater to the interests and imaginaries of foreign lifestyle migrants, tourists, and elites, whose heritage is preserved often through the marginalization of other traditions. The touristification of the square has the potential to displace vendors' work from the neighborhood that has fostered it for several generations. In turn, their displacement—even in the partial form evident in the mid-2010s—transforms the type of social space that they themselves have produced in their neighborhood (cf. Lacarriu 2016). Plaza San Francisco has a long history as a point of intersection between an indigenous, rural countryside and the urban white–mestizo marketplace (see Páez Barrera 2014). Local research participants noted that the plaza had a long history as a marketplace for rural produce, though some disagreed that this tradition was coterminous with its contemporary commercial uses.

The coloniality of urban renovation in El Centro is evident from the phenotypical whitening of uses proposed for areas like plaza San Francisco. The popular, somatically darker uses and traditions of the plaza are being displaced to make way for higher-income activity, corresponding to the phenotypically lighter centers of global accumulation. Popular commercial traditions are discarded in favor of European-oriented traditions, especially El Centro's built heritage, which represents colonial relations of exploitation. Contemporary social relations from lower classes that have developed around this aging architecture are easily cast off, their heritage destroyed to make way for heritage that fits UNESCO's colonial collection. The popular appropriation of plaza San Francisco as a market for manufactured household goods reflects recent urbanization, the transformation of indigenous and mestizo identities, and a history that includes state-led policies of import substitution industrialization. Vendors may also view their traditions as worthy of preservation, but their understanding of the space focuses more on work and daily life than on leisure and the authenticity of "old-world charm." The vision of plaza San Francisco put forward by municipal urban planners and the Universidad de Cuenca's architecture department would create a European-style open square that would fit European consultants' visions for the tourist potential of the city. Heritage revitalization under a neoliberal tourist gaze leaves little space for the open development of popular traditions, but it does not negate popular resistance. As Gloria, the shoe vendor, said, "they want a European-style plaza . . . but this is not Europe."

Heritage elites, many of whom come from privileged social

positions in Ecuador, envision heritage spaces in terms of an authentic past that must be preserved (cf. Páez Barrera 2014). While these elites often oppose free market forces that would drastically change heritage spaces, or destroy them in search of higher rents and lower-cost construction, they also often reproduce essentialized notions of indigeneity and traditional relations of domination. Páez Barrera, for instance, notes critically that the churches in plaza San Francisco and plaza San Sebastián open onto the street and not onto the square, leaving one with the impression that the traditionally indigenous market squares were used as outdoor chapels, because indigenous people were excluded from the churches themselves. However, his vision of the patrimonial square that supposedly respects the authenticity of its colonial, indigenous past reproduces the exclusion of lower-class members from the social spaces of the heritage city.

In this respect, the renovation of plaza San Francisco encapsulates the traditional Andean social relations of domination and exploitation that have long characterized El Centro and that have prevented many indigenous–mestizo workers (whether agricultural peasants, formal laborers, or informal laborers) from gaining a foothold as equals in the highly stratified colonial city. San Francisco's vendors, many of whom are perpetually in debt to pay for merchandise they buy on consignment, depend on their market for their own livelihood. As Edison put it, "the work we do is all we have, it is how we provide for our families. If we don't work, the quality of the bread we bring to our families suffers." Moreover, the social life the vendors help produce is jeopardized by a revitalization process that focuses on commercial value rather than social relations. The city's plan to privilege tourist-oriented artisan trades potentially saps the square of its function in the daily lives of the neighborhood, further gentrifying it and contributing to higher rents. This is one of the reasons why popular classes who live in the neighborhood have been quick to defend the square and also to criticize other aspects of the city's urban renewal process, including the construction of the tranvía. The potential for further displacement of popular classes and informal activities from El Centro is high in the absence of public policies that seek to eliminate inequalities of wealth and their expression in social space. Heritage preservation and tourism development seek higher rents, worsening conditions for informal and low-income workers. There can be no clearer example of accumulation by dispossession than the renovation of plaza San Francisco, which expressly benefits real estate interests and landowners.

Ultimately, this process of accumulation by dispossession seems innocuous enough to those who participate in it. North American migrants conceive of their impact on the city as minimal or even beneficial—they provide jobs and income, for instance. Yet their desire for colonial-style urban spaces and their taste for urban improvement participate in urban agendas that potentially raise rents and displace lower-income groups. The transnationalization of El Centro real estate under the impetus of lifestyle migration poses a particular challenge if new arrivals insist on "improving" urban spaces (or identify with those improvements) rather than fitting in, making use of what already exists, and fighting for greater redistribution of wealth and global social justice. The higher incomes of North Americans participate in recoding the meaning of the past in a city where colonial style is an aesthetic object that elides the brutality of colonialism.

Urban improvement in Latin America has focused on the role of the state (Janoschka and Sequera 2016), which is certainly evident in the patrimonialization of Cuenca, where landowning families have traditionally also dominated public administration (Palomeque 1990). However, the transnationalization of real estate markets also offers Latin American cities and nation-states with developmentalist incentives for arranging spaces for surplus extraction, much the way that early-twentieth-century fruit corporations rearranged the plantation economies of Latin America. State-led gentrification in Latin America is contiguous with colonial forms of domination of land and labor power. The removal of popular vendors from plaza San Francisco fits within a long tradition of symbolically and materially arranging Latin American social space in colonial, extractivist patterns, geared toward higher rents earned through trade with higher latitudes of the global division of labor. The global scaling of social space in the Latin American city reproduces the colonial pattern and thus accentuates existing inequalities rather than reducing them.

Such outcomes are anathema to the intentions of research participants, who generally hoped their effect on local price levels was minimal. As Jim (age seventy, from St. Louis) mentioned, "I think that most of us hope that [our impact] is quote, positive."[22] North American lifestyle migrants almost always showed good intentions toward local Ecuadorians, especially those whom they perceived as being the "deserving poor," that is, in poverty through no fault of their own. They wanted to help them get ahead in life. Yet the presence of higher-income migrants in the urban space of the Global South is a potential danger to lower-income residents in conditions where the former are unable (or unwilling) to integrate economically with lifestyles common at lower latitudes of the division of labor. As noted in chapter 1, North Americans identify with the material benefits of living in a "cheap" country. This economic comfort, however, exists through the exploitation of inequalities that have accumulated from the colonial period and reproduces colonial forms of dispossession—I emphasize, completely outside the remit of individual intentions. Economic forces do not require individuals to recognize their real impact to remain real.

Research participants who sold products at plaza San Francisco did not have retirement packages or social security. The seventy dollar monthly Insituto Ecuatoriano de Seguridad Social (Ecuadorian Social Security Institute; IESS) payment for the public social assistance program was unaffordable for many, according to Edison. Their situation contrasted with those from higher latitudes who have come to live with them. And an increasing number were displaced toward the city's outskirts. Vendors mentioned that they grew up within a block or two of the square, often in houses that have now been renovated and where rents are now out of reach. Alicia (Julio's wife) said that her family lived in El Vado, within a short walk of the plaza, as did many other families who worked in San Francisco while she was growing up more than thirty years ago. When she was fourteen, she said, her family moved farther out to take advantage of cheaper rents.

Likewise, Hector, a food vendor in the square, said he lived in Salado, *en las afueras* (on the outskirts). Edison also mentioned that his family now rented outside the city, where it was more affordable, demonstrating his own sort of geoarbitrage within the city whose social life has been animated by the market where his family lived and worked. Others stayed but acknowledged that renting in El Centro was very expensive. One woman, who tended the bathrooms in the middle of the mercado, mentioned that she stayed only because her daughters studied nights and she was worried about their safety over a long commute and whether they would be able to get back on the buses in the evenings if there were delays.

These displacements due to rising costs of living in El Centro hit Cuencanos from the popular classes particularly hard. Urban "revitalization" evidently made their lives more precarious and more vulnerable, a vulnerability that seemed to mirror that of the group that may displace them, the "economic refugees" from the North. Unlike these latter, there are no havens to which these lower-income classes can retreat. As the global market consumes their local one, they withdraw to outlying suburbs, their way of life and their city transformed beyond recognition.

5

The Hacienda

The urban center of Cuenca may be a World Heritage site, but its layout and built architecture cannot be separated from the relations of colonial rule that dominated the countryside. Just as North American incorporation in Cuenca intersects existing inequalities there, so too does it influence the historical relation between city and countryside. As noted in the last chapter, the heritage buildings that dominate El Centro belonged to families whose wealth was obtained by exploiting a rural labor force. For the landed classes, the arrival of North American migrants and second home owners opens new possibilities for accumulation, transforming the economic base of the countryside from agricultural production to real estate speculation. In the process, it accentuates traditional forms of appropriation through dispossession and primitive accumulation, which have long been central to European colonialism in the Americas.

North Americans who relocate to the Ecuadorian countryside often evoke the same cultural reasons as we saw with Diana in the introduction. Elise and Sandy, for instance, relocated in 2011, when care responsibilities for elderly family members were no longer an issue for them. As Elise put it, "we felt like we were getting up in age. I mean, we definitely had political reasons, economical reasons, but also, more than anything, was that we knew that we were getting up in age, that, if we wanted to do something adventurous, we had to do it then." This cultural response to aging took her and her husband first to Cuenca and then to a valley nearby, where they settled on a subdivided former hacienda, owned by a wealthy Cuencano family with important real estate interests in the city. "We could never find as perfect a spot," Elise said. "I mean, the Andes are right there, at four or

< 149 >

five o'clock, the sky changes to all kinds of colors. The beauty of this place is incredible." Her husband, Sandy, also enjoyed being out of the city. "It's a small town," he said, "and you get to know people pretty quickly, you know?" He also mentioned the beauty of the sunsets and the trees.

Like Elise and Sandy, Mary and Grant, in their mid-sixties from Houston, whom we met in chapter 1, also chose the countryside for what it offered their lifestyle. They said they were not really city people, despite a lifetime of living in American cities, and had relocated to the Ecuadorian countryside as "economic and health care refugees." Mary noted that the couple wanted to be "self-sufficient." As she put it, "we wanted the clean air, and we wanted the quiet. My early morning noise is not the fireworks, or the cars honking. . . . [My morning] is a bird chirping." She and her husband were tending to a growing garden and were learning to take care of farm animals, such as goats and ducks. While Sandy and Elise had bought their plot from the hacienda owner, Mary and Grant were renting from another important landed family with interests in Cuenca. "I had never, in my entire life, thought that I would be a farmer [in retirement]," Mary said.

Research participants in Cuenca also often appreciated the landscape, the mountains, and the sunsets. But for those participants who relocated to rural areas near Cuenca, or farther south in Loja province, landscape held special importance. Natural landscapes are coupled, often, with ideals of naturalized people and the provisory nature of the land itself. Karen, age seventy-one, had relocated from North Carolina to Vilcabamba in 2007. "When you look out the window, at this each morning," she said, pointing out the window at her trimmed lawn and garden of fruit trees next to the river with the mountains in the backdrop, "I mean . . . what a, what a way to wake up." It was not hard to agree. Kenzo, age sixty-two, who had lived most of his adult life outside of his home country of the United States, said, "It's visually stunning, beautiful, but the people, I was just meeting so many amazing, interesting people. . . . There's something very magical about this place. I feel it." The community of people, mostly other lifestyle migrants, is often discussed as a draw. But so too is the mystical power of the place, which apparently pulls people in. Younger migrants to the Vilcabamba Valley frequently mentioned the land. Katherine, age thirty-one, from southern Ontario, stated, "The land hooked me. . . . I feel like these plants and rocks, and everything, are members of the community, here, and . . . the fine point where I get why I'm here, is when I just tune in." Katherine had studied agriculture in Canada and was knowledgeable about soil science. But she felt alienated and disheartened by the corporate system of organic agriculture in Canada and felt more in tune with nature in Vilcabamba. The same could be said of Johnathan, age forty-seven, from Los Angeles. He decided he wanted to leave what he felt was a meaningless and harmful corporate lifestyle, relocating first to Costa Rica and later to southern Ecuador. He said he had "stumbled" into Vilcabamba on an *ayahuasca* tour. "Within six hours, I knew I wanted to stay here," he said. He was captivated by the community of interesting people (mostly other foreigners) and by the beautiful setting, dominated by Mandango, the mountain formation that dominates the center of the valley.

These rural areas, however, are not natural settings. The landscape is profoundly marked by institutions and historical property arrangements that enabled forms of accumulation to take place there and that have left lasting marks on the countryside and the people who live there. Indeed, the countryside remains an important location of accumulation, but also of struggle. Land reform initiatives continue to contest agro-industry's obsession with productivity and offer alternative, subsistence forms of living under the rubric of *buen vivir* (Acosta 2013; Berry et al. 2014; Pástor 2014). In many parts of Ecuador, mining also looms over mountains and lakes, threatening to unearth valuable minerals for distant markets. The southern Ecuadorian countryside is visibly divided up into plots and *caserios* (or groups of houses) specializing in different agricultural activities that are continuously changing (Rebaï 2009, 2015), reflections of new laws and new institutional formations that affect the profitability of agriculture. Historically, the hacienda has been the main institution that characterizes rural spaces (Hurtado [1977] 2010). As the principal vessels of surplus accumulation, the larger haciendas of southern Ecuador typically employed peasant laborers in various forms of precarious debt bondage. This hacienda system was dismantled relatively recently—between the second half of the 1960s and the early 1980s, when the last concessions from the 1973 land reform law were settled.

This chapter outlines how migrants from the Global North to the Ecuadorian countryside reproduce the economic interests of landholders, thereby exacerbating rural inequality and compounding the unjust legacy of a flawed agrarian reform in southern Ecuador. This latter generated the most important rural exodus in the country, stimulating a huge outflow of rural workers to the Global North and spawning networks of coyotes and people traffickers that continue to mark the region (Álvarez Velasco 2009; Borrero Vega 1996, 116–17; Kyle 2000, 45–72; Pribilsky 2007). Far from escaping social forces that they find unpalatable, North–South migrants to the Ecuadorian countryside remain firmly encased in asymmetrical global social relations. The focus of this chapter is on Vilcabamba, which in the 2010s had the largest population of North American lifestyle migrants among rural *parroquías*, or parishes. While there are North Americans relocating to valleys near Cuenca, especially in the Challuabamba neighborhood, the overall numbers of North Americans are relatively small east of the city, in Gualaceo (a city farther east and at lower altitude) and in the sugarcane valleys of Paute and Yunguilla. This made it more difficult to recruit participants in these locations. By contrast, Vilcabamba has received many more migrants from the Global North, perhaps as many as twelve hundred.[1] As a small rural community of forty-seven hundred, it has experienced the influx of foreigners from higher-income countries in ways that are much more evident. Local Vilcabambeños, or *lugareños,* as they call themselves, have developed a more critical eye toward developments in their valley and were much easier to approach and speak with about the effects of tourism and lifestyle migration. While Vilcabamba is in the south of Ecuador, it is not in Azuay, and its historical connections to Cuenca are not as important as those it has to Loja, the largest city and capital of the southern province of the same name. It is important, therefore, to bear in mind that there are certain differences between Vilcabamba and other communities of North American migrants closer to Cuenca. However, the rich history of the valley provides an interesting window into some of the same issues that North Americans moving to the countryside also face farther north (or, indeed, to varying degrees in other rural locations throughout Latin America). A focus on Vilcabamba, therefore, is meant to provoke reflection about how North–South migrants' presence in rural areas intersects histories of unequal social relations, both globally (between North and South America, for instance) and locally (between landowning classes and the families of former indentured workers).

The so-called nobles of Cuenca do own haciendas in Loja, but the large agrarian fortunes accumulated by Cuenca's landholding elites were amassed primarily through landownership in the valleys of Paute and Yunguilla, both at lower altitudes from the city of Cuenca and therefore increasingly popular with middle-class second home owners as vacation spots. Ethnographic work and interviews were also conducted in these two valleys, which are important tourist centers. Yunguilla in particular is undergoing a significant construction boom of vacation homes and gated communities, much of it oriented toward the middle classes of Cuenca but also toward North Americans looking for rural idylls at low cost. Owing to the dynamics of tourism and residential migration to Vilcabamba, however, most of the time I spent in rural areas, I spent there. Moreover, Vilcabamba shares with Paute and Yunguilla characteristics of social structure and struggle over land reform—most notably the existence of large haciendas, which used indentured workers until the late 1960s and early 1970s. Most importantly, it provides a telling window into the transnationalization of rural space in Ecuador, where lifestyle migration participates in recasting global inequalities, with important continuities with the colonial past of rural areas.

Vilcabamba, the Sacred Valley of Longevity

It is a four-hour bus trip from Cuenca to Vilcabamba, a trip that seems longer. The blue buses run across the top of the plateau at Cumbe and then drop down at Susudel to the río León before rising again to Oña. Pine plantations announce your arrival in

Loja province, and the bus stops for a time in Saraguro, the most important indigenous community in Ecuador's southern sierra. Winding roads signal your approach to the city of Loja, where you change to a smaller bus that will take you over the mountains between El Capuli and Rumishitana, and then you descend gradually to the parish of Vilcabamba, located at 1,550 meters (see Map 4). The warmer, drier climate makes Vilcabamba an important vacation destination for North Americans who have settled in Cuenca, as it is for middle-class Ecuadorians. The bus curls along a ridge as you descend into the village and stops a short walk from the town's main square in the center of the parish. The parish is composed of various *caserios*, or neighborhoods, roughly corresponding to the haciendas from the period before the agrarian reform (see Map 5). Visitors frequently remark that the place seems incredibly calm when they first arrive. But as I worked there a bit longer, I came to realize that this sense of calm masked the parish's role as a party town for young Ecuadorians vacationing from Loja, Cuenca, or even as far away as Guayaquil or Quito. Moreover, it masked a history of struggle and exploitation that intersects the growing migration of North American "economic refugees" and others from the Global North.

In the mid-twentieth century, the town gained an international reputation as the sacred valley of longevity. American explorers published popular articles in *National Geographic* and *Reader's Digest* about the long life expectancy of some of its inhabitants, many of whom claimed to be over one hundred (Leaf 1973; Payne 1954). The supposed medicinal properties of the area helped spawn a tourism industry at about the same time Vilcabamba's hacienda-based economy was going through significant transformations. Faced with the changing fortunes of the hacienda regime, landowning families sought new strategies of accumulation in relation to land and often focused on tourism development (cf. Andrade Río and Ulluari Donoso 2014). According to research participants and local informants, foreigners began relocating to the region prior to the 1980s but were few in number. One American couple who had lived in Vilcabamba since the mid-1970s said there were a few ascetic cults of North Americans living there at the time but that it became better known

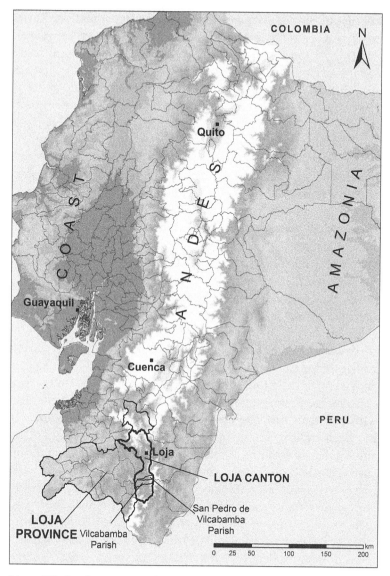

Map 4. Vilcabamba, Loja, Ecuador. Map by Joan Carles Membrado, Universidad de Valencia.

because of the publicity about its centenarian population. "It was touristy, because there was an article in the *National Geographic*, right? . . . And when backpackers really started coming to South America, this would be on the trail," Wendy said. She was in her mid-sixties, had lived in Vilcabamba for forty years, and had raised her children there. She said she had moved there initially because she wanted to "live a simple life." Their material lifestyle was humble by contrast to the more recent arrivals. More recently, the number of foreign residents and Ecuadorian second homeowners has increased dramatically. Johnathan, mentioned above, was from Los Angeles and had moved to Vilcabamba in 2009 to get away from a corporate job he said "lacked integrity." He said that since he had arrived, "wave upon wave of refugees" started arriving. After the Fukushima disaster of 2011, he said people started showing up from Hawai'i and the West Coast of the United States, afraid of the impact of nuclear fallout.[2] Having moved to Vilcabamba after what he described as a "paranormal" experience (which allowed him to realize that his life in Los Angeles was empty), he spoke of his own migration as being part of these waves. But in the six short years he had lived in the country, he felt things had changed from what he had found when he first arrived. "It is saturated to the point of absurdity," he said.

These changes are of interest especially because they intersect with a history of struggle for control over land that historically has been tightly concentrated in the hands of wealthy Lojano and Cuencano families. While academic literature has so far focused primarily on land use changes that result from tourism and lifestyle migration (cf. Borsdorf and Hidalgo 2009; Cadieux and Hurley 2011; Janoschka 2009), here I attend to a history of ownership and control of land and labor power. While scholarship in geography and rural sociology has attended to the displacement of local residents (cf. Matarrita-Cascante and Stocks 2013; Rainer and Malizia 2014; Spalding 2013), what follows focuses on the historic relations of exclusion and marginalization that mark urban–rural divides in Ecuador discussed in the last chapter. The presence of lifestyle migrants from the Global North complicates existing inequalities in the Ecuadorian countryside, offering new

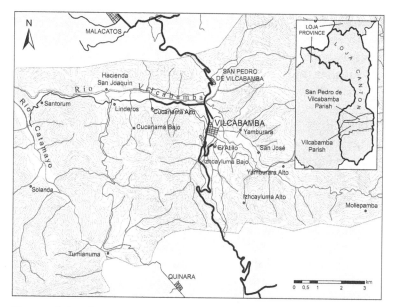

Map 5. Vilcabamba valley. Map by Joan Carles Membrado, Universidad de Valencia.

possibilities for accumulation and adding new pressures to intensify labor.

Vilcabamba was, and to a degree still is, a land of haciendas and large agricultural cash crops. The hacienda looms large as the key institution shaping the social relations of the valley, as it does in much of the south of Ecuador. Its private haciendas are owned by wealthy families from Loja and range in size from eight hundred to four thousand hectares. Most haciendas are of modest size in southern Ecuador, owing to its steep terrain (Pietri-Levy 1993). Scholarship on Ecuador's southern provinces emphasizes the region's relative isolation and the development of smaller *minifundios* (cf. Cordero, Achig, and Carrasco 1989; Hirschkind 1980; Kyle 2000). However, in Loja, as in Cuenca, the landowning elite have taken advantage of that isolation to establish their dominance over the important institutions of the valley, long holding a monopoly of administrative and professional positions in the city of Loja as well as the commanding heights of the commercial trades, which have historically linked the region with northern Peru (Espinoza and Achig 1989; Fauroux 1983; Poma and Castro 2009). While the haciendas in Ecuador's southern sierra are smaller on average than those of the north, control of the land and the labor force is no less tightly concentrated. Typically, large landowning families own important haciendas in several valleys in the south, whose sizes may be small but where there is nonetheless significant concentration of wealth. As Fierro Carrión (1991) points out, the concentration of wealth in Azuay surpasses that in the northern volcano fields, despite relatively smaller haciendas. In Loja also, relatively small haciendas in low-lying mountain valleys produce important cash crops that are the source of significant fortunes.

The largest and most important haciendas in southern Ecuador are to be found in the temperate valleys, where agricultural accumulation primarily used dependent labor on large estates. Local historians of Vilcabamba (Cabrera Azanza 2008; Vásquez Armijos 2009) as well as research participants described the haciendas of the valley as *latifundios,* or large landholdings, that focused on export crops, such as banana *(guineo),* coffee, and sugarcane, the latter supporting a *panela* (sugar) processing industry. Espinoza and Achig (1989) also note that Lojano haciendas took on proportions of *latifundios* and that landowners exercised a particularly strict control over their territory, distinct from the greater independence of the *minifundistas* apparently typical in the southern sierra. Because of the loss of indigenous population in the area due to the Inca civil war and diseases brought with the Spanish invasion in the 1530s, many of the formerly indentured peasant laborers are mestizo or identify as being of mixed indigenous and European descent.

North American lifestyle migrants to rural areas rarely expressed more than a vague notion of the place of the hacienda in Ecuador's history and culture. Their relocations were motivated primarily by projects of self-discovery or by utilitarian ideals of improving quality of life, as discussed in chapter 1. Elise and her husband, Sandy, illustrate an ideal of self-discovery through migration to the countryside. One of the bases of their relationship, Elise said, was their "sense of adventure." Sandy, like others, spoke about wanting to stretch himself out by moving into a new cultural environment. "The American culture is all too familiar," he explained. "I was ready for a change. I think that's just kinda the way I would say it. It's, like, looking for something new, and adventure." This was echoed by Elise, who described moving to Ecuador as a "big left turn," a metaphor she used to describe being "rebellious" or breaking from the established mold. "Making a left turn has been always very important," she explained. "I don't like to do, to be, to feel like I'm locked into having to be a certain way." This libertarian, individualistic spirit shows up in other ways as well. Johnathan, for instance, noted that "Ecuador has a 'Wild West' appeal to it." You are free to do what you want, he explained. "You can build a house any way you want, you are not burdened by building codes or municipal governments," he said.

These individualistic forms of self-expression, made possible by transnational lifestyle migration, were nonetheless also often tied to economic motivations. Elise pointed out, "We just thought that our little nest egg would completely dissipate in the United States, and it wouldn't be enough left over to, to live." The lower cost of living and the expectation of being able to literally move mountains to create new communities in a lower-income, Latin American country seemed to significantly enhance the agency of migrants to Vilcabamba—perhaps more so than the spiritual powers of Mandango. Karen talked about rebuilding an abandoned "farm." She had bought a former hacienda and was busy employing local people to work as wage laborers picking coffee. "We've really transformed it into something already," she said, "and we're only midstream on it, you know?" This project would not have been possible back home, where she could not have employed so many workers to build the kind of agricultural community she envisioned. Like many others, there was a spiritual quest to her labor in Vilcabamba: "If we put this little vibe out into the world, and other people do the same, we all can mutually inspire each other and maybe, just maybe, we can begin to piece together a new civilization, a garden of paradise, worldwide." Like Paula in chapter 2, Karen and others in Vilcabamba sought to align an inner sense of a calling with the external world. As Katherine from Canada put it, she and her friends in Vilcabamba sought to build a new community, one that would be more "real" than the one they had left. As she put it, "We're still stuck in our illusions and patterns and, and the things that, our cultural paradigms, like, here too, for sure." But Vilcabamba held out the possibility of learning about them and freeing themselves from them. She and her friends seemed to be experimenting with new lifestyles, perhaps before "settling down" (Amit 2011) or as a way to avoid "settling down" altogether. This is what Kenzo had done, managing to avoid, he said, ever having to work as a wage laborer. Free from the necessities of work, Kenzo and Katherine, Elise and Sandy, could spend more time thinking about what their internal ideals were, an internal desire constrained by external obligations imposed by society. This would enable them to externalize in the world around them the basis of a truer community, founded on a more authentic self—as though their inner lives and ability to transform the world around them were detached from material social relations and historical social forces.

The sense of taking control of life was often a product of material conditions that the Ecuadorian countryside made possible. As we saw in chapter 1, North Americans in Ecuador are also often escaping precarious financial conditions or attempting to leave unfulfilling careers. Kenzo was in Ecuador because he had no pension savings and said in our interview that he was not sure what was going to happen to him in a few months when his savings ran out. Isabel, a former financial services employee from Europe in her mid-forties, explained that she had relocated to Ecuador to save money, so she did not have to work as much. "It is more important to be free than to live in the First World," she said. But this sometimes came at a risk. Katherine, from Canada, became a mother in Vilcabamba, but her partner left her shortly after the baby was born. While personally enriching, her experience in Vilcabamba carried no symbolic power in North American labor markets, making it ever more difficult to return home. She had little desire to anyway. As she had explained in our interview, "Now that I've tasted this, I can't go back. Like, I've become radical. Unproductive, spiritual, seeking my own healing." She desired to stay in the more relaxed lifestyle of Vilcabamba, but when we spoke again a year later, she was unsure how she would be able to make ends meet.

Vilcabamba and Agrarian Reform

Lifestyle migrants in Vilcabamba express individualistic ideals with respect to their relocation, yet they become entwined in the historical social relations of Vilcabamba valley, dominated by the accumulation strategies of landowning elites, of which they know little. Nor do they share any historical memory with local research participants from laboring classes. This limits their ability to interact with the receiving community as organic allies in the pursuit of social justice or in an ongoing and unfinished societal process of democratization.[3] While they may see their lives as developing individually, lifestyle migrants remain embedded in social relations, evident particularly in the impact they may have on receiving communities. This is an important part of their incorporation. Vilcabamba's history as a tourism and lifestyle destination developed hand in hand with struggles for agrarian reform and the redistribution of land, which had been concentrated in the hands of a few wealthy, Spanish-descended families. Migrants from the Global North are thus not benign strangers on the land but participants in a project of modernization, largely led by the landowners, many of whom deliberately evaded attempts by the state to impose land redistribution that would have favored previously indentured workers (Fauroux 1983; Pietri-Levy 1993, 26–27). These latter and their children and grandchildren are now caught up in a process of rural gentrification, whereby land is increasingly valorized not for its agricultural uses but for the value of sublime enjoyment it provides to migrants from higher latitudes of the global division of labor. Thus lifestyle migrants from the Global North participate in transforming the economic base of Ecuador, as elites shift from agricultural land use to the secondary circuit of capital (Harvey 1978, 1985), marked by real estate investment and speculation rather than by accumulation through the productive organization of dependent workers. The result is an appropriation of space and labor that reproduces exclusion and forms of primitive appropriation that were not adequately addressed in the agrarian reforms of the third quarter of the twentieth century.

Although the hacienda system and many of its large *latifundios* were dismantled in Ecuador following the organized protests of peasant workers and agrarian reforms in the 1960s and early 1970s, the landowning elites often retained control both of the best lands and of the labor power of rural workers (Barsky 1988; Bretón Solo de Zaldívar 2012; Fauroux 1983; Guerrero 1983; Guerrero Carrión 2010; Ibarra 2002a). There are also important regional differences that played a part in the process of reform. As the literature on the Ecuadorian agrarian reforms of 1964 and 1973 points out, legislation was mostly aimed at the largest estates in the country's northern volcano fields. In the south, the problems of access to land by a predominantly yeoman peasantry were different (see Pribilsky 2007). But where indentured workers were employed, especially in valleys like Vilcabamba, redistribution was coerced by local landowners, who took advantage of the region's remoteness to evade more substantial redistributions. In the southern provinces of the sierra (Azuay and Loja, in particular), social institutions and private accumulation differed in ways that led to very different resolutions of the land reform issue.

As Bretón Solo de Zaldívar (2012) points out, each hacienda is its own tiny universe. Local conditions strongly influenced how land was redistributed following the 1964 and 1973 Agrarian Reform Laws and contribute to the pattern of lifestyle migration settlement today. In the mid-twentieth century, the largest hacienda in Vilcabamba valley was the Hacienda de Yamburara y San José, which was controlled by a monastery in the city of Loja. According to Cabrera Azanza (2008, 15) and local research participants, this hacienda was taken under control of the state in the 1950s, managed first by the Junta de Recuperación Económica and later divided up by the 1964 Agrarian Reform Law, carried through by a military government. One of the measures mandated by the reform was the distribution of land on state-run haciendas. Thus Yamburara y San José was the first hacienda where peasant workers were able to get access to their own land titles, and on terms participants found favorable.

Local research participants said that the redistribution began late in 1965 and continued through 1966. Land redistribution on this hacienda initiated the process of reform in Vilcabamba—a process that included sale of land and title to peasant workers and that legally canceled debt peonage and unpaid labor on hacienda estates. However, the 1964 Agrarian Reform Law was designed mostly for the haciendas of the northern volcano fields and was ineffective at redistributing land in the south (Abbott 2005; Hirschkind 1980). Land reform was therefore not a set piece that ended after the 1964 law, and if anything, it encouraged national peasant associations to seek more radical reforms, including collectivization of agricultural lands (Barsky 1988).

These more radical reforms were on the agenda, but their actual implementation was contained by established social classes through their control of the organs of representative democracy and their willingness to resort to force when necessary. The return to democracy from 1966 to 1972 put land reform back on the agenda, as the limitations of the 1964 law were contested. While the 1964 agrarian reform set out to end precarious forms of unpaid labor, these persisted in parts of Vilcabamba well into the 1970s, according to local research participants. Local contacts in Loja and Cuenca confirmed the findings of Hirschkind (1980), who argued that landowners in the south anticipated further agrarian reform and land redistribution and set about to protect their interests. This meant selling parts of the hacienda to unpaid workers ahead of further reforms threatened by then-president Velasco Ibarra. Further reforms were eventually carried out in a controlled, limited fashion, under another military dictatorship in 1973, designed not to upset existing class relations but nonetheless transform rural life and agriculture. In anticipation, therefore, beginning in 1966 (the year of the return to democracy), private hacienda owners in Vilcabamba began negotiating land transfers to workers referred to as *arrimados,* who were "tied" to the hacienda through debt obligation.[4]

These land transfers (paid with interest over a fixed term), however, were not without controversy in the heady days of the 1960s, only a few short years after Fidel Castro had demonstrated that violent, Cuban-style revolutions were one way of forcing the

issue of reform onto the agenda in Latin America. This geopoliti-
cal situation deeply affected the willingness of elites in Ecuador
to find a solution to problems that were framed in terms of rural
underdevelopment (Barsky 1988; Guerrero 1983). As the state-led
Instituto Ecuatoriana de Reforma Agraria y Colonización (IERAC)
initiated redistribution in Yamburara y San José, private hacienda owners sought a negotiated settlement with their indentured workers. Lurking in the background of these negotiations
were more radical solutions to the unjust, colonial appropriation
of land in the Ecuadorian countryside: the forced collectivization
of hacienda estates, turning ownership over to the workers themselves who had produced agricultural surpluses for a leisure class
of European-descended owners for generations. More radical options, however, had little traction in southern Ecuador and perhaps none in Vilcabamba—although local research participants
noted that the land reform meant the loss of collective lands,
which in turn meant they could no longer keep their animals,
a situation that compounded rural poverty after the reform. As
one woman, Berta, in her eighties, said, "That all ended, they did
not want to give space for animals after that, and we lived like
we are here in the town, because we could not have an animal—
not a goat or anything—because everything, everything was sold
and everyone already had, like, their own lot, so there was no
way to have a *campo libre* [open field for grazing]." Private land
title continues to confound agrarian reforms in Ecuador, and indigenous and peasant movements in the north often challenge
its liberal terms (fetishizing private forms of property), which
run contrary to increasingly popular principles of *buen vivir* (a
variation to which the national government feels it must pay lip
service; see Acosta 2013).

During negotiations to redistribute title, *lugareño* research
participants said that the mostly illiterate peasant workers relied on the few literate members of their communities and on
national organizations to help them formulate the terms of a
settlement with landowners. El Atillo was one of the richest private haciendas, situated right next to the San José neighborhood
and near to the town center. It was and is still today owned by
the Vivanco family of Loja, as it has been since the end of the

nineteenth century. The crest of its hill rises sharply from the eastern edge of town and climbs along a ridge all the way to what is now called Izhcayluma. At El Atillo, literate peasants (of which there were only two) led negotiations on behalf of other workers, according to several local research participants. These literate workers had received additional instruction from peasant organizations in Loja, who were helping to organize workers on private haciendas. At El Atillo, as on other private haciendas, the course negotiations took depended on the bargaining power of the *arrimados* themselves. The goodwill of *hacendados* appears to have been in short supply. Land parcels that peasants worked were often not the ones that they were allowed to buy from the *hacendado*. This served to divide peasant workers, many of whom, understandably, wanted to keep their homes. Berta mentioned how her in-laws had been allowed to keep the materials of their home, which they transported to another site. But in other cases, allowances to keep materials would have been a bargaining chip for the *hacendados,* many of whom were eager to retain their lands and to modernize their production methods, because landownership and agricultural production using an underclass of peasant workers was their main source of wealth.

Land redistribution in the late 1960s and early 1970s most often took the form of payment for land over ten years and at interest, a process that benefited landowners. Most research participants noted that this was not a very difficult debt to pay, but other sources suggest otherwise. Abbott (2005, 203), who conducted extensive fieldwork in Vilcabamba, noted that many households were unable to pay off this debt, meaning that land title was in many cases simply a new form of peonage, encouraging sales and out-migration. Wealthy families, many of them absentees who lived full time in Loja or other cities, retained control of most of the land, including the main cash crops on the *fondo de hacienda,* the main lands used by *hacendado* landowners. This land was the most productive, often on flat areas of the valley, and with access to irrigation.

Work conditions on the private haciendas were extremely demanding according to research participants, encouraging many to settle on unfavorable terms. Participants, and others with whom I spoke informally, described their work conditions on the haciendas prior to agrarian reform as slavery—a theme that was mentioned frequently at several different hacienda estates, notably El Atillo, Tumianuma, Solanda, and Santorum. Although *hacendados* did not officially own workers, there were few opportunities to move to other haciendas, because available land was already exploited. In exchange for their small plots, which tied them to the land and therefore also to the hacienda, workers were forced to work for the owners for ten to fifteen days per month on commercial crops, located on the *fondo de hacienda*. Each worker usually had a baton, or *tarjo,* which kept track of how many days they had worked each month. Yet, as in E. P. Thompson's ([1967] 1993) classic work on the introduction of time management in early industrial factories, mayordomos, who supervised peasant labor on behalf of large hacienda owners, often tampered with the tarjos. Because the workers were often illiterate and undereducated, these batons could be manipulated. Each "day" owed to the hacienda owner was paid by accomplishing three "tasks," tabulated on the *tarjo.* However, as research participants pointed out, not all tasks could be completed in a day, such that workers often ended up spending almost all of their time working for the *hacendado,* and in situations where demanding mayordomos could extract additional labor and threaten them with the accumulation of debts to the *fondo de hacienda.*

Research participants from different haciendas said that at the time of the land reform, negotiators for the *arrimados* advised against individual settlements, and national organizers urged *arrimados* to resist together and to fight for just terms. But hacienda owners held all the cards and could wear the workers down. They offered the best parcels first to those who would settle first. I was told of a few at El Atillo who refused. But by dividing the workers and playing favorites, the *hacendados* effectively threatened those who held out with being left with the worst-quality land—or with nothing at all. On the private haciendas, it seems, there was intense pressure for the *arrimados* to settle and to accept inferior land on terms that in most cases would subsequently make it impossible for them to remain on the land as independent peasants. The parcels the *hacendados* were willing to part with were often very small relative to the total agricultural area, resulting in minimal effective redistribution, or less than 10 percent of the total area of the hacienda. One research participant from Cucanamá mentioned receiving a parcel of one-half of a hectare, though others from that hacienda mentioned receiving about two. These were too small to survive on, and often, especially in the western end of Vilcabamba, from Cucanamá Alto to Santorum, and down toward Solanda and Tumianuma, where there is far less rain, former *arrimados* were unable to earn a living if they lacked access to irrigation.

By treating each family as an individual case, private landowners could undermine the solidarity of workers and thereby deprive them of land claims against the *fondo de hacienda*. This enabled the *hacendados* to hold on to their best lands. As Marcelo, a teacher in his early sixties, told me, "the worst, driest, unirrigated land was redistributed, while they [the *hacendados*] kept the best for themselves." The land *arrimados* received was often of poor quality, forcing them to return to the hacienda as paid laborers. While there was tension in the years during and immediately after agrarian reform, research participants noted that *campesinos* (or farmers) often continued to work on the haciendas after agrarian reform (or moved to work the fields of other *hacendados*), such that landowners also retained control over their labor power. As Marcelo put it, "the agrarian reform was a real disaster." Those who resisted the unequal distribution of the land, as on Hacienda La Palmira, he said, were chased away and received nothing. "The law was on the side of the boss," he said.

Those who were organized or who resisted the *hacendados* faced reprisals, a process that was often violent throughout southern Ecuador. At Hacienda Santa Ana, in Cariamanga, Loja, in 1968, workers attempting to access water resources during a drought were massacred by paramilitaries organized by the *hacendados*. In Solanda, the far western edge of Vilcabamba parish, where workers had held together, every last *arrimado* was marched off the hacienda into a landless and uncertain future. On Vilcabamba's private haciendas, research participants talked about how *hacendados* worked actively to demobilize workers, denying them access to education and punishing perceived union sympathizers and agrarian reform activists, sometimes throwing them off the hacienda and burning their crops or even their houses. I met Diego, a slender man in his seventies, who participated in the *lucha campesina* (peasant struggle) and who was active in organizing for just redistribution of land in the 1960s and 1970s. Taking a break from his work in the garden, he invited me to talk under the veranda of his small adobe home and offered me cola and crackers. A dog sat on the concrete floor under a small wooden table, nursing a bad leg. Diego said he faced torture (which has left him with permanent headaches), destruction of his home and crops, forced eviction, and multiple arrests before finally being granted a plot in the early 1980s. For twelve years, he fought for just distribution on his hacienda. "We suffered bitterly" during that struggle, he said. While some redistribution took place on private estates, it left the *fondo de hacienda* intact, enabling *hacendados* to continue to draw agricultural profits from the land.

Not all research participants narrated the land reform in terms of its injustices—though these are clear to see. Knowledge of agrarian reform and land redistribution in Vilcabamba is shaped by common discourses that emphasize the social gains *arrimados* made through the elimination of unpaid, precarious positions on the hacienda rather than on how current material inequalities are the product of an unjust distribution of land. Diego himself said that though it had not resolved everything, "at least it did something." Camilo, a man in his eighties who still did farmwork, stated, "Now everyone is free already, there are a lot of young professionals now from Vilcabamba, men as well as women, with good professions." Many were glad to be able to work on their own and therefore viewed the reform as a watershed in their lives and in the class relations of the valley. Others seemed to want to let bygones be bygones and not disturb a past now apparently so remote as to seem irrelevant to the lives of those who live in Vilcabamba today. I met Valentino, a man in his seventies, after he finished his afternoon work in his fields. He lived with one of his children in a modern two-story house. We sat in front of the door, under a concrete sun porch, which the sun already crept beneath. I asked him if he thought the reform was just. His response was emphatic: "*claro que sí*" (of course it was), he told me. Yet, when pushed for a justification, his response focused mostly around work conditions and not around redistribution of wealth. "From then on," he said, "they [the workers] were property owners, they worked for themselves." Berta recalled that from the reform on, you could take your time when you were eating, something you couldn't do as an *arrimado* working for *"los ricos"* (the rich)—the women had to get up extra early to prepare meals the men barely had time to consume. Similarly, Rafael, a *lonjevo* of 102, said that the agrarian reform "gave us a way to live." Our short interview took place on the porch of his small home, where he lived with his extended family. Though his eyesight and hearing were failing, he remembered the land reform period well and talked about his youth working on Hacienda San José. Like other research participants who were old enough to have full memories of work on the haciendas in the 1950s and 1960s, he noted how, after the reform, they were able to live in peace, without being bothered by the demands of the *hacendado*. "There was no one messing with us," he said.

Local research participants often mentioned to me that young people were not interested in this history and viewed their "slavery" as a thing of the past. Yet the lack of affordable land for young people and the ongoing politics of access to it and to opportunities beyond Vilcabamba are a product of social positions inherited from this turbulent period in Ecuador's history. In the absence of an egalitarian redistribution of arbitrarily acquired wealth—a project that may have been utopian or that lacked social actors capable of carrying it through in the 1960s—southern Ecuador has developed as a sharply unequal society, one divided between landowning families who have had continued access to the cultural and economic capital generated by the haciendas and a large mass of poor workers whose children and grandchildren continue to struggle (sometimes with success, but as the exception and not the rule).

Land Redistribution and Real Estate Development

In contrast to the resistance to reform on the part of private hacienda owners, land redistribution was swifter and more peaceful on the state-run Yamburara and San José haciendas.

This ultimately affected the future development of tourism and the appropriation of land by foreigners since the 1980s. According to local research participants who were involved in the land reform movements, workers on the state-run hacienda at Yamburara y San José were better organized and participated in protests leading up to agrarian reform in the early 1960s. Evidently, in addition to this organization, they benefited from the lighter hand of state administrators, who, after 1964, were empowered to speedily sell title to the land to those who worked it. Workers had more autonomy in some parts of the hacienda and were able to pay for their land in rent rather than through labor. Even the workers themselves were often referred to as *colones* rather than *arrimados,* implying significantly more agency over their land tenure. At the time of the reform, they crucially benefited from access to more land. The Junta de Recuperación kept very little of the main *fondo de hacienda* where the cash crops of the hacienda were grown, allowing more land to be redistributed and enabling the workers to buy much larger plots, usually eight or ten hectares but in some cases as much as sixteen or twenty hectares, according to research participants. Not only were the sizes of the redistributed plots much larger than those on private haciendas but the terms of payment carried a lower interest rate and they were in a better-irrigated and more humid part of the valley.

These relatively large plots enabled the owners to divide up the land, often giving their children sizeable properties as well. But Yamburara and San José are also significant because they are the two neighborhoods where, until recently, most lifestyle migrants settled. Yamburara in particular has so many foreigners living within its boundaries that locals say there are more gringos there than *lugareños.* Parts of San José have been turned into small, gated communities. In other cases, the parcels were bought by foreigners and have been transformed into large private *fincas* or vacation properties. The concentration of foreign landowners in this part of the valley is due in part to the form that agrarian reform took there. No doubt, it is also due to its relative proximity to water and (at least in its western portions) to the main town center. Yet historically, land purchases in Yamburara and San José are facilitated by the relative cash poverty of rural agricultural workers who have larger landholdings as a result of the redistribution of the 1960s. Families in Yamburara have a tradition of selling off parcels of their land to pay off debts (including debts to the state to buy the original parcel), to make investments (including buying more land somewhere else where costs are lower), or to meet other expenses (such as buying building materials). After more than a generation, most of the original plots have now been split at least once among family members, reducing the sizes of the originally redistributed parcels. Nonetheless, they remain on average larger than those in other parts of Vilcabamba valley, which in some cases have also been divided by sale or inheritance.

The relatively larger parcels, coupled with the ability of foreign buyers to convince cash-poor families to sell entire sections of several hectares at a time for what seem to *lugareños* like astronomical prices, have contributed to extensive real estate development and construction in the neighborhood (see Figure 7). Larger lots allow smaller-scale foreign developers to subdivide and sell at markup prices to other foreigners. But what was an

Figure 7. Entry and exit of heavy machinery. Photograph by the author.

advantage—larger lots, the product of agrarian struggle—has turned into somewhat of a liability. The larger plots are now too expensive for locals to buy. But they are enticing to real estate companies, who will subdivide the land and sell lots or finished houses to foreigners at markup prices that reflect the spending power of higher latitudes of the global division of labor.

While some small landholders have benefited from the inflow of foreign residents and tourists, the benefits to rural workers are uneven and, for most, detrimental. Rather, large landowners are those who stand most to benefit as a result of ongoing development. While some lands were divided and sold—either to family members or other wealthy Lojano families—after the 1973 agrarian reform, the bulk of lands remained tightly concentrated. Furthermore, the World Bank–promoted Agrarian Development Law of 1994, which set up a state-guaranteed land title registry, furthered the interests of landowning classes relative to those of former *arrimados*. The law facilitated the creation of land markets, which, after the agrarian reforms of the 1960s and 1970s, had been stifled by regulations designed to ensure a modicum of fairness for income-poor families whose lands had been wrested from a flawed redistribution. Prime land in the Vilcabamba valley, especially the *fondos de hacienda* of the private estates, has since been divided into lots and sold to foreigners and wealthier professionals from Loja for vacation homes or investment properties (see Figure 8), in a process similar to what can be found in other Ecuadorian locations, notably in Cotacachi (cf. Gascón 2016; Viteri 2015).

Disproportionately, it is the landowning elites who are capitalizing on the cultural and economic shifts driving national and transnational residential migration to the "Valley of Longevity." In this respect, the effect of lifestyle migration in the countryside mirrors that of the city and its historic neighborhoods. The landowning classes are best positioned to take advantage of the shift toward real estate development. The hillside of El Atillo is easily one of the most privatized spaces in Ecuador, with large pasturelands marked off by barbed wire or large walls, atypical of other parts of southern Ecuador. Parts of the hillside have

Figure 8. Gated community, El Atillo, Vilcabamba. Photograph by the author.

been sold for luxury lots, while another large section has been developed for a sizable gated community, with thirty-seven lots (starting at $35,000 for seven hundred square meters). According to *lugareños*, the owners rent luxury houses short term to foreigners who may be looking to relocate to the valley. Other wealthy families are similarly cashing in on the inflation of land prices in other parts of the valley—land they inherited from an unequal and unjust redistribution process.

In a few cases, families who inherited haciendas have sold them to wealthy foreigners who have themselves done the developing. The most notable case in this respect is the large gated community of Hacienda San Joaquín across the río Vilcabamba in San Pedro de Vilcabamba. It contains ninety-four lots over 270 hectares, including space for private horse-riding trails.[5] Foreign real estate speculators enjoyed the possibility of huge price markups on land, justifying their profits under the ideological and cultural guise of private landownership and market demand. With relatively little capital, small or midsize developers can make very large sums of money selling land to foreigners via the internet, enabling them to speculate in transnational real estate, abetted by new and perverse forms of arbitrage.

Foreigners have bought parcels throughout Vilcabamba and neighboring San Pedro and are also buying parcels in Malacatos and Quinara to the north and south of the Vilcabamba valley, all with the aim of reselling at markup prices to wealthy foreigners. In the process, they have succeeded in driving up land prices—the deliberate intent of their original purchases and subdivisions— pursuing economic interests that do not often correspond to those of local workers, most of whom inherited land from their parents, who were *arrimados* on the hacienda estates.

Rural Gentrification and Displacement

Just as agrarian reform has changed the social relations of the valley, so too has the influx of foreigners. *Lugareño* research participants saw new opportunities for social mobility as a result of tourism and real estate development, and they pointed to signs of improvement in their material livelihood as measures of progress. As Valentino noted, "they have improved Vilcabamba by bringing money for [environmental] preservation." Rodrigo, a schoolteacher, echoed this, saying, "For the most part, they [the lifestyle migrants] have helped economic development." As noted, money gained from land sales also enables families to invest in education or in urban property in Loja. The decline in agriculture as an important economic activity in the valley (Reyes-Bueno et al. 2016) forces younger *lugareños* to think of their future else- where. Some younger Vilcabambeños did not seem to be particu- larly upset about this. One man with whom I spoke, perhaps in his late thirties, said that he remembered the fields being full of corn when he was young but he was now more interested in working in the tourist sector than as a farmer. The decline of agriculture in Vilcabamba has accelerated these sales. As Pilar, a retired farmworker, noted, "the land is worth more sold than sowed." In an environment in which access to land was, in the first place, highly restricted due to the regime of accumulation of southern Ecuador, it is clear that these changes do not affect all social classes evenly. North–South migrants are pushing up the cost of land and are further restricting access to it for the descendants of *arrimados* and *colones,* just as the economic base of Ecuador's rural economy undergoes important transformations.

As foreign buyers increase their share of the overall land market in Vilcabamba (Reyes-Bueno et al. 2016), the increase in prices has produced new hardships on rural workers. As Alejandro, a semiretired agricultural worker, noted, "there are no advantages without disadvantages." Most research participants and local residents approached in casual conversation expressed concerns about rising costs of living. Gabriela, a mother who operated a small business in the town, said, "Prices are exaggerated, let me tell you." Manuel, a local faith worker, said, "You have to perform miracles to get by [on $320 a month]. Most people have two jobs." Marcelo, mentioned earlier, noted that the price of land had shot up such that "people from here can no longer buy land." And some of those who have already sold, he said, "are left with nothing." Two *lugareño* men, both in their early thirties, who participated in an informal group discussion about the migration in 2014, had moved to Spain twelve years prior. They said they wanted to move back but could not afford to buy property. According to them, property that would have sold for $1,000 per hectare a decade and a half ago now starts at $30,000. Online, properties in Vilcabamba are listed at more than $200,000 for less than an hectare, far beyond the means of local residents.[6] The basic salary in Ecuador was $375 per month in 2017, according to the Instituto Nacional de Estadística y Censos (INEC). Moreover, Loja province has an underemployment rate measured in the range of 75 percent, with nearly 60 percent of residents in the parish of Vilcabamba categorized as poor, with incomes below what would enable them to buy the basic basket of goods (just over $700 per month in early 2017).[7] Younger workers in Vilcabamba usually migrate in search of work, either to Loja, larger cities in Ecuador, or abroad.

In conditions of already low wages and casual work, it is difficult for *lugareños* who wish to remain in the town to keep pace with the real estate boom. Research participants noted that many of the descendants of *arrimados* who sell land are subsequently forced to migrate elsewhere (sometimes abroad) or search for lower-cost housing farther out, in more remote parts of the valley. Other local participants say they cannot afford to buy. Gabriela mentioned, "I don't have a property because I can't save enough money. Who knows, maybe in fifteen or twenty years, Vilcabamba will belong only to foreigners, because we can't afford to buy." Their inability to remain in place contrasts with the experiences of North–South migrants, who are able to live economically less restricted lives in Ecuador.

These disparities illustrate the distinct but increasingly interrelated positions of a global social field, evident in Vilcabamba in the form of a transnational real estate market. The disparities between current residents and newcomers are stark, particularly because many of the valley's poor are themselves elderly pensioners living a retirement remarkably different from those North Americans who have arrived recently. Most worked as unpaid *arrimados* in a labor regime very different from that of North American retirees and now live on pensions that top out at fifty dollars per month. Rosita participated in one of my focus groups in 2015 at a center that provides services for the local elderly. She lives not far from where a foreign real estate developer is building a small, gated community. Her daughter and granddaughter both suffer from developmental disabilities, and at seventy, she was the primary caregiver, somehow getting by on a limited income and with help from social services. During a visit to her home, she complained about a relative who frequently robbed her. Her house, which sat by the road, was built by the government for poor families. It lacked a door.

The inflation in land prices has drawn transnational real estate agencies into the market for properties not entirely dissimilar to Rosita's, offering North American and European transnational retirees and second home buyers opportunities similar to those displayed on popular reality television shows like *House Hunters International*. The influx of North American retirees, attracted by the low cost of living advertised in international lifestyle publications like *CNN Money* and *International Living*, drives the demand for new, gated communities, if not in Vilcabamba, then elsewhere in Ecuador or Latin America. In the process, land has become a new form of commodity, valorized for its intangible, aesthetic quality rather than its agricultural productivity—the main use that can be derived from it for Ecuadorians who would remain in place. As real estate, land in Vilcabamba is heavily marketed online by international lifestyle marketers, alternative health entrepreneurs, and interests tied to the tourism industry.[8]

While the influx of foreigners creates certain employment opportunities, most of these are unskilled service jobs. "They take advantage of our labor," one woman told me. Construction may have provided good jobs, but, as she noted, "once the construction ended [at San Joaquín], there was nothing left for us." These jobs can only be recovered through more residential development on large gated estates. Gladys was a middle-aged homemaker and part-time worker who lived with her family in a bungalow they owned in the town. She told me about her brother who used to work at one of the construction sites but who is now unemployed and going into debt. Low-skilled construction workers also had to compete with workers willing to relocate either from other parts of Ecuador to work on a project or from across the border in Peru, where wages are even lower than they are in Ecuador's dollarized economy. The work is short term, and while at the moment there is lots of it, it is premised on the arrival of yet more North–South migrants and wealthier second home owners, making it less and less possible for workers to remain in place.

In addition to rising living costs and changing work conditions, research participants also noted the *malos costumbres* (bad habits) that lifestyle migrants brought with them, which also contributed to a sense of displacement and alienation. Some migrants from the Global North battled addictions such as alcoholism and drug use. Ecuadorian research participants lamented the exposure their children had to scenes and experiences that were foreign to their own upbringing in what was a quieter, more remote, rural valley. As Marcelo pointed out, "kids are having sex at a very young age." This was something he saw as the result of foreign influences rather than as the result of changing sexual mores within Ecuador itself. Gloria noted, "Before, kids didn't know what drugs were, but now people talk about drugs at a young age." For her, this was also a result of the influx of foreigners, who introduced problems and crime (though it may also have a great deal to do with how international drug networks have redeployed in the early twenty-first century around new production centres in the Peruvian Amazon). Unable to critique tourism and lifestyle migration trends on which their livelihoods depend, frustration over the process transforming their lives often seems to be expressed by identifying certain types of migrants who should be kept out. Yet the main mechanism of social exclusion operating in the valley remains the real estate market. Increasingly, the houses Ecuadorian workers build are not for them but for foreigners and second home owners (see Figure 9).

Even those who sell often find themselves in vulnerable positions, usually requiring that they move outside the valley. As Enrique stated, "properties pass into the hands of foreigners, which requires people to . . . look for other possibilities elsewhere in the country." Gabriela said, "We have to migrate . . . you have to leave to wherever you can find a way out." Alejandro concurred, noting that the effect of the foreigners settling in Vilcabamba was

Figure 9. New home construction, El Atillo, Vilcabamba, 2013. Photograph by the author.

that local people had to leave. Pilar mentioned that her twelve children now live in Quito, Loja, and Guayaquil. One had even moved abroad. Their remittances supplemented her fifty dollar per month pension. The rising price of land in Vilcabamba has enticed many *lugareños* to sell, but in doing so, some have also forced themselves into migration or into permanent dependence on landowning foreigners or wealthy locals. Just like the foreign migrants to Vilcabamba, not all those who have left in search of better lives have fared well. As Enrique put it, "they [*lugareño* migrants] benefit from selling the land, but there is a lot of poor investment. There is a lack of foresight, and people are left with no money, no land, nothing."

Coloniality, Inequality, and Migration

Like migration to Cuenca, lifestyle migration to the countryside offers an ethnographic window through which to explore "globalization," a concept that can sometimes be amorphous and abstract. In Vilcabamba, the acceleration and extension of transnationalism of people, commodities, and capital take concrete, material forms. Places once distant and isolated from one another are now only a few clicks and a flight away. Ecuadorian workers demonstrate resourcefulness in the face of the migration process now transforming the social and economic fabric of the valley. Many participate in their own transnationalism, leaving for global regions where they can earn higher incomes, albeit often forfeiting citizenship rights due to restrictive immigration rules and border regimes. For those who remain in Vilcabamba, the opportunities to benefit from the arrival of lifestyle migrants are not shared evenly. Those who own the most land are best positioned to benefit from the transnationalization of real estate and housing markets. The best businesses catering to higher-income foreigners and tourists are also owned by other lifestyle migrants.

The inflow of people from higher latitudes of the global division of labor injects new global inequalities into the internal colonial relations of the valley, as speculators exploit rent gaps, displacing and even impoverishing those with fewer resources.

This migration is a contemporary continuation of settler forms of colonialism, which clearly persist in various forms of "land grabbing" (cf. Mollett 2016; Zoomers 2010) and take new forms in an increasingly interconnected world of globalized lifestyles. North–South migrants, often with ostensibly good intentions or projects of self-fulfillment, participate in processes of appropriation by dispossession, in part because they lack a critical vocabulary and moral grammar to understand material, social–structural inequalities and their implication in them. Their lifestyles are the product of global social relations that deprive other people of the means of subsistence and that perpetuate high levels of poverty and underemployment. Vilcabamba should remind us of the apparent banality of colonialism and the conversion of a violent social process into something that appears peaceful, orderly, and inevitable.[9] It also illustrates how diverse forms of colonialism from different historical periods intersect in ways that multiply or exacerbate inherited inequalities. Lifestyle migrants intent on buying land and building new lives are also displacing working people, whose families struggled to obtain land on which they may have worked without wages for generations. The key commodity being sold in Vilcabamba is no longer peasant labor power but rather commodified land, which the *hacendado* class largely retained in a flawed process of land reform that occurred within the lifespans of most North American research participants.

Lifestyle migrants do not all act like neocolonials, nor do they understand their actions in Vilcabamba as participating in colonial-style dispossession.[10] As noted here, they employ individualistic cultural narratives of their migration, which prevent them from recognizing the collective processes in which their actions are embedded. The touristification of Vilcabamba valley, and the sale of land to foreign lifestyle migrants, no doubt offers some benefits to some local workers, at least some of the time. However, it does not offer workers greater ownership or direction over their lives, which ostensibly was what social movements for agrarian reform had hoped for in the 1960s and 1970s (and, indeed, what migrants like Elise, Katherine, and Johnathan desire for themselves). While there has been social mobility for rural Ecuadorians over the last generation, further advances for families of former *arrimados* seem mortgaged to land speculators in the name of economic growth and "development." Lacking the ability to relocate to lower rungs of the global division of labor, the best young *lugareños* can hope for is often a chance to relocate to the Global North, where they might earn more money, often in service industries catering to wealthier North Americans and Western Europeans.

The coloniality of contemporary migration becomes visible through an analysis of Vilcabamba, which serves, perhaps, as a microcosm of neoliberal globalization. Lifestyle migration is a colonial pathway, and to a certain extent, in Cuenca and Vilcabamba, North Americans act as settlers. To walk the dusty roads of El Atillo, or the steep paths of Yamburara, is to be at the heart of a colonial, capitalist economy, encapsulating the injustices of contemporary, global society.

6

Lifestyle Migration, Transnational Gentrification, and Social Justice

Lifestyle migration to locations in southern Ecuador illustrates how our emerging global society remains deeply entangled in social structures of inequality, many of them inherited from the colonial period. An ethnographic approach to lifestyle migration in southern Ecuador draws our attention to global social inequalities, their complexity, and how they are mutating under complex social circumstances, occurring at multiple scales and locations. North American migration to Latin American destinations, such as Cuenca and Vilcabamba, reproduces colonial patterns of domination in the absence of concerted and collective responses to them.

Contemporary processes of globalization demand more focused analysis on how historically unequal social relations and spatial injustices are morphing in a transnational, globalized world, marked by neoliberal social restructuring. In this respect, the greater economic insecurity facing a growing number of North American retirees can produce further insecurity and precarity in the Global South, where their migrations intersect existing inequality and internal colonialism and potentially reproduce unequal relations with respect to labor and space. This concluding chapter reflects on the intersection of lifestyle migration and gentrification, seeing in the changes afoot in Cuenca and Vilcabamba one of the main challenges facing a deeply unequal, highly mobile, and increasingly integrated global society: the power of higher latitudes to usurp and appropriate social space at lower latitudes of the global division of labor, activating global rent gaps and accentuating geographies of inequality

< 183 >

and spatial injustice on a global scale reminiscent of a history of colonial/global economic integration. These relations illustrate coloniality—the persistence of arbitrary, colonial forms of domination in neoliberal globalization, marked by increased transnational networks of social and economic integration mediated by free markets.

The changes taking place in Cuenca and Vilcabamba are familiar to scholars of spatial transformations on a global scale. They are contiguous with global gentrification (Atkinson and Bridge 2005; Lees, Shin, and López-Morales 2016; Shin 2018; Slater 2017) and intricately entwined with the consequences and crisis of the neoliberal capitalism of recent years (Duménil and Lévy 2011). The spatial arrangements described in chapters 4 and 5 are the product of a specific moment of capitalist accumulation. However, they are also the product of particular lives that have played out in historically specific material settings and cultural ideals. Much has been written in gentrification literature about whether culture or capital is the main motive force of gentrification (Atkinson and Bridge 2005; Lees, Slater, and Wyly 2008; Ley 1996; Smith 1996). The process currently under way in Cuenca underscores the importance of both, demonstrating how economic forces and cultural shifts at multiple scales and latitudes of global society produce social relations in local space that can be highly unequal and unjust.

The contiguity between urban gentrification and processes of colonialism has been hinted at before (cf. Atkinson and Bridge 2005; Blomley 2003), but often with respect to urban centers in the Global North. The coloniality of contemporary global society has not been entirely absent from migration scholarship either (see, e.g., Grosfoguel, Oso, and Christou 2015); however, the turn toward transnationalism in migration scholarship, which explicitly sought to embed studies of migration in global relations of surplus extraction and labor exploitation (Castles 2010; Glick Schiller 2009; Glick Schiller and Faist 2010; Hansen 2016; Hansen and Jonsson 2011), has often undertheorized North–South migration in ways that limit analyses of global mobility regimes (Glick Schiller and Salazar 2013). As Lundström (2017) points out, the experience of racialized white migrants from high-income countries in Europe decenters many of the core assumptions and problems of migration scholarship, which, as transnational scholars have pointed out, tends to focus too much on an "immigrant problem" and on the agendas of nation-states (Knowles 2017; Lundström 2017). An attempt to integrate not only privileged bodies moving across borders (cf. Amit 2007; Croucher 2012) but also their spatial effects helps to bring to the fore a global sociology grounded in sociohistorical forces and processes within which individual lives play out. The migration of North Americans to southern Ecuador enables us to appreciate how contemporary migration and regimes of mobility are embedded in historical, asymmetrical relations of exploitation and capital accumulation.

Moreover, in the period when formal colonial administration has lapsed, the economic crises that accompany enhanced global competition undermine the social conventions of countries in the Global North and thereby open new avenues not only to geoarbitrage and lifestyle migration but also to accumulation through real estate speculation aimed at taking advantage of historically produced rent gaps between the Global North and the Global South. These are the very rent gaps that make North–South migration desirable for a growing number of people seeking to escape the competitive environment of capitalist labor markets. Given that the baby boomer generation began to retire at the same moment as the most significant financial crisis since 1929, the potential for international lifestyle marketers to promote the idea and ideal of different forms of lifestyle arbitrage is obviously quite large. As Toyota and Xiang (2012) pointed out with respect to the Japanese retirement industry, national governments also have interests in dumping the social costs of an aging population onto other lower-cost regions in the Global South or in modifying transnational care chains such that care work itself is exported to lower-income countries (cf. Bender et al. 2014; Böcker, Horn, and Schweppe 2017; Ormond and Toyota 2016; Yeates 2012). Those who are no longer—or no longer wish to be—useful to the system of surplus production are compelled to either search for lower-cost environments or age into poverty. An international lifestyle industry now opens up new locations for settlement, recognizing the value of its growing market. While lifestyle migrants to Ecuador, on the whole, had little investment in colonialist social relations, they nonetheless embodied the coloniality of contemporary global society. They desired to escape capitalist social relations—in a few cases, explicitly so, though mostly they spoke of wanting to spend their remaining healthy years doing things that were more meaningful to them. Yet, they were the forces of capitalist real estate extractivism in the places they went. Their mobility and the advantages they obtained from it were contingent on a history of arbitrary injustices, with which a cosmopolitizing global civil society has not yet fully reckoned.

I develop this conclusion in three main parts. First, I attend to the concept of latitudes of the global division of labor and look at how powerful actors and institutions are able to appropriate spaces at lower-income latitudes. Next, the compression of these latitudes in an accelerated historical phase of globalization produces new opportunities for rent gaps that have been noted in some academic literature, and which I work out here under the rubric of transnational gentrification—the peculiar place effects of late capitalist appropriation of lower-income spaces, which can be transformed for higher-income activities. Finally, I discuss how the activation of global rent gaps, and their proliferation through international lifestyle marketers promoting lower-cost international retirements to economically insecure North American baby boomers, changes the meaning and character of local place and urban "revitalization." Local places can more easily be captured in a more globalized, mobile, and compressed environment. This leads to asymmetrical patterns of displacement.

Global Inequality in Local Place

I have borrowed Aihwa Ong's concept of latitudes as a way to enter into an analysis of global inequalities. I have done so because Ong's (2006) work draws attention to the symbolic and material inequalities at global scale, which are the result of an unequal global division of labor formed through a history of European colonial domination. North American migration to Cuenca draws our attention to a complex entanglement of different latitudes of the global division of labor, even as it also draws our attention to how the relations between latitudes are fundamentally shifting in ways that are producing new logics of transnational mobility. This section uncovers how the latitudes of a global division of labor help structure broader, global economic forces along hierarchical lines, such that the dislocating effects of neoliberal austerity are visited differently upon different populations, stratified across the global division of labor.

Over the last generation, North American workers have become more vulnerable to economic shocks that threaten to reposition them within the class systems of their home countries. This has had the effect of reducing their economic position without, however, really reducing their transnational mobility rights, at least not yet. As Ong (2006) points out, higher-value activities in the global division of labor are rewarded not merely in monetary terms but also in mobility rights and neoliberal citizenship. Ong calls these latitudes of citizenship, because the rights and privileges that are accorded to individuals in the global social field are unequally distributed according to social position and the core–periphery asymmetries of the global political economy. Although growing inequality in North America has reduced quality of life for some workers, many of my research participants were able to maintain material lifestyles because they had moved to a lower-income country. They could remain what Ong calls "exceptions to neoliberalism" only because the logic of the market, ever more harshly applied in Cuenca's urbanism, did not apply to them in the same way that it applied to the vendors of plaza San Francisco or to the former *arrimados* of Vilcabamba or Yunguilla.

While citizenship has usually been conceived as a claim on a territorially bounded polity which simultaneously constructs its excluded Other (Cresswell 2013; Isin 2002), North–South lifestyle migration demonstrates the asymmetrical ways that certain citizens of high-income countries can enhance their rights through mobility and how their "Otherness" can be almost seamlessly included in spaces they are able to appropriate and transform. A new generation of "global citizens" now shops around for the best set of resident rights or extraterritorial benefits—including residency requirements, health care, travel, and transit subsidies—in low-income countries (Bantman-Masum, forthcoming), just as corporations and tax avoiders have done for decades (see Deneault 2012). Lifestyle migrants practicing geoarbitrage, however, also draw our attention toward other migrants, whose bodies are much more tightly regulated by revanchist border regimes (Jones 2016). Citizens of higher latitudes of the global division of labor—usually located in countries in the Global North—are lightly regulated relative to those from lower latitudes in the Global South. This is one of the central organizing principles of contemporary global mobility regimes (Glick Schiller and Salazar 2013). It facilitates the development of utilitarian transnationalism at higher latitudes of the global division of labor, where individuals search for ways to better profit from historically inherited asymmetries of wealth and income. It is also a product of global coloniality, whereby citizens of countries that have traditionally been at the center of transnational networks of accumulation have acquired access to higher incomes and greater material resources, as a by-product of colonial administrations that subordinated nonwhite, colonized "Others." While the rights and advantages North–South migrants obtain through mobility across latitudes could potentially change in the future (and are therefore unstable), national governments in the South are unlikely to curtail them under current transnational financial regimes, in which tourists and foreign residents represent sources of foreign currency, perceived as necessary for other development goals or for debt repayment.

International institutions like the United Nations (through the United Nations World Tourism Organization) and the World Bank (through structural adjustment loans and the targeted development loans of the Inter-American Development Bank [IADB]) have promoted increased North–South tourist mobilities for several decades. Since the late 1970s, Latin American governments have sought—and been encouraged—to think of their historic El Centro neighborhoods as potential tourism assets. The IADB has facilitated loans, and development consultants have promoted urban redevelopment, especially in large metropolitan cities (Lees, Shin, and López-Morales 2016), but increasingly in smaller ones. The IADB also targeted UNESCO-designated sites with loan facilities aimed at heritage preservation and offered cities like Cuenca free consulting advice on how best to create more income from heritage assets and integrate them into modern urban plans. A growing market for urban heritage can be exploited across latitudes of the global division of labor, just as new land around these cities can be opened up for real estate development and secondary accumulation. As new technologies and low-cost airfares improve intercontinental communications and reduce their cost, the resulting time and space compression has helped transnationalize Latin American real estate markets, activating rent gaps on a global scale. It is not certain that financial interests have deliberately intended for global rent gaps to be appropriated by North–South migrants and real estate speculators, but it is one effect of neoliberal modes of development over the last generation. International financial institutions have promoted urban competitiveness and exacerbated global gaps between rich and poor, while investing in transportation and telecommunications infrastructure that has diminished relative distance in global space.

Multilateral development agencies, private corporations (including engineering and investment firms), and the IADB have collaborated to help Cuenca become a globalized city, able to access higher ground rents by attracting tourists, lifestyle migrants, and other activity from higher-paying latitudes of the global division of labor. With the help of international lifestyle marketers like *International Living,* the process has pulled Cuenca out of its provincial obscurity and positioned it as a global destination for tourists and lifestyle migrants alike. As in other midsize cities in emerging-market countries, the IADB and other bilateral development agencies have encouraged investment in large infrastructure projects, particularly a costly light-rail public transportation system, which required extensive consulting and engineering expertise from corporations in Europe, North America, and Japan. They have also invested in improving the aesthetic quality of Cuenca's public spaces, transforming them from useful places (for the people who live in them) into spaces whose usefulness comes from the exchange value of what they can symbolize (for the owners of real estate capital): "colonial style" without so many visible signs of colonialism.

Infrastructure projects are designed and guided by financial logic that conceives of emerging cities as competitive zones, which can be pulled into economic relations at a global scale and thereby made more useful to capital. Large infrastructure projects do resolve real problems that are the result of contemporary social processes in Latin America: congestion, traffic, and urban pollution, in this case. However, they also require financing and loan repayment, which obligates new relations of exploitation based on economic development. Cities must become more competitive—and increase ground rents and the public tax base to afford the loans. In Cuenca's case, this tax base has long been controlled by the landowning families who most benefit from policies that raise ground rents and that force informal workers and rural peasants into more intensive relations of exploitation.[1] In an economy dominated by low-income informal workers and shaped by a history of racial hierarchy, ground rent increases do not produce development; they produce inequality. The transnationalization of real estate in cities like Cuenca and its environs exacerbates these inequalities. The competitiveness of cities in the Global South is often premised on financial support from institutions in the Global North, which, thereby, are able to intensify exploitation, appropriating higher rents in the form of interest payments. Lifestyle migrants can pay higher rents and are attracted by infrastructure designed to improve the livability of cities. These improvements can be appropriated, especially in conditions where North Americans need a low-cost retirement destination to live up to the cultural ideal of "successful aging." This appropriation can broadly be termed as *gentrification*, which, in midsize Latin American cities like Cuenca, is a truly transnational phenomenon.

Transnational Gentrification

Though latitudes are the scaffolding of a sociology of global inequality, it is important to understand how geographies of difference and the opportunities, meanings, and uses of relative exchange values across latitudes are shifting as a result of the capitalist compression of space and time described earlier. This compression activates new opportunities to exploit rent gaps as spaces in the Global South are reimagined for higher-rent activities derived from offshoring lifestyles or activities previously located in the Global North. In many cases, attracting higher-income buyers from higher latitudes of the global division of labor is the only way to make investment in urban "revitalization" in lower-income countries profitable.[2] The spatial consequences of this type of urban intervention are well known in the North American context and go by the name "gentrification," whereby the population of a neighborhood is replaced by higher-income groups and activities (Clark 2005). Latin American studies of gentrification have pointed out that the class dynamics of the region do not favor the same types of gentrification processes as the Global North (Betancur 2014; Janoschka and Sequera 2016; Janoschka, Sequera, and Salinas 2014; Lees, Shin, and López-Morales 2016). The large number of informal workers with insecure incomes and the relatively small size of the middle class have meant that transnational actors and the state are much more important in supporting and financing higher-rent activities in historic centers than they are in North American cities. Moreover, the hollowing out of many of these historic centers in Latin America and the "regeneration" of these spaces through state investment in tourism has led to debates about what forms of dispossession, exclusion, and dislocation actually take place in these contexts and how they may differ from classical cases in urban studies (Delgadillo 2016; Gonzalez 2016). While Latin American studies of gentrification tend to focus on large metropolitan areas (Atkinson and Bridge 2005; Betancur 2014; Carrión Mena 2007; Durán 2015; Janoschka and Sequera 2016; Manrique Gómez 2013), and to a lesser degree on rural ones (cf. Bastos 2014; Gascón 2016; Rainer and Malizia 2015; Spalding 2013), the same processes also play out in smaller historical cities, such as Cuenca (for a study of San Miguel de Allende in Mexico, see also Pinley Covert 2017; Gárriz Fernández 2011). In these cities, as in larger ones, the potential to increase ground rents through support for "colonial-style" heritage preservation has drawn the IADB into the ambit of funding municipal intervention projects going back to the 1990s. Clearly, accumulation through land and real estate speculation has spread far beyond the big city "usual suspects" even in Latin American urban research.

Cuenca has become a globalized social space through a combination of transnational networks that entangle wealthy Ecuadorian landowners, Anglo-American international lifestyle marketers, developers and bankers from the Global North, and North American lifestyle migrants, most of whom are retirees in search of lower-cost retirement options. The transnational processes now changing the city also include remittances from Ecuadorian migrant workers in the Global North as well as return migrants—although these transformations tend to be on the city's edges more so than in its historic center (cf. Klaufus 2009). While a series of factors have combined to make the city the most expensive in Ecuador, heritage preservation and transnational lifestyle migration are now the main drivers of urban transformation.[3] This is because they represent demand for the higher-rent activity that the Municipio de Cuenca is intending to generate through intervention projects, often identified by foreign or IADB consultants. Since 2013, this latter has been working with Cuenca through its Emerging and Sustainable Cities program, part of its Housing and Urban Development loan portfolio. The intentions of this program are to make cities in Latin America and the Caribbean—many of them midsize cities like Cuenca—more competitive and integrated into an emerging global economy. Consultants have deliberately focused on growth strategies that will help Cuenca increase ground rents through urban improvement projects—but they do so in the absence of any program aimed at increasing local incomes. Thus the higher-rent activities will have to be supported by external forces, namely, tourism and lifestyle migration.

This promotion of urban "revitalization" in Cuenca's El Centro is, therefore, a form of urban colonialism (Atkinson and Bridge 2005), connected not only to processes of globalization but also to the coloniality of global structures of accumulation centered on new types of exploitation of urban land in the Global South. Just as in New York or London, where a global superelite have generated ground rent increases that no longer bear any relation to local incomes (Butler and Lees 2006; Fernandez, Hofman, and Aalbers 2016), so too has North–South migration to midsize cities and towns—like Cuenca and Vilcabamba—generated transnational processes of gentrification, displacement, and exclusion. These lifestyle migrants from higher-income countries—many of them a new type of economic migrant—are often seen as benign and are not perceived as competition for local laborers. However, they activate global rent gaps and help produce gentrification processes that displace them. Even in relatively small numbers, North American lifestyle migrants can have a very significant impact, as Cuenca and Vilcabamba demonstrate. As pension savings and financial security are undermined, baby boomer retirees seeking more livable, walkable urban spaces (which North American developers and municipalities singularly fail to produce) end up appropriating improvements that may be conceived of and justified as benefiting local populations.

This is not merely a free market process. As elsewhere in Latin America, the activation of rent gaps and the expansion of secondary circuits of accumulation have depended on heritage preservation in which local and national governments play an important part (Betancur 2014; Hylton 2007; Lees, Shin, and López-Morales 2016; López-Morales 2010). As noted in chapter 4, international financial institutions have also supported local government. In Cuenca's El Centro, IADB loans funded "intervention" projects designed to "revitalize" central plazas with the intention of raising ground rents. While attempts were made to provide services for workers who would soon be displaced, nothing was done to support the livelihood of, increase employment opportunities for, or improve the incomes of informal vendors— social justice policies that would require much more substantial economic reforms and global economic redistribution. Thus, as in other heritage cities targeted by the IADB and World Bank, attempts to improve competitiveness and aesthetics of downtown neighborhoods have promoted gentrification and displacement (Betancur 2014; Carrión 2007; Lees, Shin, and López-Morales 2016, 100–103; Sigler and Wachsmuth 2016). Moreover, this displacement overlaps the marginalization of rural and indigenous traditions in shaping the modern heritage city and reproduces caste systems that exacerbate income inequalities.

Increasing the market value of heritage sectors is consistent with national developmentalist programs, which are increasingly called into question, in the Ecuadorian context in particular, through the politics of *sumak kawsay* or *buen vivir.* These principles seek to enhance quality of life outside of traditional economic growth models. But the existing emphasis on growth and heritage tourism also marginalizes alternatives. The national government's support for Cuenca's urban heritage redevelopment and its *tranvía* project intended to extract more exchange value from existing space, positioning Cuenca as an important part of its national tourism strategy. While the migration of North American retirees to the city has been crucial to actually realizing ground rent increases, the process of gentrification was both state led and promoted by international financial institutions. The latter's ability to compel the action of the Ecuadorian state, obliging it to pursue policies that maximize foreign exchange earnings, is a reflection of neoliberal developmentalism, which was consolidated in the debt crisis of the early 1980s—a crisis created by banks located and owned in the Global North (which overlent for projects that were sometimes never going to be profitable) but which was paid for by workers in the Global South (who lost decades of development as their countries repaid loans to the Global North at the usurious interest rates of the Carter and Reagan administrations). Tourism and heritage gentrification in Cuenca fit within a colonial history of accumulation through dispossession and depends on the epistemic coloniality of developmentalist thinking (Escobar 1995; Quijano 2000), which presumes that economic growth in the Western, Eurocentric pattern provides better lives for everyone.

In Cuenca, state-led urban gentrification is also an elite-driven process, dependent on local architects and developers, many of them from wealthy, landed families. Their interests in increasing ground rents also work to favor appropriation of lower-income spaces by higher-income latitudes and thus perpetuate a long history of urban colonialism. Municipal participation in urban "interventions" and infrastructure upgrades stimulated large private construction sites that have supplanted formerly lower-income housing in central areas of the city (see Figure 10). Large

Figure 10. New condominium construction, Cuenca, 2015. Photograph by the author.

private developments of luxury condo apartments are sold advertising modern, European appliances in English (see Figure 11). These urban interventions are conducted under the guidance of the IADB, whose Emerging and Sustainable Cities program specifically calls for a change in Cuenca's model of urban growth toward a denser urban layout.[4] The new condominiums are marketed to the professional classes and to foreign lifestyle migrants who can pay the rents that make these projects profitable. For Ecuadorian middle and upper-middle classes, units might be purchased as an investment, with the intention of renting to foreign residents. In Gringolandia and elsewhere in the central areas of Cuenca, North American tenants are the main driving force of increased rents on land and condominium units, much as tenants have been the leading force in other Latin American gentrifications (Inzulza-Contardo 2012).

Moreover, as Sigler and Wachsmuth (2016) note of Panama's Casco Viejo, the urban transformations taking place in Cuenca could not be sustained on the basis of local income and investment

Figure 11. Condominium construction, advertising amenities, Cuenca, 2015.
Photograph by the author.

alone. Growth and ground rent increases depend on demand from
higher latitudes of the global division of labor. Thus local improvements always risk being appropriated by people from higher latitudes, who are able to pay to sustain higher-rent activities. Such
appropriation is the indirect outcome of the institutional politics
at the core of transnational gentrification. As heritage tourism
in Latin America and other regions of the Global South begins
to attract transnational lifestyle migrants (including those motivated by economic factors, as seen in chapter 1), more analytical
attention must be focused on coloniality and transnational appropriation of space as well as the intersections of lifestyle ideals
and place imaginaries that move across latitudes of the global division of labor and activate global rent gaps. Whereas much of
the existing literature on "land grabbing" and *extranjerización* (or
foreignization) of land has focused on agricultural land or natural resources (Borras and Franco 2012; Borras et al. 2012; Glauser
2009; Kaag and Zoomers 2014; Zoomers 2010), there is a growing
need to analyze these processes in urban settings as well (see van
Noorloos 2011; van Noorloos and Steel 2016).

The ability to attract higher-income demand to urban areas
of the Global South is a product of historically specific material
circumstances and contingent lifestyle ideals. In the case of life-

style migration to Ecuador, cultural ideals are an important factor in configuring the emerging forms of neoliberal globality, which shape social hierarchies at different latitudes. The cultural ideal of successful aging (Boudiny 2012; Dillaway and Byrnes 2009; Katz 2005; McHugh 2000) was readily visible in the discourses of North Americans in Cuenca, who assigned moral worth and social distinction to themselves (as adventurous) and others like them (as brave), as noted in the introduction, often on the basis of staying active and avoiding signs of aging or of slowing down. Echoing Diana and Rick, Brett, (age seventy, Vancouver) whom we met in chapter 2, mentioned that the "adventure" of living in a different culture "keeps you young . . . and you don't fossilize." North Americans have internalized the ideal of taking individual responsibility for an aging process that is supposed to maximize health, welfare, and sociability through independent action, instead of relying on entitlement welfare programs, which the ageist discourse on health care reform in the United States has framed as unaffordable. While North American lifestyle migrants appear to be breaking new ground and experimenting in novel lifestyles, these latter also follow socially sanctioned cultural codes and prescribed paths that are shaped by policy debates from the 1980s and 1990s (cf. Dillaway and Byrnes 2009), increasingly packaged by an international lifestyle industry and effectively rendering them conformist, even as they may appear unorthodox.

It is easy to identify with the cultural ideals and lifestyle experiments articulated by Diana, Rick, and Brett. Their lives do seem exciting and full of potential, in part because so many people today identify with travel and personal growth as the ends of successful living and aging. Often, they are the lives we would want for ourselves. They inspire us to find our own sources of adventure. But they are also culturally and politically produced ideals that play out in the tension between a utilitarian accumulation of intense experiences (e.g., living in a way that produces as much "true" inner happiness as possible; cf. Bellah et al. 1985) and the enforced conformity of prescribed consumer lifestyles, promoted by marketers (like *International Living*) and corporate interests whose vision of global society is one of increasing competitiveness and profitability. They individualize responsibility for health and sociability in aging at the expense of a more holistic approach that would recognize and address social inequalities. Lifestyle migration to Ecuador is an experiment with life, but one that is increasingly a mass-produced, catered phenomenon, with a market of individuals searching (and sometimes needing) to partake in it.[5] As an ideal of adventurous aging, it is the product of a competitive, neoliberal culture of constant self-evaluation and comparison that leads us to be dissatisfied with lives that seem to fade out.

Coloniality and Displacement

Being able to fall back on lower latitudes of the global division of labor doesn't merely facilitate experimentations in new lifestyles for North American migrants. As Ipsita Chatterjee (2014) suggests, it also implies the exploitation of other lifestyles, which otherwise made use of the spaces being occupied by North–South migrants. Working Ecuadorians, especially those in informal sectors, working as small agriculturalists or as street vendors (and often as both), are put to work in support of the lifestyles of others at higher latitudes of the division of labor. Their lives are also resettled in new spaces that allow for higher levels of accumulation—accumulation that also means exploitation for workers made more vulnerable and whose choices about how and where to work are further limited. Furthermore, the national institutional setting in which the lifestyles of lower-income Ecuadorians play out is influenced by the epistemic colonialism of Eurocentric development projects, which seek to create higher-income activities that also require higher levels of economic exploitation and appropriation of labor power. The problem has long been that capitalist markets have had little use for the excess labor power of informal workers in the Global South, meaning that exploitation takes other forms, including physical and symbolic displacement and exclusion from the places where higher profits can be realized as accumulation strategies shift from extraction of labor power to extraction of ground rent.

Popular social classes on lower incomes in Ecuador have different uses and needs for the spaces of El Centro and harbor decidedly different imaginaries of what these spaces mean to them. They often lack incomes necessary to maintain properties and have a decidedly more pragmatic relationship to heritage. Instead of a collective process of maintenance and upgrading, lower-income people are displaced by private hopes of increased ground rent made possible by North American lifestyle migrants who can pay higher rental prices for renovated properties. This is, of course, just one more way that "heritage" is socially constructed. In Cuenca, higher-income migration enables renovation of older properties that, without this migration, would fall into ruin or be destroyed. Of course, the heritage of lower-income groups is often marginalized or lost, unless it can attract higher rents. When it does, it ceases to belong to lower-income groups and is appropriated by higher latitudes.

Moreover, the economic limitations to lower latitudes' ability to care for heritage is a product of the extreme forms of historically accumulated exploitation, in which North Americans in Ecuador may have little investment but from which they benefit all the same in terms of the availability of low-income workers for low-income domestic work. While some North Americans may wish to counter this history by establishing paternalistic relations with their service class workers (or attempt to improvise less paternalistic and more egalitarian forms), for instance, by paying them higher than normal rates, such one-to-one solutions to global inequality do nothing to challenge or change established hierarchies of class and status—though they are no doubt much appreciated by the individuals who are helped. Indeed, in many cases, North Americans identify with and promote changes intended to beautify the city, but often at the expense of lower social classes, whose priorities for limited public funds may be different.

The spatial injustices of lifestyle migration also play out through the widespread support North American migrants express for urban infrastructure projects that will help "modernize" the city and bring it into line with their tastes and lifestyle desires. New projects like the light-rail *tranvía* construction align the city's "European-style" heritage with the imaginaries of North Americans. Of course, this imaginary is sustained by the global boom in heritage cities (Brumann 2014), which

increasingly follow similar and proscribed forms of urban management and "upgrading" (D'Eramo 2014). In the heritage city,
even public transportation increasingly takes a symbolic form.
Its value comes not from the usefulness of transporting the public through the city (since the Cuenca *tranvía* plan actually sacri-
fices the system's transportation utility and increases its cost for
a predominantly low-income ridership) but from its potential to
increase ground rents along the *tranvía* route, in the historic district of El Centro, which is increasingly arranged to make higher-
income travelers feel like they are in Europe. The effects are,
potentially, new forms of spatial apartheid, as Cuenca's El Centro
becomes increasingly difficult to access or to move through for
the majority of the city's workers. Taxi drivers and others dependent on access to El Centro worried about new plans for pedestrian streets and for laneways dedicated to the *tranvía*.[6] During
construction, which required what can only be described as her-
culean civil tolerance of an open construction zone in the heart of
the city, some two hundred businesses in El Centro closed along
the *tranvía* route, fomenting speculation about what might follow.[7] Some of the buildings along the route are owned by the city
and are being renovated for new tourist purposes, relying, therefore, on foreign demand. Streetscapes that used to be dominated
by popular *tiendas,* bakeries, restaurants, offices, and so on, are
now transformed into higher-end cafés, restaurants, and bars.
In a context marked by the transnationalization of Ecuadorian
real estate, urban improvements that help market the city to international travelers and residential tourists have the potential
to produce spatial exclusions and "territorial disqualifications"
(Angelicos and Méndez 2017) on the basis of housing affordability, popular commercial practices, streetscape uses, and even mobility across the city. Other urban revitalization projects, such
as the very popular and extensively used Parque de la Madre, in
El Vergel opposite the Tomebamba from El Centro, have drawn
new investment from transnational retailers like McDonald's.
Similar investments can be expected in El Centro as the *tranvía*
and urban "improvements," such as the renovation of plaza San
Francisco, are completed.

As Cuenca has transnationalized into a lifestyle hub, a growing number of middle- and lower-income Ecuadorians have been

displaced from neighborhoods where they could most easily access work, schools, and city services, which are sparse in the outlying areas. Local media have begun to comment regularly about the rise in real estate prices and the lack of affordability in central neighborhoods, where the municipality claims most North Americans are now living—in El Centro and along the main avenues leading from it—avenida Odroñez-Lasso (Gringolandia) to the west and avenida Remegio Crespo to the south of El Centro (García Álvarez, Osorio-Guerrero, and Pastor Herrera 2017). Rental listings in local newspapers explicitly solicit foreign renters for central properties, which are listed at prices that are unaffordable to locals but which local owners claim represent the real costs of their investments.[8] Despite an increase in condo supply in central neighborhoods, lower-income Ecuadorians have not gained access to housing there, and social housing projects financed through Ecuadorian state companies are located far from El Centro. One young mother, who worked as a housecleaner, was interviewed by *El Tiempo* about how difficult it is to find housing in central neighborhoods, a theme that I also heard from Ecuadorian research participants. She was quoted as saying, "It seems like housing is only for foreigners."[9] The article went on to say that she and her family were forced to rent further out from the city, north of the airport and the industrial zone, where they had less access to bus lines and where a lack of lighting contributed to feelings of insecurity. Their modified lifestyles, marked by commuting, safety fears, and new household compositions, are the corollary of North American lifestyle experiments in transnational social space.

It is not merely physical space that is appropriated but also symbolic space. A study by the Universidad de Cuenca noted that much of the activity directed toward the expanding heritage tourism and foreign resident population has clustered in El Centro (Rey et al. 2017),[10] significantly changing the character of certain parts of the downtown. Wealthier than many middle-income Ecuadorians, gregarious North American expats who can take in the orchestra or the local arts scene have also fundamentally transformed these scenes in ways that are significant for a city that has long prided itself on its artistic production. One Cuencana research participant in her thirties who was active in the arts scene said that North Americans had come to dominate certain arts institutions and had increasingly pushed artists themselves further into the suburbs, where rents were affordable, but potentially limiting their access and exposure to networks in El Centro. One 2014 arts event integrated short documentaries by Cuencanos and North Americans about the indigenous heritage of one of the historic neighborhoods abutting plaza Otorongo. Ostensibly an event that demonstrated cross-cultural integration and cooperation, it also reproduced colonial patterns of misrecognition of indigenous culture that have long plagued Cuencano society. One video discussed the natural healing powers of indigenous medicine, essentializing indigenous subjects and locating indigenous people in an idealized nature—thus perpetuating a history of spatial marginalization within the city. Another told the history of one of Cuenca's neighborhoods where indigenous people who managed to free themselves from the hacienda system historically settled. But it provided no context of the exploitation of indigenous labor forces in the countryside nor of the forced assimilation and discrimination that indigenous people faced in the city. Instead, it repeated existing tropes in which indigenous people in Cuenca are mobilized by elites as decorative figures, much as the folkloric chola Cuencana (Mancero Acosta 2012; Weismantel 2001) (see Figure 12). Significantly, I noted a dearth of participants who seemed to identify as indigenous, making the tone of conversations about indigeneity decidedly more objectifying and exoticizing than discussions that might foster greater knowledge of the complexities of indigenous identities in Ecuador and the consequences of ongoing colonial violence, epistemic devaluation of indigenous knowledge, and the occupation of indigenous land (Becker 2010; Bravo Díaz 2013; Bretón Solo de Zaldívar 2015a, 2015b; Célleri 2016; Kingman 2006; Meisch 1995; Noroña 2006; Roitman 2009; Weismantel 2001).

These spatial and social impacts reproduce colonial patterns. The integration of Cuencano real estate into global markets amounts to a phenotypical whitening of transnationalized social space (Mollett 2016), reproducing the racialized caste system that has long characterized class inequalities in Ecuador, which relegates indigenous heritage and tradition to the margins of a "civilizing" project—this time in the guise of urban renewal through heritage preservation (see Figure 13). While the remittance

Figure 12. The decorative chola Cuencana, a symbol of Cuenca. Photograph by the author.

economies and South–North migration patterns of previous decades may have militated in the direction of greater equality and spatial transformations favoring popular classes, North–South migration often inverts this.[11] North Americans may desire to appreciate Ecuador "as it is" rather than trying to make it "like it was back home" (see also Hayes and Carlson 2018), but their presence in Ecuadorian space most often transforms it in ways that suit their lifestyle ideals, their notions of a "colonial-style" city, and their tastes. This is not a product of "obnoxious gringos" or of the moral dispositions (or lack thereof) of individual North Americans. It is a product of inherited structural asymmetries that provide North–South migrants with significant economic and symbolic advantages in Ecuador.

Moreover, transnational gentrification produces new geographies of gendered exploitation. The thousands of North Americans relocating to Cuenca often wish to employ part-time "help," one of the main ways that they interact with local Cuencanos. As rents become prohibitive in neighborhoods in and near El Centro, the feminized labor force of low-cost caregivers and domestic workers who cater to the foreign population of lifestyle

Figure 13. Restoration work in El Centro, Cuenca, 2015. Photograph by the author.

migrants live increasingly far from where they work, where they can afford rents. The lifestyle experiments of North American migrants are often related to other lifestyle experiments involving the long commutes of working mothers and to new relationships of care in low-income communities. Even in outlying suburbs, like Challuabamba, real estate development for upper-class gated communities and suburban *fincas* threatens lower-income workers with displacement to areas even farther out from El Centro. This spatial separation for domestic workers is a long-standing tradition in Cuenca, where wealthy families have always sought out domestic workers from dependent families on their haciendas in the countryside. As the demand for this type of labor increases, potentially providing more employment to women, they are also increasingly relocated from central neighborhoods to ones farther out. This has a significant impact on the commute times of women and children and on their safety and security in a city that, while relatively safer than many American cities, nonetheless has significant problems with violent criminality.

There was a real desire on the part of most migrants with whom I spoke to avoid negative outcomes for Ecuadorians . After all, they themselves often just wanted to be able to retire or to avoid "genteel poverty" in their retirement years, check out from divisive American politics, or escape the insane work lives of a hypercompetitive labor market. Though they often identified with the privileges of being wealthier patrons in a low-income country (which warrants further critique and reflection), they most often showed little conscious desire to lord privilege and status over Ecuadorians of any class background and held genuine and sometimes deep egalitarian intentions. One might draw some hope from these dispositions. The problems I have identified in this book are not an argument for excluding people from transnational migration and travel—though, following Valentine (2008), I am under no illusion that this on its own will produce more cosmopolitan, egalitarian outlooks on the part of North–South migrants. Quite aside from what are often good intentions, North American participation in transnational gentrification is the product of structural forces that are often overlooked and for which research participants often lacked a language even to describe.

Neoliberalism, Migration, and Global Social Justice

As North American social relations morphed after 2008 under pressures of neoliberal austerity and rapacious logics of accumulation and expulsion, countries like Ecuador welcomed to their shores thousands of economic migrants with higher incomes than most local residents. These self-proclaimed "refugees" have activated local rent gaps that provide a few with opportunities for profitable investment. But they also produce gentrification, residential exclusions, and the displacement of informal workers from spaces rezoned for higher-income activity, a process so often called "development." In addition to potential future cuts to public health insurance in the United States, workers throughout the Western capitalist liberal democracies face increasingly casualized careers and unstable work and family lives. Since the free market neoliberal consensus offers nothing by way of resolution to these structural problems but only exacerbates them, one can expect citizens from the high-income countries of the Global North—increasingly left to their own devices to support themselves in conditions they can neither choose nor completely control—to continue experimenting with new lifestyles in affordable, lower-cost locations. Though some of these locations will be in the United States or Canada, many will continue to be in Latin America.

Despite the social costs, the desire for profitable investments and higher rents ensures that cities and towns will have to compete to become lifestyle enclaves. Even areas that don't actively seek lifestyle migrants might receive them, as higher latitudes undergo structural changes that prevent an increasing number of people from maintaining their livelihoods in regions zoned for high productivity and high incomes and that require the disciplined bodies of a competitive capitalist workforce. This is not for everyone, as the high rates of depression and dropout in the Global North make only too clear. Perhaps southern Ecuador will continue to be a key refuge. From a certain perspective, its mountains and rivers are becoming ever more powerful actors on the global social scene, attracting different types of migrants from around the world, a growing number of whom are drawn to the siren songs of its *duendes,* or spirits, like the ones that inhabit the lakes of the nearby Cajas Mountains.[12] In a world of ever-increasing and rapacious extractivism (mining must also keep up with the frenetic, competitive pace of the machines), the *duendes* may sense that their best chance of survival depends on turning the city they have fostered over centuries into a global safe haven for higher-paying customers. Perhaps they will be the last before climate change silences all these other spirits and returns the Earth to the mountains and the lakes—the true sovereigns in Andean epistemology.

The *duendes* may, of course, call another tune. There are workable alternatives to global neoliberalism. The current encounter between North American lifestyle migrants and Ecuadorian informal workers in places like Vilcabamba and plaza San Francisco is mediated by unequal global social relations, but relations can be contested and changed. As chapters 1 and 3 pointed out, lifestyle migrants often identify with existing inequalities, which place them in more powerful social positions. As chapter 2 discussed, they also often (though not always) assign responsibility for this inequality to the backwardness and lack of work ethic of Ecuadorian workers, which belies the real social forces disrupting the lives of all the players on this stage. An alternative encounter would have to be based on more egalitarian global social structures, ones that bring the sharply unequal latitudes of the global division of labor much closer together rather than merely relying on whatever good intentions individuals can muster on their own. In the absence of institutions and collective representations that might enforce global social relations based on solidarity, care, and mutual aid, these intentions cannot counter the destructive force of the market. In contrast to the morality of the market, the values of altruism and solidarity remain marginal to the macrostructures driving global neoliberalism, despite their importance in the lives of so many of my research participants (and of my students in Canada, most of whom want careers that would allow them to give of themselves in ways that are recognized by others). The apparently natural demands of free market competition, profit imperatives, and the continuous push for ever greater productive efficiency are the very forces generating economic insecurity and subjective feelings of stress and "frenetic standstill" (Rosa 2013). Cleary lifestyle migrants who desire to escape the cultural and economic excesses of late capitalist life are not crazy. However, in an unequal global society, they can be the carriers of the very forces they seek to escape, as discussed in chapters 4 and 5.

As carriers of powerful but destructive social forces, the gringos of Cuenca give rise to powerful counternarratives of their emplacement, ones that take a variety of different forms. One day, I had the good fortune of being able to join a group of North Americans whom Eileen (age fifty-seven, from North Carolina) brought along to one of the popular markets to teach how to communicate in Spanish with the vendors and ask for certain fruits and vegetables. While Eileen was dutifully explaining something to the small group she'd brought along, I briefly wandered off, and encountered an older woman wearing a checkered apron— typical of the market women of Cuenca at this time—and whose hands seemed to me to suggest intimate familiarity with the soil in which her vegetables grew. She looked at me quizzically. I said hello to her in Spanish and we talked briefly. She, now the interviewer, asked me what I was doing there, and I explained. She paused, squinted, and looked past me to the small group and then back. "Ah, yes, there are a lot of gringos coming here now," she said. "They are sick. They work too much," she added without rancor. It struck me that this interpretation held more than a kernel of truth. North Americans, like Paula in chapter 2, narrated their relocations in terms that were not always very dissimilar. Perhaps this woman's attention to overwork and health problems referenced her own knowledge of Ecuadorian laborers who move to the United States to work in precarious conditions and who return with their own narratives of global inequality. Her words could no doubt be interpreted in other ways, but they left me thinking that North Americans in Cuenca could not count on being the writers of their own stories for much longer. Below the powerful positions they (we) currently occupy seems to loom another story, which will be uncomfortable to hear.

Acknowledgments

This book is the product of many serendipitous trajectories. I first thought about taking on research about North Americans on tight budgets relocating to Ecuador at the very beginning of 2011, while visiting my friend Gabriela Molina in Cuenca. On the edge of a lake in the Cajas Mountains, I had the good fortune of running into a couple from Oregon, who told me about why they had decided to move to Ecuador. At the time, I was not a scholar of this type of migration. I was, I thought, an economic sociologist, interested in a new research project (something more empirical than my dissertation work, I told myself). I was interested in how the Great Recession had produced new lifestyles in the shadow of growing inequalities. From there, this project morphed a thousand times, and I am lucky to have met so many fantastic people along the way who collaborated in it, who challenged me, and who helped me grow as a person and as a scholar.

The book itself passed through many places. First conceived in Alicante and Madrid, much of it came out between Cuenca and Fredericton, with significant stops in Berlin, Marrakesh, Valencia, Toronto, and Kamloops.

I am therefore deeply indebted to many people who have influenced this work in different ways. First, I would never have visited Cuenca without the friendships I forged as a student in Salamanca, especially with Gabriela Molina. I am particularly indebted to her family for their generosity and encouragement to pursue this research and to her husband, Thommy, for great discussions and friendship. My yearly visits to Cuenca were undertaken eagerly knowing we would keep up our reflections on the world and our lives in it.

I am grateful to colleagues in Ecuador who shared their knowledge and perspectives on their country and on Ecuadorian scholarship. I am particularly grateful to Ana Borrero, Andrea Bravo, Patricio Carpio, Daniela Célleri, María Mercedes Eguiguren, Gioconda Herrera, Israel Idrovo, Michel Levi, Pablo Osorio, Monserrath Tello, and María Amelia Viteri for their discussions, help, and encouragement. I am also indebted to Ann Miles and Lynn Hirschkind, American scholars of Cuenca who generously shared their experiences and knowledge of a place they love. I hope my own work demonstrates something of the care and affection I learned from them for a city and region that faces perennial challenges stemming from its colonial history and the unequal organization of the global economy.

Many others were integral to shaping this project. Daniela Paiva taught me a great deal about Latin American cities. Our reflections on inequality, privilege, and discrimination greatly influenced my work in Ecuador. Emmanuelle Piccoli taught me of her love for the Andes and its people and opened windows I may otherwise have passed over. Her suggestions for readings, her brilliant conversations, and her wonderful friends are integral to this book. I am deeply indebted also to Alejandro Campos-García for his friendship and for introducing me to scholarship on decoloniality. Our discussions about critical race theory and global sociology have shaped my outlook and this book.

Others read earlier versions of my work and provided critical and supportive comments, either at conferences or more informally. Thank you to my colleagues in the Canadian Network for Critical Sociology, especially Fuyuki Kurasawa and Marcia Oliver. In addition, I am indebted to Michaela Benson, who challenged me intellectually in the conceptualization of this work, provided stimulating feedback, and pushed me in new directions, especially during a visiting fellowship at Goldsmiths University of London in May 2017. Kristi Allain helped fine-tune late drafts of my chapters. Her exceptional theoretical breadth and knowledge of key literatures helped make this a more coherent piece of work. Luin Goldring provided helpful comments, suggestions, and encouragement, which was important to me as I began this work. Raquel Huete and Alejandro Mantecón enhanced my understanding of the spatial and environmental effects of lifestyle migration during a visiting fellowship at the Universidad de Alicante in 2015. They also introduced me to Joan Carles Membrado, from the Universidad de Valencia, who graciously produced maps that are reproduced in this book. Lola Arteaga Revert produced maps of urban Cuenca, for which I am very grateful. Despite all their great advice and help, I remain responsible for the shortcomings in this work.

My research was primarily the product of small grants at a small university and, I would like to think, an example of how more egalitarian granting structures can help scholars do research that is meaningful to them and interesting to others and that informs the teaching they bring to the classroom. It was a more egalitarian granting structure at St. Thomas that allowed my research in Ecuador to get off the ground. I am grateful to my colleagues there who helped to support my work, and especially to Shaun Narine, who led the St. Thomas Global and International Studies Initiative, and Danielle Connell and Mike Dawson, who have backstopped our Research Office. Their help has since led to other grants that will help me continue my work. Tri-Council funding guidelines require that I recognize funding from the Canada Research Chair in Global and International Studies, which began in 2016. By that time, the bulk of the work represented in this book was done and funded by small grants at St. Thomas.

These grants helped employ a talented group of undergraduate students who participated in various ways in this research: Rachael Arseneault, Rheanna Bibby, Ella Henry, Mary-Dan Johnson, Mai López, Julia Roul, Keith Van Every, Riley Williams, and Alexandra Woodworth. I am also grateful for the help of University of New Brunswick graduate students Erfan Mojib, for his excellent help with data coding, and Tracy Glynn, for her research. Stephanie Dotto, a PhD candidate from Trent University, provided invaluable editorial help. Most of all, I am indebted to my transcriber, Jesse Carlson, then a PhD candidate at York University, whose expertise helped push me as an interviewer and whose insightful comments helped guide coding.

Of course, this book is about the stories of the people who participated in my research, starting with the people I met in Cuenca from 2011 to 2016 and who captured my attention with their friendliness and fascinating life stories. I found myself pulled into the stories of so many of the people with whom I spoke—not all of whom could be adequately included in this book. I tried to be true to the stories they told me, both in terms of how they narrated their experiences and in terms of some of the things they talked about and controversies to which they drew attention. These latter often spoke to issues that were not always immediately present in our conversations. I hope most lifestyle migrants in Cuenca will recognize the issues I speak about here, though no doubt there is such a wide variety of experiences, backgrounds, and ideas about what it means to live and age in Cuenca that it would be impossible to capture everyone's experience fully without writing a much longer book whose value might be lost in the expansive detail on which it could draw. I am especially appreciative of the friendships I formed with some of my participants and of our conversations about what life looks like from different age points. These will stay with me.

In this book, I tried to lay out what I think are important issues lifestyle migrants from higher-income countries might want to think about. These thoughts are not intended to discourage people from living abroad, or from living in lower-income countries. But they are a call to reflect on the consequences of lifestyle mobilities in a highly unequal world. The facility with which people like myself can move across borders and settle in lower-income communities like Cuenca and Vilcabamba warrants reflection. These unequal mobilities show how our very own successes and failures are partly the product of unfair and arbitrary social forces that warrant care and critical attention. I am sure some of the innovative and thoughtful migrants who have relocated to Cuenca or communities like it will find new ways to address some of the issues I bring up in this book, or may already be doing so.

I am greatly indebted to Ecuadorians from diverse backgrounds who participated in this study. Initially, I did not set out to study how Ecuadorians saw the arrival of North Americans, but as my research expanded and as I became more knowledgeable of Ecuadorian history, I began to realize that the topic of life-style migration was broader than I initially thought. I hope that this book reflects my solidarity with their ongoing work to build a better city and better region for all members of their community as well as my desire to continue to learn from them.

Appendix

Methodology

This book is based on six field site visits to Cuenca from 2011 to 2016. Events at plaza San Francisco discussed in chapter 4 are ongoing at time of writing, and material was included from fieldwork on a seventh visit conducted in Cuenca in December and January 2017–18. In all, I spent thirty-nine weeks in Ecuador, with visits ranging from three weeks to three months. During this time, I conducted ethnographic research, participating in the social life of North Americans in Cuenca, and coupled this with semistructured qualitative interviews, through which I asked questions regarding migrants' motivations and the meanings they gave to their transnational relocations. The results of my study are not intended to be representative of the population of migrants in Cuenca as a whole—a population that, in any case, has grown and changed over the course of the study and that contains a diversity of lifestyles, life stories, and social positions. I was more interested in the ways North Americans talked about their lives and their community in Ecuador and aimed to gather socially significant narratives rather than merely representative ones. Participants and other lifestyle migrants to Ecuador might recognize, therefore, that certain elements of their experience have been omitted or overlooked. I sought mostly to reflect on how North Americans in southern Ecuador gave meaning to their migration and how they made sense of cultural and ethnic differences and inequalities. Although I used a diversity of sampling techniques (convenience, snowball, and reputational), individuals who participated in civic organizations or in the social life of the North American migrant community dominate my sample. My results may, therefore, underrepresent socially isolated individuals, who are usually overrepresented in the retirement age population (see Klinenberg 2001).[1] I did hear of socially isolated or "shut-in" migrants but, despite attempts, was not able to interview anyone I felt to be truly cut off from other social relations in the community of expatriates. When isolated people were mentioned, those with whom I spoke alluded to people who were "too afraid" to come down into the street—a social anxiety perhaps also mixed with racial awareness.

In Cuenca, I conducted 83 semistructured qualitative interviews with 108 separate individuals (55 men, 53 women, and 23 couples interviewed together). Of these interviews, eleven were with Canadians. I interviewed ten participants a second time. Interviews ranged in length from just under thirty minutes to longer than two hours, with most interviews lasting about an hour. The vast majority of participants are in their sixties ($n = 57$); however, they ranged in age from twenty-nine to eighty years. In addition to this, I opened a separate field site in 2013 in Vilcabamba to assess landscape impacts of lifestyle migration in a rural community (Hayes 2015a). Over four field site visits from 2013 to 2016, totaling three weeks in Vilcabamba, I conducted sixteen interviews with twenty-one lifestyle migrants (twelve men, nine women).[2]

In the book, I avoid making statistical generalizations about the overall population, whose numbers are also difficult to estimate because no government agency keeps official statistics of North American residents living in Ecuador. In fact, a recent Municipality of Cuenca report funded by the United Nations Development Programme was unable to find a precise number of lifestyle, or residential, migrants (García Álvarez, Osorio-Guerrero, and Pastor Herrera 2017). The number of residency visas (of which there were more than eighty-two hundred in the 2010 census) serves as a proxy number, but it does not account for people who may have migrated irregularly (quite a few North Americans enter the country and overstay their visas) or who may have obtained a visa and subsequently left, either returning to their home country or moving on to other destinations, which is a frequent occurrence (see Bantman-Masum 2015a).

Table 1. Numbers of North American research participants by age (in years)

	Under 45	45–54	55–64	65–74	75+
Cuenca	11	6	40	34	5
Vilcabamba	4	7	4	6	–

Note. I interviewed 108 participants in total (including couples interviewed together) and did not record ages for 12. Their approximate ages would have been fifty years or older.

In addition to these interviews in Cuenca, I also conducted forty-one interviews with Cuencanos (thirteen men, twenty-eight women). These interviews began in 2013 and focused on people who either worked with North American migrants or were involved in promoting or resisting processes of gentrification in the city's historic El Centro. These interviews differed in content and scope from those focused on experiences of migrants and also varied based on the social position of the participant. I wanted to learn about Ecuadorian perceptions of the new arrivals[3] but, more importantly, to receive informed accounts of specific aspects of the migration (e.g., its effect on the real estate market; the experiences of people working with or for North Americans as teachers, translators, or facilitators). Drawing on my ability to speak Spanish, I always conducted interviews with Ecuadorians in that language. I recruited these interview participants in a variety of different ways, relying in part on convenience sampling but also dipping into the community of Cuencanos who provide intermediary services for lifestyle migrants (n = 12) using snowball sampling from two separate contacts whom I met initially because their contact information was available online. These interviews lasted approximately an hour and most often occurred at private residences or, occasionally, in coffee shops.

Because one of the issues that came up frequently was the impact of North–South migration on the cost of living and on the transformation of places in the city, I often relied on ethnographic methods and informal conversation to gather information about the perceptions of Ecuadorians. Sometimes, I was able to arrange short interviews with research participants with their consent to participate. At other times, I merely mentioned in conversation that I was a Canadian sociologist looking at the effects of North–South migration on changes in urban or rural land uses and asked questions. My ethnographic notes cover a great many of these informal conversations and shape my understanding of how Ecuadorians view this migration, especially Ecuadorians in the middle and upper-middle classes, with whom I associated most frequently. I also approached working-class Ecuadorians in public places, especially small shops *(tiendas)*, *mercados,* and taxis. In rural areas, I approached local construction workers or agricultural laborers at community gathering points or as I walked along the side of the road. They were very valuable sources of information about the city and its culture. During these informal contacts, I always mentioned that I was a Canadian researcher doing work on North American migrants. In a few cases, this was enough to end their willingness to talk with me, and in those cases, I did not press the point. In one case, I was told that Canadian lawyers had been through a neighborhood looking to buy real estate, and I suspected that a woman who refused to talk with me may have been approached previously for those purposes. Interviews in the popular market at plaza San Francisco (*n* = 13) and in rural areas around Cuenca (*n* = 9) focused on specific issues, especially the impact participants felt North American migrants were having on their lives. In rural areas, I was particularly interested in how the landscape was changing, including for agriculture, and I also asked about the history of agrarian reform and what life was like there before the late 1960s. I usually did not record these interviews, instead transcribing from notes shortly after the interviews.

In addition, I conducted twenty-nine interviews with Ecuadorian residents of Vilcabamba (nineteen men, ten women) using a mix of convenience and reputational sampling to get a sense of their perceptions of the effect the migration was having on their lives and their community. Some of these interviews were shorter, averaging twelve to fifteen minutes, but approximately half lasted between forty-five minutes and an hour, with one lasting several hours. I interviewed four of these research participants twice, and I did not record most of the Ecuadorian interviews in Vilcabamba.

Research assistants helped with the transcriptions of recorded interviews, which I then coded using a Word document and search terms chosen on the basis of themes and topics that came up in the interviews. Additional coding was conducted by reading through interviews once key themes had been identified. Often, the questions I asked determined the themes I picked out for coding, but in a few instances, other themes emerged quite unexpectedly. For instance, during my third visit in 2013, I began reflecting on "obnoxious gringo" narratives as indicative of a concern about whiteness that occurs throughout the North American population in Ecuador and which forms the basis of chapter 3. This led to additional coding work, but also, more importantly, it led to changes to the interview questions, such that I did not always ask all research participants exactly the same questions, in the same order, or in the same way. However, I attempted to make the main themes and topics as constant as possible.

In addition to semistructured qualitative interviews, I spent most of the rest of my time in Cuenca and Vilcabamba doing participatory observation or ethnographic analysis. I went to bars, restaurants, social events, house parties, dinners, and cultural events (the orchestra, art openings, festivals, etc.), where I met some North American lifestyle migrants and tourists with whom conversation was both enjoyable and fascinating. I participated in "gringo nights," making friends with people older and more experienced than me. I also made many Ecuadorian friends and spoke with a variety of people with whom I otherwise would not have had the opportunity to speak. Though I can speak Spanish very well, I do so with an accent that positions me in the Global North, reflecting both my Anglo-Canadian origins and my time learning the language in Spain. In speaking with Ecuadorian workers, I was often confronted with the real manifestations of what Pierre Bourdieu (1989) calls *social distance*. My ability to bridge this distance (when I was able to do so) was partly due to the fact that in most circumstances, both Ecuadorians and other North Americans tended to view my whiteness and masculinity positively, allowing me the privilege to define situations and my own presentation of self with greater ease than might be the case for people from other embodied positions. I also drew on my experiences growing up in a socially diverse, bilingual, largely rural Northern New Brunswick community, at the margins of the global economy, where I learned a lot about the social and moral codes that circulate in stratified social fields. This book is, therefore, partly a product of what it seeks to critique. My findings reflect my social position in the higher latitudes of an increasingly stratified global division of labor. No doubt, the migration of North Americans to Ecuador looks different viewed from other angles, representing other social identities and other latitudes of the global division of labor. I hope, however, that the perspective represented here offers something of value to how we think about both global migration and global inequality and that it might contribute to work on this topic undertaken by colleagues in other locations, representing other social positions. A fuller understanding of how global inequalities play out in the local places of lifestyle migrant communities deserves attention from multiple angles, many of which I have tried to learn from in the process of this research.

Notes

Introduction

1. All names are pseudonyms to protect the identities of the research participants.
2. In this book, I refer to "racialized white" people to draw attention to a process of identifying a group on the basis of shared somatic features, in this case, phenotypical whiteness, which suggest a natural, or biological, basis to the group's identity (Miles and Brown 2003, 99–103). These categories, formed historically by scientific experts searching for natural bases of apparent differences in human "evolution" or "development," have become commonsense categories to refer to others and to identify the self, a form of racial "subjectification" (Foucault 2005; Miles and Brown 2003), through which individuals assign belonging to a collective entity stabilized by inherited biological or genetic features. Race categories, however, lack stable biological markers to which they purport to refer, such that even to talk about "racialized white" people seems to assume there is a "white" that corresponds to or stabilizes the racialization. Whiteness may be ontologically unstable; however, it also operates as a social fact (one that may vary from place to place and over time), and as I point out throughout, it currently carries important social and symbolic power, a product of its historical position as a marker of European ethnic and racial origin in violent and exploitative colonial social relations that benefited places in what came to be called "Europe." Europe has historically defined itself in relation to its modernity as against the nonmodernity and backwardness of all other places (Mignolo 2000; Quijano 2000).
3. Joan was one of just two non–North Americans interviewed in Cuenca, both of whom were from Sydney, Australia.
4. Because "Rick" is a pseudonym, I had to be creative with the name of his peppers. Rick actually had a much better name lined up.
5. For further reading on the topic of coloniality as articulated by the modernity–coloniality–decoloniality school, see Lugones (2007), Mignolo (2000), Quijano (2000, 2007), and Santos (2014).
6. See "Foreign Ministry Studies Impact of Foreign Residents on Cuenca: Says Some Regulation May Be Required due to Affect on Local Population," Cuenca High Life, February 28, 2017, http://cuencahighlife.com/foreign -ministry-studyies-the-impact-of-foreign-residents-on-cuenca-suggests -some-regulation-may-be-required-due-to-affect-on-local-population/,

and "En Cuenca vive más de 8000 estadounidenses," *El Tiempo,* February 25, 2015, http://www.eltiempo.com.ec/noticias-cuenca/158349-en-cuenca-viven-ma-s-de-8-000-estadounidenses/. More recently, Cuenca's mayor has said publicly that there are between eight thousand and ten thousand U.S. citizens resident in the city. See "Entre 8,000 y 10,000 estadounidenses viven en la ciudad de Cuenca," *Andes Info,* March 7, 2018, https://www.andes.info.ec/fr/noticias/actualidad/15/entre-8000-y-10-000-estadounidenses-viven-en-la-ciudad-de-cuenca. The numbers from the Ecuadorian Foreign Ministry do not include migrants who have returned (of whom there are reportedly quite a few) or those who overstay their tourist visas. Such numbers are, therefore, estimates.

7. Other studies of whiteness also note an ambivalence on the part of white migrants to nonwhite places, including French European retirees in Senegal (Quashie 2016b) and Euro-American corporate expatriates in Jakarta (Fechter 2005).

8. There is now a growing English-language literature on lifestyle and privileged relocations to non-Western locations, particularly to former European colonies. Many of these migrations have been to former British colonial interests in East and Southeast Asia, India, or the Persian Gulf (see, in particular, Fechter 2007; Knowles and Harper 2009; Korpela 2009a, 2009b; Lehmann 2014; Leonard 2008; Walsh 2010, 2012). In a similar fashion, French-language studies have focused on experiences in former French colonies and protectorates (see Berriane and Janati 2016; Fabbiano 2016; Louveau 2016; Peraldi and Terrazzoni 2016; Quashie 2016a, 2016b). There have also been studies of Portuguese labor migrants in Angola (Dos Santos 2016) and of British migrants in Beijing (Knowles 2015). Studies on Latin American destinations inspired by postcolonial critiques have focused primarily on Mexico (Bantman-Masum 2015a, 2015b; Bastos 2014; Croucher 2009; Gárriz Fernandez 2011), Nicaragua (Mollett 2016), and Panama (Benson 2013, 2015; Spalding 2013). Given the rapid growth of migration to destinations in Latin America, North Africa, Turkey, Thailand, and Vietnam, it is likely that this research will continue to proliferate.

9. The increase in number of refugee and asylum seekers moving to Europe since 2014 has been represented variously as a migrant or refugee crisis (Goodman, Sirriyeh, and McMahon 2017). While ostensibly a crisis for the existing social relations of a highly unequal European polity, which appears unable to deal with the costs associated with incorporating the migrants, it might be more accurate to describe the situation as a crisis of global justice, since war, climate change, and economic stagnation are as much (if not much more so) the responsibility of failed Euro-American foreign and economic policies designed to serve Euro-American interests as they are the product of political failure in lower-income parts of the world.

10. Much of the existing literature in lifestyle migration emerged from studies of North Europeans (often retirees) moving to the Mediterranean coast, especially to Spain (Casado-Díaz 2006; Huete 2009; King, Warnes, and Wil-

liams 2000; Mantecón 2008; Membrado 2013; Oliver 2008; O'Reilly 2000, 2007; Rodriguez, Fernandez-Mayoralas, and Rojo 2004), Mediterranean islands (Åkerlund 2017), or rural France (Benson 2011, 2016; Lawson 2017). More recent theoretical reflections have highlighted the core cultural aspects of lifestyle migration and have increasingly integrated issues of power and inequality (see Benson and O'Reilly 2016, 2018; Benson and Osbaldiston 2014). In this respect, the scholarship in this subfield has produced solid sociological approaches combining analyses of cultural meanings and understandings with economic and political structures that also shape understanding and experience.

11. See Mawuna Remarque Koutonin, "Why Are White People Expats When the Rest of Us Are Immigrants?," *Guardian,* March 13, 2015, https://www.theguardian.com/global-development-professionals-network/2015/mar/13/white-people-expats-immigrants-migration.

12. Following Picard (2003), *touristification* refers to the conscious production of place and culture by receiving societies in a context of tourism development. Picard argues that it is not merely a matter of external forces reshaping receiving communities. It is primarily an internal process designed to attract outsiders to a collection of cultural artifacts and practices.

13. *Mestizo* refers to a racialized category of mixed European and indigenous origin (see Roitman 2009).

14. The selection of heritage objects is linked to contemporary processes of surplus extraction, which create value through manipulation of the symbolic meaning of collections and associations between objects (see Boltanski and Esquerre 2014; Franquesa 2013; Greffe 2011; Kingman 2004).

15. Acosta, López Olivares, and Villamar (2006) put the amount of remittance income invested in residential real estate at 4 percent for the whole of Ecuador.

1. Geoarbitrage and the Offshoring of Retirement

1. For Ecuadorian research participants, the idea of moving away from friends and family on one's own in retirement was anathema. One Spanish-language teacher who was familiar with North American retirees in Cuenca and admired them for their independent lifestyle nonetheless said that she and her friends sometimes felt sorry for them and wanted to check in on them or invite them to family events to make sure they were not too lonely.

2. See "Americans Find More Affordable Paradise for Retirement," *ABC News,* May 15, 2013: http://abcnews.go.com/Travel/americans-find-retirement-paradise-ecuador/story?id=19187268. See also the study on relocation to Baja California by Lardiés (2011), where similar narratives emerge from lifestyle migrants there.

3. As Robert Bellah et al. (1985) assert, Benjamin Franklin's famous "Advice to a Young Tradesman" best illustrates this type of self-interested individualism, one that assumes that what is good for a person is the pursuit of

what is most useful to him or her, particularly the accumulation of material benefits. Utilitarian individualism is also sometimes combined with what Bellah et al. call "expressive individualism," that is, a form of individualism based on knowing and expressing one's apparently true, inner self. This combination may take the form of individual attempts to maximize the number of opportunities for self-discovery and personal growth.

4. King, Warnes, and Williams (1998), for instance, discuss economic motivations but do not find them to be very important as a reason for transnational relocation. Several studies, however, anticipate the importance of North American economic migration to Latin American destinations (Dixon, Murray, and Gelatt 2006; Sunil, Rojas, and Bradley 2007; Otero 1997; Zeltzer 2008).

5. Tim Parker, "Retire in Ecuador with $200,000 Worth of Savings?," *Investopedia*, July 27, 2015, http://www.investopedia.com/articles/personal-finance/072715/retire-ecuador-200000-savings.asp?partner=mediafed.

6. Like many participants, Mary and Grant supported their lifestyle abroad through pension benefits they received from the government of their home country. Their home country, therefore, remained particularly relevant to their lives in Ecuador. The transnational portability of these pensions stems from their institutional design, which assigns rights on the basis of having paid into the pension (as though these savings were a form of property) rather than on residency or citizenship alone.

7. For instance, 48 percent of non-college-educated women were employed below $15 per hour according to 2017 data, as compared with 29 percent for non-college-educated men. College-educated women were twice as likely as college-educated men (22 percent vs. 11 percent) to be employed at wages below $15 per hour. See "The Precarious Economic Lives of Older Women," New School SCEPA, December 8, 2017, http://www.economicpolicyresearch.org/jobs-report/november-2017-unemployment-report-for-workers-over-55-2.

8. Ecuadorian participants did not necessarily share this characterization, however. Some Ecuadorians did see these women as adventurous, but others I interviewed or spoke with felt consternation at the prospect of women (and men) moving on their own at the end of their lives and often took pity on them.

9. Ecuador's Ministerio de relaciones exteriores was using the statistics in an internal debate about what type of migrants were being attracted to the country under its residency visa requirements. A copy of part of the unpublished report was shared with me during a meeting in 2013.

10. See Avery Shenfeld, "Punch Drunk," for an assessment of heavily indebted households over age fifty-five in Canada: http://research.cibcwm.com/economic_public/download/eijan12.pdf.

11. See Peter Whoriskey's "America's Reluctant Septuagenarian Workforce," *The Week*, January 21, 2018, http://theweek.com/articles/749428/americas-reluctant-septuagenarian-workforce.

12. For an example, see Suzan J. Haskins, "Are You Cut Out for the Expat Life?,"

International Living, July 10, 2014, https://internationalliving.com/are-you
-cut-out-for-the-expat-life/, and Jim Santos, "6 Reasons Why Salinas,
Ecuador Isn't for Everyone," *International Living,* November 26, 2016,
https://internationalliving.com/6-reasons-salinas-ecuador-isnt-everyone/.
Both provide lists of the qualities a successful "expat" needs to "thrive."
They include warnings about what to expect, as in Haskins: "Does it drive
you crazy when things don't happen at the appointed hour? Get used to it if
you're thinking of moving overseas." Santos states, "We don't really notice
the noise or crowds most of the time anymore."

2. Migrant Imaginaries

1. See Bryan Haines, "Cuenca, Ecuador: The Complete Guide to Living and Traveling in Cuenca," *Gringos Abroad* (blog), July 3, 2017, http://gringosabroad
   .com/cuenca-ecuador/.
2. See Fundación Municipal de Turismo de Cuenca, "Cuenca's French Route.
   A Testimony of France's Legacy in Cuenca," Gringo Tree, April 12, 2017,
   https://www.gringotree.com/cuencas-french-route-testimony-frances
   -legacy-cuenca/.
3. See Dan Austin, "Living in Cuenca? Retirees Say It's Like the 1950s," Gringo
   Tree, May 23, 2016, https://www.gringotree.com/cuenca-ecuador-retirees
   -say-its-like-living-in-the-1950s/.
4. Andrea had spent decades living outside the United States, and this certainly may have affected her perceptions and imaginary of Ecuador. Further
   research might identify how participants who remain longer in Ecuador
   change perspectives and viewpoints with increasing experience of the realities of Cuenca. However, it is also possible that spending more years in
   the country makes little difference, especially given that North Americans
   who had lived in the city for four or five years often shared tropes relative
   newcomers also discussed.
5. To protect the anonymity of the research participant, I have deliberately
   hidden her country of birth and place of work in the United States. She
   mentioned in her interview that she had seen four other African American
   women who lived in Cuenca, and other expats continuously mistook them
   for each other.
6. This is a frequent topic of debate and discussion in the North American
   community, and many research participants also mentioned it. See Deke
   Castleman, "Punctuality: Gringos and Ecuadorians Have a Different Perception of Being 'On Time,'" Cuenca High Life, July 22, 2017, https://
   cuencahighlife.com/punctuality-the-differences-in-whats-considered-on
   -time-between-north-and-south-america/.
7. See "Cuenca—It's Like the Good Ol' Days of the 1950's," *Ahhh Cuenca* (blog),
   June 5, 2015, http://danoinec.blogspot.ca/2015/06/cuenca-its-like-good
   -ol-days-of-1950s.html. Websites like Gringo Tree later recirculated this
   post.

3. Gringo Identities

1. In this chapter and throughout the book, references to "white" and "whiteness" refer to racial categories that are a product of the coloniality of power or the colonial ranking of different forms of labor on the basis of their proximity to the metropolitan centers of accumulation in Europe. To refer to individuals who are "racialized as white" draws attention to a social process of racial "subjectification" (Miles and Brown 2003). See footnote 2 in the introduction.

2. Some North American women in Ecuador referred to themselves as *gringas,* modifying the gender of their perceived racial category in Spanish, something not usually done in English. This gendered and racialized identity is worthy of further study. North American women's bodies and femininity are coded differently in the Andes, even as they age, and while most retired women I asked said they were no longer interested in pursuing romantic relationships, this narrative did not always match up with reality. Moreover, white female North American retirees commented on receiving better service and attention in Ecuador and appeared to expect that their professional experience and expertise would not be ignored, as they often seemed to be in North America. For a discussion of privileged white women in the context of lifestyle migration, see Croucher (2014).

3. Examples of paternalism are readily evident among charity organizations run by North American expatriates, who often frame paternalistic acts of giving as morally good rather than as claims for social justice and redistribution of wealth. At their worst, paternalistic notions of charity prey on aging North Americans' desires to remain useful and productive and reinforce harmful neoliberal ideologies about the "deserving poor," evolutionary understandings of "underdevelopment," and perceptions of global poverty that neglect histories of racist exclusion, colonialism, and contemporary transnational corporate plunder.

4. For an interesting and important discussion of how lifestyle migrants become accustomed to the racialized social order of receiving communities in Latin America, and adjust their own behavior and expectations to the established "rules" of the field, see Benson (2015).

5. North American or "expat" online bulletin boards mention this issue, both in Latin America and elsewhere. For a recent discussion on Cuenca, see David Morrill, "Gringo Prices, Viveza Criolla, and How to Survive Economically in the Latin Culture," *Cuenca High Life,* March 23, 2017, https://www.cuencahighlife.com/gringo-prices/.

6. An important subset of North Americans argue in deprecating tones in private conversation or online about the high spending practices of their compatriots, claiming that Cuenca should be a destination only for those of "meager means." These latter are also often seen by higher-income migrants from North America as people who are relocating to Cuenca "for the wrong reasons."

7. This is not universally the case. There are evidently many instances, as the previous chapter illustrated, where ethnocentric and racist ideas about Ecuador and Ecuadorians circulate. These latter often offend more egalitarian and antiracist North Americans and, as discussed later in this chapter, are a source of anxiety for them.

8. For an example of earlier discussions about "ugly Americans," a less racialized but sometimes interchangeable descriptor of North Americans, see Lee Dubs, "The Ugly American Revisited," Cuenca High Life, February 10, 2012, https://www.cuencahighlife.com/lee-dubsthe-ugly-american-revisited-arrogance-plus-ignorance-is-a-recipe-for-trouble-as-more-n-americans-move-to-ecuador/.

9. To be sure, transplanted racism and white supremacy are also important concerns. Although North Americans are relocating to a different ethno/cultural milieu, racist imaginaries and rejections of cultural pluralism may nonetheless circulate more widely than I was able to ascertain. For an interesting account of the cultural imaginaries of British migrants who rejected multiculturalism and cultural pluralism through migration to Turkey, see Ertuğrul (2016).

4. Transforming the City

1. LeBlanc, a French urban planner who has worked on Cuenca for UNESCO, is quoted in Dante Angelo, "Tram and San Francisco Plaza Redesign Set the Stage for More Big Changes to Cuenca's Historic District, Urban Planner Says," Cuenca High Life, June 19, 2016, http://www.cuencahighlife.com/tram-and-san-francisco-plaza-construction-are-the-perfect-time-to-make-big-changes-to-cuencas-historic-district-urban-planner-says/.

2. Many Cuencanos blame the fall in sales on traffic chaos caused in part by construction on the *tranvía* (or tram project), which shut down much of El Centro during June and July 2016 and which was still disrupting traffic into 2018. But stallholders in the building, several of whom I spoke with, said the drop was due to the move into a building that made them invisible to their clients. See "Centro Comercial 9 de Octubre, sus comerciantes desesperan," *La Tarde,* July 12, 2016, http://www.late.com.ec/2016/07/12/centro-comercial-9-de-octubre-sus-comerciantes-desesperan/.

3. See "Enfrentamientos entre comerciantes y Guardia Ciudadana," *El Tiempo,* December 13, 2016, http://www.eltiempo.com.ec/noticias/sucesos/9/404200/enfrentamientos-entre-comerciantes-y-guardia-ciudadana. Clashes have been sporadic since; see "Nuevo incidente entre Guardia Ciudadana y vendedores deja heridos," *El Tiempo,* September 27, 2017, http://www.eltiempo.com.ec/noticias/sucesos/9/421868/nuevo-incidente-entre-guardia-ciudadana-y-vendedores-deja-heridos.

4. Landowning and manufacturing elites' traditional and familial attachments to the distinction practices of this stratified field often motivate their expansionary business projects and can be understood as a product

of their social position. Their distinction projects often create work for other social classes, but, just as with the projects of social elites elsewhere, these are often at service levels that reinforce class and racial hierarchies and frequently have negative social effects for those who are exploited and displaced, negative effects that are not always appreciated by those who occupy overly privileged positions. A more democratic alternative would need to focus on collaborative forms of labor and enterprise and might include shared ownership and rewards. Such business organization gets short shrift not just in Cuenca but around the globe.

5. See "En diciembre del 2017 debe entregarse el Parque De La Libertad," *El Mercurio*, December 11, 2016, http://www.elmercurio.com.ec/575442-en -diciembre-del-2017-debe-entregarse-el-parque-de-la-libertad/. Also see coverage in the English-language news for lifestyle migrants, as in "New Historic District Park Will Include Recreation Areas, Shops, Restaurants, a Theater, and an Observation Tower," Cuenca High Life, September 16, 2017, https://www.cuencahighlife.com/new-historic-district-park-will -include-recreation-areas-shops-restaurants-theater-observation-tower/.

6. There has been ongoing local coverage of informal workers' demands for fixed selling points in the city's squares, demands the Municipio has resisted. See Lineida Castillo, "Los vendedores informales de Cuenca amenazan con protestas si se retoman los controles," *El Comercio*, May 12, 2015, http://www.elcomercio.com/actualidad/vendedores-informales -cuenca-protestas-ordenamiento.html.

7. See "La plaza San Francisco atesora una historia de personajes y formas de ocupación," *El Tiempo*, July 18, 2016, http://www.eltiempo.com.ec/ noticias/cuenca/2/378226/la-plaza-san-francisco-atesora-una-historia -de-personajes-y-formas-de-ocupacion.

8. For a full overview of the different projects, see "Plaza San Francisco suma más de siete diseños," *El Mercurio*, December 14, 2015, http://www .elmercurio.com.ec/507262-plaza-san-francisco-suma-mas-de-siete-dise nos/#.V1iDVDf1_dk.

9. See "Nuevos puestos para la plaza San Francisco," *El Tiempo*, January 11, 2017, http://www.eltiempo.com.ec/noticias/cuenca/2/405813/nuevos-puestos -para-la-plaza-san-francisco.

10. All names of Ecuadorian research participants are pseudonyms.

11. For a discussion of the traditions of textile production and weaving in Otavalo, see Korovkin (1998). For discussion of Western imaginaries of indigenous Andean spaces, see Gómez-Barris (2012) and Meisch (2002).

12. "Editorial: Objeciones a proyecto San Francisco," *El Mercurio*, June 13, 2016, p. 4A. My translation.

13. See http://www.turismo.gob.ec/resultados-del-2015-ano-de-la-calidad -turistica-en-ecuador/.

14. The impact of the *tranvía* project on traffic flow is hotly contested. Many taxi drivers with whom I spoke feared it would cripple access to an already congested El Centro, and commuters said it would increase their commute

times. Local media have reported on these matters; see "New Traffic Restrictions, Pedestrian and Bike Plans, Anger Historic District Business Owners," Cuenca High Life, July 29, 2016, https://www.cuencahighlife .com/new-traffic-restrictions-pedestrian-bike-plans-anger-historic-district -business-owners/. See also "Frentistas rechazan las restricciones vehiculares," *El Tiempo,* July 29, 2016, http://www.eltiempo.com.ec/noticias/ cuenca/2/378997/frentistas-rechazan-las-restricciones-vehiculares. Like the renovation of plaza San Francisco, the *tranvía* project valorizes public space for the commercial uses of higher-income groups, especially foreign lifestyle migrants. People who worked in El Centro viewed it as a major disruption and resisted it in occasional public mobilizations, ongoing at the time of writing. What may follow the opening of the line (planned sometime in 2018, but already three years behind schedule) is also debated. See "Tranvía, de receta del éxito a dolor de cabeza," *El Tiempo,* January 1, 2017, http://www.eltiempo.com.ec/noticias/cuenca/2/405230/tranvia-de -receta-del-exito-a-dolor-de-cabeza. For foreign consultants and specula tors, it offers the possibility of real estate accumulation; see Liam Higgins, "While Some See a Real Estate Melt-Down in Ecuador, Others See Opportunity," Cuenca High Life, June 27, 2016, https://www.cuencahighlife.com/ see-real-estate-melt-ecuador-others-see-opportunity/. The transformation of Cuenca's urban transit over the last few years has participated in forms of spatial exclusion and embellishment that are partly the result of internal dynamics, particularly Cuencano elites' strategies to distinguish themselves from Quito and Guayaquil by approximating European styles and tastes, and by coordinating—through the municipality, which they largely control— infrastructure projects intended to position the city within European modernity (Mancero Acosta 2012). The city constantly evokes European heritage cities when referring to the potential for urban "rehabilitation" offered by the *tranvía* project, a project whose consultants and engineers are drawn from higher-income countries like France, Spain, and Japan. Fernando Salazar, director of Cuenca's transportation department, said that Cuenca's *tranvía* system most resembled Bordeaux; see "Cuenca Looks to Bordeaux to Integrate Tram into Its Public Transit Network," Cuenca High Life, July 18, 2016, https://www.cuencahighlife.com/cuenca-looks-bordeaux -integrate-tram-public-transportation-network/. At the time of writing, Medellín is the only Andean city with a similar tram system.

15. The projects to rehabilitate public squares announced in June 2016 are a good example; see "Plan para reactivar el Centro Histórico de Cuenca," *El Mercurio,* June 11, 2016, https://www.elmercurio.com.ec/533421-plan -para-reactivar-el-centro-historico-de-cuenca/#.V1-KQjf1_dk. However, the *tranvía* light-rail project, which is being built by Spanish and French engineering firms, with loans coming from European governments and multilateral institutions, is also a good example. See Sylvan Hardy, "Cuenca's Tram Project Has Left the Station, but Opposition to It Continues," Cuenca High Life, December 29, 2014, https://www.cuencahighlife.com/

cuencas-massive-tram-project-has-left-the-station-but-opposition
-continues-el-centro-property-owners-city-officials-and-expats-weigh-in/.

16. See John Keeble, "Cuenca Could Become an International Events Destination," Cuenca High Life, February 4, 2017, https://www.cuencahighlife.
com/cuenca-poised-become-national-international-events-destination/.
On the construction of a Sheraton Hotel, see "Ampliación del Mall del Río
con sector bancario y hotel," El Mercurio, January 29, 2015, http://www
.elmercurio.com.ec/465554-ampliacion-del-mall-del-rio-con-sector
-bancario-y-hotel/. The powerful Grupo Ortíz, which owns several Cuenca-
area malls and supermarkets and is well connected with Cuenca's leading
noble families, is carrying out the project.

17. I interviewed a total of eleven vendors for this research, four in 2015 and
seven in 2016. Further interviews were conducted in 2017–18.

18. At time of writing, the roadway along calle Padre Aguirre, to which vendors
were temporarily moved, was also being renovated, temporarily displacing
vendors yet again. Some were very nervous they would not be able to return. In early 2018, several interview participants mentioned that stress
levels were high and that uncertainty and lack of communication of a plan
to relocate to the renovated plaza had begun to take a toll on their mental
health.

19. This trend is noted in Liam Higgins, "Larger Businesses Are Relocating Outside the Historic District, but Some Say That Is a Good Thing," Cuenca High
Life, November 27, 2017, https://cuencahighlife.com/larger-businesses-are
-relocating-outside-of-the-historic-district-but-some-say-its-a-good
-thing/. The article also quotes a UNESCO consultant about the changing
character of El Centro: "As we have seen elsewhere, the historic district will
become more residential and include more boutique businesses, especially
restaurants, coffee shops and gift shops. We will see an increasing number
of renovation projects, converting old buildings in modern housing that
will attract young professionals as well as foreign expats." These changes
were already evident in the changing streetscape of El Centro during a field
site visit in early 2018.

20. "El cuencano tiende a dejar el centro," El Tiempo, January 2, 2017, http://
www.eltiempo.com.ec/noticias/cuenca/2/405292/el-cuencano-tiende-a
-dejar-el-centro.

21. In September 2016, more than seven hundred street vendors were removed
from the area around El Arenal, the large feria libre market, to a new location on the city's outskirts provided for them, the plataforma Narancay.
Local newspapers have reported that sales in the area, however, are low,
and there have been several protests by vendors. See "Narancay tiene 50
espacios libres para comerciantes," El Tiempo, October 20, 2016, http://
www.eltiempo.com.ec/noticias/cuenca/2/399838/narancay-tiene-50
-espacios-libres-para-comerciantes. There have been ongoing police operations to clear out remaining street vendors from the streets around feria
libre, because sales are much better there. See "Nuevo operative en la feria

libre," *El Tiempo*, April 11, 2018, http://www.eltiempo.com.ec/noticias/
sucesos/9/432652/operativo-feria-libre. Security, antidrug operations, and
"clearing traffic" from around the existing market facility have been priorities of the municipal government. One particular area, which municipal
authorities and police named the "callejón de la muerte" or "alley of death,"
was occupied by almost one hundred vendors who resisted displacement by
sleeping at their workplace. See "Comerciantes duermen en el 'Callejón de
la muerte,'" *El Tiempo*, January 12, 2018, http://www.eltiempo.com.ec/
noticias/sucesos/9/427836/comerciantes-duermen-en-el-callejon-de-la
-muerte. A woman in the article is cited saying that sales have dropped
since municipal authorities began using the nickname. The big box chain
Coral is building a large new shopping facility only a few blocks away.

22. The potential impact North Americans have on the price level gets "discussed a lot," as Simone, from San Francisco, put it. For a more thorough
discussion of how North Americans conceive of their economic impact, see
Hayes (forthcoming).

5. The Hacienda

1. This was the number reported by *El Telegrafo* in early 2013, based on census data collected by INEC in 2011. See "Extranjeros cambiaron la vida de
Vilcabamba," *El Telegrafo*, February 25, 2013, http://www.eltelegrafo.com
.ec/noticias/sociedad/1/extranjeros-cambiaron-la-vida-de-vilcabamba. See
also "Extranjeros adoptaron costumbres y cambiaron el estilo de vida en Vilcabamba," Andes: Agencia Pública del Ecuador y Suramérica, February 23,
2013, https://www.andes.info.ec/es/noticias/no-se-pierda/1/extranjeros
-adoptaron-costumbres-cambiaron-estilo-vida-vilcabamba.

2. Vilcabamba has a long history of attracting countercultural migrants, con-
spiracy theorists, and hippies. In addition to noting the influx of North
Americans, I also met a large number of young Argentinians who referred
to the town as Vilcawawa, referring to a common South American term for
children (wawa). Several young couples in their twenties had settled in the
town to have children together or to live collectivist lifestyles on the land
while selling artisanal items to tourists.

3. Such projects are equally unfinished in Canada and the United States.

4. *Arrimados* had access to a small plot of land for subsistence, which they paid
for in labor on the hacienda. Though these workers could not formally be
bought and sold, their debts could be inherited.

5. http://www.haciendasanjoaquin.com/. The property was bought by an
American developer in 2005. It is located immediately across the río Vilcabamba from the barrio Linderos, in San Pedro de Vilcabamba parish.

6. Land prices in Vilcabamba and nearby Malacatos are significantly higher as
a result of tourism development. In Quinara, they were approximately $50
to $75 per square meter in 2013, compared to $150 to $320 per square meter
in Vilcabamba, according to a report in *El Comercio*. This price difference

has had the effect, however, of drawing migrants toward less expensive areas. See "El extranjero quiere vivir a Quinara," *El Comercio,* September 23, 2013, http://www.elcomercio.com/actualidad/ecuador/extranjero-quiere -vivir-quinara.html.

7. For data on underemployment, see MCPEC (2011, 32). Poverty data for Vilcabamba canton is from the INEC Censo de población y vivienda 2010. The basic basket of goods, or *canasta básica,* is reported monthly by INEC: http://www.ecuadorencifras.gob.ec/canasta/.

8. One interesting and informative observer of the comings and goings of spirituality and health entrepreneurs, as well as real estate speculators, is a member of the community of lifestyle migrants, the passionfruitcowgirl: https://passionfruitcowgirl.wordpress.com/category/vilcabamba/.

9. The violence of this process should not be underestimated and can include the consequences of social exclusion and marginalization visible in the large inequalities in Ecuadorian health and education statistics, for instance. It is also experienced in the personal miseries inflicted on individuals living in poverty, including criminalization and mental illness.

10. Such dispossession is not only founded on an economic basis. Cultural narratives are also important, especially the extent to which symbolic boundaries are used to separate undeserving people from desirable commodities, such as land. There was a tendency on the part of some research participants to discuss the landscape as "wasted" or as having been ill treated by Ecuadorian peasants and landowners. The land, I was told on several occasions, had to be "healed." This imaginary of "natives" making poor use of natural resources, and being in need of tutelage from Europeans, has a long history in North American culture, where it conjures excuses for diverse forms of economic dispossession and epistemological devaluation stretching back to the beginning of European settlement (see Tuck and Yang 2012). Such ideas are echoed among wealthy Ecuadorian landowners, such that North American participants reproduce colonial relations of appropriation and exploitation in the countryside. While visiting one rural location in Azuay, I met a *hacendado* from Cuenca who insisted that indigenous people could not run a productive dairy farm. While insisting he was not racist (because he did not "hate" "other" races), he stated that they were inherently less productive, justifying their continued subordination to him, as well as his colonial inheritance: ownership of the productive capital of the dairy operation and much of the grazing land in the area.

6. Lifestyle Migration, Transnational Gentrification, and Social Justice

1. In a context led by real estate speculation and investment, more intensive exploitation takes the form not only of more intensive labor but also of spatial displacement onto more peripheral urban and rural lands that increase in value through residential subdivision and denser settlement. In a few

cases, such land is owned by lower-income Ecuadorians or by migrants and return migrants from Ecuador to the United States or Europe. But most lands being subdivided on the outskirts of Cuenca and in Vilcabamba belong to the landed classes and are the remnants of large haciendas.

2. Transnational real estate speculation also relies on financial derivatives, which supercharge construction markets for second homes and tourism properties, because profits stem not from regular loans taken out against real estate but from the sale of financial derivatives and mortgage-backed securities, which simultaneously free up more money for fresh mortgage loans (Aalbers 2008; Sassen 2017). In the process, risks are transnationalized and globalized in new ways.

3. Heritage preservation and lifestyle migration are important drivers of transnational gentrification in other locations as well. See especially Sigler and Wachsmuth (2016) and the very interesting study of the Baka neighborhood of Jerusalem in Zaban (2015, 2016). Though his current work only tangentially touches on lifestyle migration as such, Cócola Gant (2016) also mentions new housing types that cater to short-term visitors and heritage tourism as important aspects of gentrification in Barcelona. In Cuenca, the tourism mobilities of prospective lifestyle migrants are also an important part of the transformation of key neighborhoods. There is growing interest in tourism gentrification as a specific context of urban social injustice (see also Cócola Gant 2018; Gotham 2005; Gravari-Barbas and Guinand 2017), which in Latin American heritage cities is highly oriented toward tourists from higher-income countries in North America and Western Europe (see Scarpaci 2005).

4. See "Cuenca, Ecuador: Del diagnóstico al Plan de Acción para un crecimiento sostenible," *Ciudades Sostenibles* (blog), January 9, 2015, https:// blogs.iadb.org/ciudadessostenibles/2015/01/09/cuenca/.

5. It is, however, not a free market, as the experience of refugees and economic migrants from the Global South would clearly demonstrate. It is a market imbued with coloniality, whereby downward mobilities are encouraged but upward ones are tightly regulated, especially for racialized bodies.

6. See "New Traffic Restrictions, Pedestrian and Bike Plans, Anger Historic District Business Owners," Cuenca High Life, July 29, 2016, https://www .cuencahighlife.com/new-traffic-restrictions-pedestrian-bike-plans-anger -historic-district-business-owners/. See also footnote 15 in chapter 4.

7. See "Almost 200 El Centro Businesses Close Doors," Cuenca High Life, June 5, 2016, https://www.cuencahighlife.com/almost-200-el-centro-businesses -close-doors-noise-ordinance-needs-teeth-quake-moves-manta-toward -ocean/. See also "Tranvía, de receta del éxito a dolor de cabeza," *El Tiempo,* January 1, 2017, http://www.eltiempo.com.ec/noticias/cuenca/2/405230/ tranvia-de-receta-del-exito-a-dolor-de-cabeza. Also see comments by a foreign real estate speculator in "While Some See a Real Estate Melt-down in Ecuador, Others See Opportunity," Cuenca High Life, June 27, 2016, https://www.cuencahighlife.com/see-real-estate-melt-ecuador-others-see

-opportunity/. It is not clear to me that speculator Ryals Arberger is a real person (an online search failed to locate him), but even if it is "fake news," Cuenca High Life is a vehicle for transnational real estate speculation, and the intent of the article is to drum up publicity for it.

8. See Lineida Castillo, "Las casas y servicios aumentan en Cuenca por los extranjeros," *El Comercio*, September 11, 2015, http://www.elcomercio.com/actualidad/casas-y-servicios-aumentan-cuenca.html.

9. See "La especulación desordena y segrega," *El Tiempo*, December 26, 2016, http://www.eltiempo.com.ec/noticias/cuenca/2/404900/la-especulacion-desordena-y-segrega.

10. The report, commissioned by the Dutch Ministry of Education in collaboration with the Universidad de Cuenca, and authored by Cuencano researchers, absurdly notes that "indigenous" informal vendors were a greater danger to the architectural heritage of El Centro, despite also admitting that it was foreign residents, with limited knowledge of this heritage, who were the ones often restoring it to suit their own residential tastes (Rey et al. 2017, 89). Certainly poverty and necessity have created new living patterns in El Centro, which have changed the uses of elite architecture enshrined as heritage by UNESCO in 1999. Popular uses, thereby, became a new type of problem, justifying their displacement by the city and wealthier landowners.

11. The impacts of remittances on economic development are highly contested in the academic literature (see Binford 2003; Faist 2008; King, Mata-Codesal, and Vullnetari 2013; Mata-Codesal 2018). The World Bank Group, however, has long trumpeted remittances' ability to drive development, at least under the right conditions (see World Bank 2006, 2008).

12. The social agency of nonhuman actors is increasingly of interest to social scientists working from a variety of theoretical perspectives, notably actor-network theory (Latour 2005), object-oriented ontology approaches (Harman 2016), the "new animism" (Harvey 2014), and anthropologies grounded in "traditional" or "indigenous" knowledge (cf. Cruikshank 2005; de la Cadena 2010; Descola 1994; Smith 2013). These approaches reject the Western cultural split between acting subjects (who so often seem powerless to change social structures) and nonacting objects (who so often appear to be the real initiators of social forces). Western empiricism has, for centuries, separated subjects and objects and pursued their study under entirely different traditions (social vs. natural sciences). The preceding approaches reject that this separation is ever really possible and see Western empiricism as culturally specific. Quijano (2000) and other decolonial scholars in Latin America refer to the hegemony of this Western empiricist worldview as Eurocentrism, which arbitrarily separates the knowing subject from the object that is known and orders them in hierarchical relation, such that rationality supersedes corporality. For a discussion of indigenous epistemology as it pertains to the Andes, see de la Cadena (2010), Velásquez (2018), and, in the Ecuadorian Amazon, Descola (1994).

Appendix

1. It is likely that relocation to Ecuador might contribute to such isolation, a topic my sampling methods would not have captured. Ecuadorian research participants frequently made mention of individual "shut-ins," perhaps indicating cultural differences in expectations about being single and alone in later life. As one Ecuadorian research participant told me in 2015, "they come here to die by themselves." During my fieldwork contacts with North Americans, I also heard about these "other" migrants, some of whom may have been too afraid to venture out in public, ostensibly because they felt they would be targeted for their relative wealth, a topic I touch on in chapter 3. The topic has also been addressed in more recent online discussions; see "Reaching Out to Those Who Are Alone," Cuenca High Life, April 10, 2018, https://cuencahighlife.com/reaching-out-to-those-who-are-alone/.

2. My interview participants in Vilcabamba included two Western Europeans, five South Americans, three Canadians, and eleven U.S. Americans.

3. García Álvarez, Osorio-Guerrero, and Pastor Herrera (2017) have documented these perceptions quantitatively.

Bibliography

Aalbers, Manuel. 2008. "The Financialization of Home and the Mortgage Market Crisis." *Competition and Change* 12: 148–66.

Abbott, J. Anthony. 2005. "Counting Beans: Agrobiodiversity, Indigeneity, and Agrarian Reform." *Professional Geographer* 57, no. 2: 198–212. https://doi.org/10.1111/j.0033–0124.2005.00472.x.

Acosta, Alberto. 2013. *El Buen Vivir: Sumak Kawsay, una oportunidad para imaginar otros mundos*. Barcelona: Icaria.

Acosta, Pablo A., Pablo Fajnzylber, and Humberto Lopez. 2007. "The Impact of Remittances on Poverty and Human Capital: Evidence from Latin American Household Surveys." eLibrary World Bank Group. https://doi.org/10.1596/1813–9450–4247.

Acosta, Alberto, Susana López Olivares, and David Villamar. 2006. "La contribución de las remesas a la economía ecuatoriana." In *Crisis, migración y remesas en Ecuador ¿Una oportunidad para el codesarrollo?*, edited by Alberto Acosta. Madrid: CIDEAL. http://www.flacsoandes.edu.ec/agora/la-contribucion-de-las-remesas-la-economia-ecuatoriana.

Aguilar, Victor, Jorge Luis Palacios, and Santiago Pozo. 2007. "Análisis de la migración en la provincia del Azuay (I Parte): Destino de las divisas." *Boletín del observatorio económico del Azuay* 10: 60–65.

Åkerlund, Ulrika. 2017. "Strategic Lifestyle Management in Later Life: Swedish Lifestyle Movers in Malta Seeking the 'Best of Both Worlds.'" *Population, Space, and Place* 23, no. 1: e1964. https://doi.org/10.1002/psp.1964.

Alcoff, Linda. 2015. *The Future of Whiteness*. Malden, Mass.: Polity Press.

Allain, Kristi, and Barbara L. Marshall. 2017. "Foucault Retires to the Gym: Understanding Embodied Aging through Leisure Fitness in the Third Age." *Canadian Journal on Aging* 36, no. 3: 402–14.

Allan, Theodore. 1994. *The Invention of the White Race: Racial Oppression and Social Control*. Vol. 1. London: Verso.

Álvarez Velasco, Soledad. 2009. "Transitando en el clandestino: Análisis de la migración indocumentada en tránsito por la frontera sur mexicana." *Andina Migrante* 4: 2–10. http://repositorio.flacsoandes.edu.ec/bitstream/10469/849/1/BFLACSO-AM4.pdf.

Álvarez Velasco, Soledad. 2016. "¿Crisis migratoria contemporánea? Complejizando el vínculo migración irregularizada, violencia y Estado capitalista a partir de la dinámica de dos corredores migratorios globales." *Ecuador Debate* 97: 155–71.

Amit, Vered. 2007. "Structures and Dispositions of Travel and Movement." In *Going First Class? New Approaches to Privileged Travel and Movement,* edited by Vered Amit, 1–14. New York: Berghahn Books.

Amit, Vered. 2011. "'Before I Settle Down': Youth Travel and Enduring Life-course Paradigms." *Anthropologica* 53: 79–88.

Andrade Río, María Augusta, and Narcisa Ulluari Donoso. 2014. "Historia del Agroturismo en el canton Cuenca, Ecuador." *PASOS: Revista de Turismo y Patrimonio Cultural* 13: 1199–212.

Angelicos, Nicólas, and María Luisa Méndez. 2017. "Struggles against Territorial Disqualification: Mobilization for Dignified Housing and Defense of Heritage in Santiago." *Latin American Perspectives* 44, no. 3: 100–112.

Apostolopoulos, Yorgos, Lila Leontidou, and Philippos Loukissas, eds. 2001. *Mediterranean Tourism: Facets of Socioeconomic Development and Cultural Change.* London: Routledge.

Appleby, Roslyn. 2013. "Singleness, Marriage, and the Construction of Heterosexual Masculinities: Australian Men Teaching English in Japan." *PORTAL Journal of Multidisciplinary International Studies* 10, no. 1. http://dx.doi.org/10.5130/portal.v10i1.2334.

Arce Abarca, Ignacio. 2016. "Contestaciones a la ciudad global: La cuestión urbana en el siglo XXI. Un diálogo con Teresa Caldeira." *Íconos: Revista de Ciencas Sociales* 56: 149–55.

Atkinson, Rowland. 2015. "Losing One's Place: Narratives of Neighbourhood Change, Market Injustice and Symbolic Displacement." *Housing, Theory, and Society* 32, no. 4: 373–88.

Atkinson, Rowland, and Gary Bridge. 2005. Introduction to *Gentrification in Global Context: The New Urban Colonialism,* edited by Rowland Atkinson and Gary Bridge, 1–17. London: Routledge.

Avila, Eric, and Mark H. Rose. 2009. "Race, Culture, Politics, and Urban Renewal." *Journal of Urban History* 35, no. 3: 335–47.

Bantman-Masum, Eve. 2011. "'You Need to Come Here . . . to See What Living Is Really About': Staging North American Expatriation in Merida (Mexico)." *Miranda: Multidisciplinary Peer-Reviewed Journal of the English-Speaking World* 5. https://doi.org/10.4000/miranda.2494.

Bantman-Masum, Eve. 2015a. "Lifestyle Transmigration: Understanding a Hypermobile Minority in Mérida, Mexico." *Journal of Latin American Geography* 14, no. 1: 101–17.

Bantman-Masum, Eve. 2015b. "Migration Machine: Marketing Mexico in the Age of ICTs." In *Digital Labour and Prosumer Capitalism: The US Matrix,* edited by Mathieu O'Neil and Olivier Fraysse, 106–24. London: Palgrave Macmillan.

Bantman-Masum, Eve. Forthcoming. "Enjeux politiques de la migration entre États-Unis et Mexique: Citoyenneté contractuelle et marchandisation de la souveraineté." In *Mobilités contemporaines des nord(s) vers les sud(s),* edited by Giulia Fabbiano, Michel Peraldi, Alexandra Poli, and Liza Terrazzoni. Paris: Karthala.

Barsky, Osvaldo. 1988. *La reforma agraria Ecuatoriana.* Vol. 3. Quito: Corporación Editora Nacional.

Bastos, Santiago. 2014. "Territorial Dispossession and Indigenous Rearticulation in the Chapala Lakeshore." In *Contested Spatialities, Lifestyle Migration and Residential Tourism,* edited by Michael Janoschka and Heiko Haas, 47–59. London: Routledge.

Beck, Ulrich. 2011. "We Do Not Live in an Age of Cosmopolitanism but in an Age of Cosmopolitisation: The 'Global Other' Is in Our Midst." *Irish Journal of Sociology* 19, no. 1: 16–34.

Beck, Ulrich, and Elisabeth Beck-Gernsheim. 2004. "Families in a Runaway World." In *The Blackwell Companion to the Sociology of Families,* edited by Jacqueline Scott, Judith Treas, and Martin Richards, 499–514. Malden, Mass.: Blackwell.

Becker, Marc. 2010. *Pachakutik: Indigenous Movements and Electoral Politics in Ecuador.* Lanham, Md.: Rowman and Littlefield.

Bellah, Robert, Richard Madsen, William M. Sullivan, Ann Swidler, and Steven M. Tipton. 1985. *Habits of the Heart: Individualism and Commitment in American Life.* New York: Perennial.

Bender, Désirée, Tina Hollstein, Vincent Horn, Lena Huber, and Cornelia Schweppe. 2014. "Old Age Care Facilities and Care-Seeking Elderly on the Move." *Transnational Social Review: A Social Work Journal* 4, no. 2–3: 290–93.

Benson, Michaela. 2011. *The British in Rural France: Lifestyle Migration and the Ongoing Quest for a Better Way of Life.* Manchester: Manchester University Press.

Benson, Michaela. 2012. "How Culturally Significant Imaginings Are Translated into Lifestyle Migration." *Journal of Ethnic and Migration Studies* 38: 1681–96.

Benson, Michaela. 2013. "Postcoloniality and Privilege in New Lifestyle Flows: The Case of North Americans in Panama." *Mobilities* 8, no. 3: 313–30.

Benson, Michaela. 2015. "Class, Race, Privilege: Structuring the Lifestyle Migrant Experience in Boquete, Panama." *Journal of Latin American Geography* 14, no. 1: 19–37.

Benson, Michaela. 2016. "Deconstructing Belonging in Lifestyle Migration: Tracking the Emotional Negotiations of the British in Rural France." *European Journal of Cultural Studies* 19, no. 5: 481–94.

Benson, Michaela, and Karen O'Reilly. 2016. "From Lifestyle Migration to Lifestyle in Migration: Categories, Concepts and Ways of Thinking." *Migration Studies* 4, no. 1: 20–37.

Benson, Michaela, and Karen O'Reilly. 2018. *Lifestyle Migration and Colonial Traces in Malaysia and Panama.* New York: Palgrave.

Benson, Michaela, and Nick Osbaldiston. 2014. "New Horizons in Lifestyle Migration Research: Theorising Movement, Settlement and the Search for a Better Way of Life." In *Understanding Lifestyle Migration: Theoretical Approaches to Migration and the Quest for a Better Way of Life,* edited by Michaela Benson and Nick Osbaldiston, 1–23. London: Palgrave Macmillan.

Benson, Michaela, and Nick Osbaldiston. 2016. "Toward a Critical Sociology of Lifestyle Migration: Reconceptualizing Migration and the Search for a Better Way of Life." *Sociological Review* 64, no. 3: 407–23.

Berriane, Mohamed, and M'hammed Idrissi Janati. 2016. "Les résidents européens de la médina de Fès: Une nouvelle forme de migration nord-sud." *Autrepart* 77: 87–105.

Berry, Albert, Cristóbal Kay, Luciano Martínez Valle, and Liisa North. 2014. *La concentración de la tierra: Un problema prioritario en el Ecuador contemporáneo.* Quito: Abya-Yala.

Betancur, John J. 2014. "Gentrification in Latin America: Overview and Critical Analysis." *Urban Studies Research* 14: Article 986961. http://dx.doi.org/10.1155/2014/986961.

Bhambra, Gurminder K. 2014. *Connected Sociologies.* London: Bloomsbury.

Binford, Leigh. 2003. "Migrant Remittances and (Under)development in Mexico." *Critique of Anthropology* 23, no. 3: 305–36.

Blackburn, Robin. 2006. "Finance and the Fourth Dimension." *New Left Review* 39: 39–70.

Blackburn, Robin. 2011. *Age Shock: How Finance Is Failing Us.* London: Verso.

Blomley, Nicholas. 2003. *Unsettling the City: Urban Land and the Politics of Property.* New York: Routledge.

Boatcă, Manuela. 2016. *Global Inequalities beyond Occidentalism.* London: Routledge.

Böcker, Anita, Vincent Horn, and Cornelia Schweppe. 2017. "National Old-Age Care Regimes and the Emergence of Transnational Long-Term Care Arrangements for the Elderly." In *Transnational Social Policy: Social Welfare in a World on the Move,* edited by Luann Good Gingrich and Stefan Köngeter, 222–42. New York: Routledge.

Bode, Inga. 2008. *The Culture of Welfare Markets: The International Recasting of Pension and Care Systems.* New York: Routledge.

Boltanski, Luc, and Arnaud Esquerre. 2014. "La 'Collection,' une forme neuve du capitalisme: La mise en valeur économique du passé et ses effets." *Les Temps Modernes* 679: 5–72.

Borras, Saturnino M., and Jennifer C. Franco. 2012. "Global Land Grabbing and Trajectories of Agrarian Change: A Preliminary Analysis." *Journal of Agrarian Change* 12, no. 1: 34–59.

Borras, Saturnino M., Jennifer C. Franco, Sergio Gómez, Cristóbal Kay, and Max Spoor. 2012. "Land Grabbing in Latin America and the Caribbean." *Journal of Peasant Studies* 39, no. 3–4: 845–72.

Borrero Vega, Ana Luz. 1996. "Impacto de la migración en el Azuay." In *Estudios, cronicas y relatos de nuestra tierra,* edited by María Rosa Crespo, 107–25. Cuenca: Universidad de Cuenca.

Borsdorf, Axel, and Rodrigo Hidalgo. 2009. "Searching for Fresh Air, Tranquility and Rural Culture in the Mountains: A New Lifestyle for Chileans?" *DIE ERDE* 140, no. 3: 275–92.

Boudiny, Kim. 2012. "'Active Ageing': From Empty Rhetoric to Effective Policy Tool." *Ageing and Society* 33, no. 6: 1077–98.

Bourdieu, Pierre. 1989. "Social Space and Symbolic Power." *Sociological Theory* 7, no. 1: 14–25.

Braverman, Harry. 1974. *Labor and Monopoly Capital: The Degradation of Work in the Twentieth Century.* New York: Monthly Review Press.

Bravo Díaz, Andrea Elizabeth. 2013. "Cuando los saberes se hace audibles: La transmisión del conocimiento en el Ecuador del siglo XXI." MA thesis, FLACSO Ecuador.

Bretón Solo de Zaldívar, Victor. 2008. "From Agrarian Reform to Ethno-development in the Highlands of Ecuador." *Journal of Agrarian Change* 8, no. 4: 583–617.

Bretón Solo de Zaldívar, Victor. 2012. *Toacazo: En los Andes equinocciales tras la Reforma Agraria.* Quito: FLACSO Sede Ecuador y Abya-Yala.

Bretón Solo de Zaldívar, Victor. 2015a. "Tempest in the Andes? Part 1: Agrarian Reform and Peasant Differentiation in Cotopaxi (Ecuador)." *Journal of Agrarian Change* 15, no. 1: 89–115.

Bretón Solo de Zaldívar, Victor. 2015b. "Tempest in the Andes? Part 2: Agrarian Reform and Peasant Differentiation in Cotopaxi (Ecuador)." *Journal of Agrarian Change* 15, no. 2: 179–200.

Bromley, Rosemary. 1998. "Informal Commerce: Expansion and Exclusion in the Historic Centre of the Latin American City." *International Journal of Urban and Regional Research* 22, no. 2: 245–63.

Bromley, Rosemary, and Peter Mackie. 2009. "Displacement and the New Spaces for Informal Trade in the Latin American City Centre." *Urban Studies* 46, no. 7: 1485–506.

Bruder, Jessica. 2017. *Nomadland: Surviving America in the Twenty-First Century.* New York: Norton.

Brumann, Christoph. 2014. "Shifting Tides of World-Making in the UNESCO World Heritage Convention: Cosmopolitanisms Colliding." *Ethnic and Racial Studies* 37, no. 12: 2176–92.

Bureau of Labor Statistics. 2010. *Record Unemployment among Older Workers Does Not Keep Them Out of the Job Market.* Issues in Labor Statistics 10-04. Washington, D.C.: U.S. Department of Labor.

Bureau of Labor Statistics. 2011. *The Employment Situation, November 2011.* USDL 11-1691. Washington, D.C.: U.S. Department of Labor. http://www.bls.gov/news.release/pdf/empsit.pdf.

Bush, Melanie E. L. 2004. "Race, Ethnicity, and Whiteness." *SAGE Race Relations Abstracts* 29, no. 3–4: 5–48.

Butler, Tim, and Loretta Lees. 2006. "Super-Gentrification in Barnsbury, London: Globalization and Gentrifying Global Elites at the Neighbourhood Level." *Transactions of the Institute of British Geographers* 31: 467–87.

Cabrera Azanza, Luis. 2008. *Valle de Vilcabamba: Sinopsis histórica.* Loja: Editorial ObraViva.

Cadieux, Kirsten V., and Patrick Hurley. 2011. "Amenity Migration, Exurbia, and Emerging Rural Landscapes: Global Natural Amenity as Place and as Process." *Geojournal* 76: 297–302.

Carrión Mena, Fernando, ed. 2007. *El financiamiento de los centros históricos de América Latina y del Caribe*. Quito: FLACSO Ecuador.

Carrión Mena, Fernando. 2010. *Ciudad, memoria y proyecto*. Quito: Organización Latinoamericana y del Caribe de Centros Históricos.

Carrión Mena, Fernando, and Manuel Dammert Guardia. 2011. "Quito's Historic Center: Heritage of Humanity or of the Market?" In *Selling Ethnicity: Urban Cultural Politics in the Americas*, edited by Olaf Kaltmeier, 171–88. Surrey, U.K.: Ashgate.

Casado-Díaz, Maria Angeles. 2006. "Retiring to Spain: An Analysis of Differences among North European Nationals." *Journal of Ethnic and Migration Studies* 32, no. 8: 1321–39.

Castles, Stephen. 2010. "Understanding Global Migration: A Social Transformation Perspective." *Journal of Ethnic and Migration Studies* 36, no. 10: 1565–86.

Célleri, Daniela A. 2016. "La pertenencia étnica en contextos migratorios: Jóvenes indígenas migrantes en una comunidad rural de Otavalo-Ecuador." PhD diss., Gottfried Wilhelm Leibniz Universität.

Chatterjee, Ipsita. 2014. *Displacement, Revolution, and the New Urban Condition: Theories and Case Studies*. London: Sage.

Clark, Erc. 2005. "The Order and Simplicity of Gentrification: A Political Challenge." In *Gentrification in a Global Context: The New Urban Colonialism*, edited by Rowland Atkinson and Gary Bridge, 256–64. London: Routledge.

Cócola Gant, Agustín. 2016. "Holiday Rentals: The New Gentrification Battlefront." *Sociological Research Online* 21, no. 3: 10. http://www.socresonline .org.uk/21/3/10.html.

Cócola Gant, Agustín. 2018. "Tourism Gentrification." In *Handbook of Gentrification Studies*, edited by Loretta Lees and Martin Phillips, 281–93. Cheltenham, U.K.: Edward Elgar.

Cócola Gant, Agustín, Gustavo Durán Saavedra, and Michael Janoschka. 2016. "La ciudad del siglo XXI: Políticas públicas urbanas, desplazamientos y contestaciones." *Íconos: Revista de Ciencias Sociales* 56: 11–18.

Coleman, Daniel. 2006. *White Civility: The Literary Project of English Canada*. Toronto: University of Toronto Press.

Coleman, Daniel. 2008. "From Contented Civility to Contending Civilities: Alternatives to Canadian White Civility." *International Journal of Canadian Studies* 38: 221–42.

Cordero, Claudio, Lucas Achig, and Adrián Carrasco. 1989. "La región centrosur." In *La sociedad azuayo-cañari: Pasado y presente*, vol. 1, edited by Leonardo Espinoza, 15–35. Quito: El Conejo.

Cresswell, Tim. 2013. "Citizenship in Worlds of Mobility." In *Critical Mobilities*, edited by Ola Soderstrom, Didier Ruedin, Shalini Randeria, Gianni D'Amato, and Francesco Panese, 105–24. New York: Routledge. https:// www.researchgate.net/profile/Tim_Cresswell/publication/260869717_

Citizenship_in_Worlds_of_Mobility/links/0046353288282dd168000000/
Citizenship-in-Worlds-of-Mobility.pdf.

Crispin, Jessa. 2017. "The Unsettled." *The Outline.* https://theoutline.com/
post/1910/the-unsettled.

Crossa, Verónica. 2012. "Disruption, Yet Community Reconstitution: Subvert-
ing the Privatization of Latin American Plazas." *GeoJournal* 77, no. 2: 167–83.

Croucher, Sheila. 2009. *The Other Side of the Fence: American Migrants in Mexico.*
Austin: University of Texas Press.

Croucher, Sheila. 2012. "Privileged Mobility in an Age of Globality." *Societies* 2,
no. 1: 1–13.

Croucher, Sheila. 2014. "The Gendered Spatialities of Lifestyle Migration." In
Contested Spatialities, Lifestyle Migration and Residential Tourism, edited by
Michael Janoschka and Heiko Haas, 15–28. New York: Routledge.

Croucher, Sheila. 2016. "Rooted in Relative Privilege: US 'Expats' in Granada,
Nicaragua." *Identities: Global Studies in Culture and Power.* http://dx.doi.org/
10.1080/1070289X.2016.1260022.

Cruikshank, Julie. 2005. *Do Glaciers Listen? Local Knowledge, Colonial Encounters,
and Social Imagination.* Vancouver: University of British Columbia Press.

Debnár, Miloš. 2016. *Migration, Whiteness, and Cosmopolitanism.* Cham, Swit-
zerland: Springer.

de la Cadena, Marisol. 2000. *Indigenous Mestizos: The Politics of Race and Culture
in Cuzco, Peru, 1919–1991.* Durham, N.C.: Duke University Press.

de la Cadena, Marisol. 2010. "Indigenous Cosmopolitics in the Andes: Conceptual Reflections beyond Politics." *Cultural Anthropology* 25, no. 2: 334–70.

de la Torre, Carlos. 1999. "Everyday Forms of Racism in Contemporary Ecuador:
The Experience of Middle-Class Indians." *Ethnic and Racial Studies* 22, no. 1:
92–112.

Delgadillo, Victor. 2016. "Selective Modernization of Mexico City and Its Historic Center: Gentrification without Displacement?" *Urban Geography* 37, no.
8: 1154–74.

Deneault, Alain. 2012. *Offshore: Tax Havens and the Rule of Global Crime.* New
York: New Press.

Deneault, Alain, and William Sacher. 2012. *Imperial Canada Inc.: Legal Haven of
Choice for the World's Mining Companies.* Vancouver: Talonbooks.

Dennie-Filion, Gabrièle. 2013. "The Economics of Lifestyle Migration: A Study
of Western European Migration to Marmaris, Turkey." Unpublished mas-
ter's thesis, University of Amsterdam. http://dare.uva.nl/cgi/arno/show
.cgi?fid=543523.

D'Eramo, Marco. 2014. "UNESCOcide." *New Left Review* 88: 47–53.

Descola, Philippe. 1994. *In the Society of Nature: A Native Ecology in Amazo-
nia.* Cambridge: Cambridge University Press and Maison des Sciences de
l'Homme.

Dillaway, Heather E., and Mary Byrnes. 2009. "Reconsidering Successful Aging:
A Call for Renewed and Expanded Academic Critiques and Conceptualiza-
tions." *Journal of Applied Gerontology* 28, no. 6: 702–22.

Dixon, David, Julie Murray, and Julia Gelatt. 2006. "America's Emigrants: U.S. Retirement Migration to Mexico and Panama." Migration Policy Institute. http://www.migrationinformation.org/feature/display.cfm?ID=416.

Donoso Correa, Mario Ernesto. 2016. "Análisis crítico de la planificación urbana de la Ciudad de Cuenca." *Maskana: Revista Cientifica* 7, no. 1: 107–22.

Dos Santos, Irène. 2016. "L'Angola, un Eldorado pour la jeunesse portuguaise? Mondes imaginés et expériences de la mobilité dans l'espace lusophone." *Cahiers d'études africaines* 221: 29–52.

Doucet, Andrea, Robyn Lee, Alana Cattapan, and Lindsay McKay. 2016. "Consuming Intimacies: Bodies, Labour, Care and Social Justice—Guest Editors' Introduction." *Studies in Social Justice* 10, no. 2: 194–98.

Drost, Nadja, and Keith Stewart. 2006. "EnCana in Ecuador: The Canadian Oil Patch Goes to the Amazon." In *Community Rights and Corporate Responsibility: Canadian Mining and Oil Companies in Latin America*, edited by Liisa North, Timothy David Clark, and Viviana Patroni, 113–38. Toronto: Between the Lines.

Duménil, Gérard, and Dominique Lévy. 2011. *The Crisis of Neoliberalism*. Cambridge, Mass.: Harvard University Press.

Durán, Lucía. 2015. "La Ronda: Olvidar el barrio, recordar la calle." MA thesis, FLACSO Ecuador.

Echtner, Charlotte M., and Pushkala Prasad. 2004. "The Context of Third World Tourism Marketing." *Annals of Tourism Research* 31, no. 2: 469–71.

Ehrenreich, Barbara. 1989. *Fear of Falling: The Inner Life of the Middle Class*. New York: Pantheon.

Ekerdt, David J. 1986. "The Busy Ethic: Moral Continuity between Work and Retirement." *The Gerontologist* 26, no. 3: 239–44.

Engemann, Kristie M., and Howard J. Wall. 2010. "The Effects of Recessions across Demographic Groups." *Federal Reserve Bank of St. Louis Review* 92: 1–26. https://files.stlouisfed.org/files/htdocs/publications/review/10/01/Engemann.pdf.

Ertuğrul, Gökçen. 2016. "British Migrants in the Turkish Countryside: Lifestyle Migration, Loss of Social Status and Finding 'True Life' in Difference." *METU Studies in Development* 43, no. 2: 475–96.

Escobar, Arturo. 1995. *Encountering Development: The Making and Unmaking of the Third World*. Princeton, N.J.: Princeton University Press.

Escobar García, Alexandra. 2008. "Tras las huellas de las familias migrantes del cantón Cañar." In *America Latina migrante: Estado, familias, identidades*, edited by Gioconda Herrera and Jacques Rámirez, 243–58. Quito: FLACSO Ecuador.

Espinoza, Leonardo, and Lucas Achig. 1989. "Aspectos socio-economicos de la sierra centro-sur en el siglo XVIII: Formas de produccion y estructuracion social." In *La sociedad azuayo-cañari: Pasado y presente*, vol. 1, edited by Leonardo Espinoza, 111–25. Quito: El Conejo.

Fabbiano, Giulia. 2016. "'Expats,' 'installés' et 'pionniers': Mobilités contemporaines, mondes sociaux et dynamiques postcoloniales des Français en Algérie." *Autrepart* 77: 17–33.

Fabian, Johannes. 1983. *Time and the Other: How Anthropology Makes Its Object.* New York: Columbia University Press.

Faist, Thomas. 2008. "Migrants as Transnational Development Agents: An Inquiry into the Newest Round of the Migration-Development Nexus." *Population, Space, and Place* 14, no. 1: 21–42.

Fauroux, Emmanuel. 1983. "Poder regional e instituciones regionales en la provincia de Loja desde principios del siglo XX: Ejes de una investigación." *Cultura (Quito: Banco Central del Ecuador)* 5, no. 15: 235–54.

Fechter, Anne-Meike. 2005. "The 'Other' Stares Back: Experiencing Whiteness in Jakarta." *Ethnography* 6, no. 1: 87–103.

Fechter, Anne-Meike. 2007. *Transnational Lives: Expatriates in Indonesia.* Aldershot, U.K.: Ashgate.

Fechter, Anne-Meike, and Katie Walsh. 2010. "Examining 'Expatriate' Continuities: Postcolonial Approaches to Mobile Professionals." *Journal of Ethnic and Migration Studies* 36, no. 8: 1197–210.

Fernandez, Rodrigo, Annelore Hofman, and Manuel Aalbers. 2016. "London and New York as a Safe Deposit Box for Transnational Wealth Elite." *Environment and Planning* 48, no. 12: 2443–61.

Ferriss, Timothy. 2007. *The 4-Hour Workweek: Escape 9–5, Live Anywhere, and Join the New Rich.* New York: Crown.

Fichtner, Jason, John Phillips, and Barbara Smith. 2012. "Retirement Behavior and the Global Financial Crisis." In *Reshaping Retirement Security: Lessons from the Global Financial Crisis,* edited by Raimond Mauer, Olivia Mitchell, and Mark Warshawsky, 81–97. Oxford: Oxford University Press.

Fierro Carrión, Luis. 1991. *Los grupos financieros en el Ecuador.* Quito: Centro de educación popular.

Foucault, Michel. 2005. *Hermeneutics of the Subject: Lectures at the Collège de France, 1981–82.* New York: Palgrave Macmillan.

Fournier, Gary M., David W. Rasmussen, and William J. Serow. 1988a. "Elderly Migration: For Sun and Money." *Population Research and Policy Review* 7, no. 2: 189–99.

Fournier, Gary M., David W. Rasmussen, and William J. Serow. 1988b. "Elderly Migration as a Response to Economic Incentives." *Social Science Quarterly* 69: 245–60.

Frankenburg, Ruth. 1997. "Introduction: Local Whiteness, Localizing Whiteness." In *Displacing Whiteness: Essays in Social and Cultural Criticism,* edited by Ruth Frankenburg, 1–34. Durham, N.C.: Duke University Press.

Franquesa, Jaume. 2013. "On Keeping and Selling: The Political Economy of Heritage Making in Contemporary Spain." *Current Anthropology* 54, no. 3: 346–69.

Freund, David M. P. 2006. "Marketing the Free Market: State Intervention and the Politics of Prosperity in Metropolitan America." In *The New Suburban*

History, edited by Kevin Michael Kruse and Thomas J. Sugrue, 11–32. Chicago: Chicago University Press.

Freund, David M. P. 2010. *Colored Property: State Property and White Racial Politics in Suburban America*. Chicago: University of Chicago Press.

Furtado, Celso. (1959) 2006. *Formação econômica do Brasil*. Sao Paulo: Companhia Das Letras.

Gago, Verónica. 2018. *Neoliberalism from Below: Popular Pragmatics and Baroque Economies*. Durham, N.C.: Duke University Press.

Galeano, Eduardo. (1971) 2010. *Las venas abiertas de América latina*. 5th ed. Buenos Aires: Siglo Ventiuno Editores.

Gambold, Lisl. 2013. "Retirement Abroad as Women's Aging Strategy." *Anthropology and Aging* 34, no. 2: 184–98.

Garcia, Fernando Almeida. 2014. "A Comparative Study of the Evolution of Tourism Policy in Spain and Portugal." *Tourism Management Perspectives* 11 (July): 34–50. https://doi.org/10.1016/j.tmp.2014.03.001.

García Álvarez, Milton, Pablo Osorio-Guerrero, and Luis Pastor Herrera. 2017. *Estudio sobre los impactos socio-económicos en Cuenca de la migración residencial de Norteamericanos y Europeos: Aportes para una convivencia ármonica local*. Cuenca, Ecuador: Ilustrada Municipalidad de Cuenca and the United Nations Development Programme.

Gárriz Fernández, Iranzu. 2011. "The Right to the City as a Conceptual Framework to Study the Impact of North–South Migration." *Recreation and Society in Africa, Asia, and Latin America* 2, no. 1: 3–33. https://journal.lib.uoguelph .ca/index.php/rasaala/article/view/1553.

Gascón, Jordi. 2016. "Residential Tourism and Depeasantisation in the Ecuadorian Andes." *Journal of Peasant Studies* 43, no. 4: 868–85.

Gibson, Heather. 2002. "Busy Travelers: Leisure-Travel Patterns and Meanings in Later Life." *World Leisure Journal* 44, no. 2: 11–20.

Gilleard, Chris, and Paul Higgs. 2011. "The Third Age as a Cultural Field." In *Gerontology in the Era of the Third Age: New Challenges and New Opportunities*, edited by Dawn C. Carr and Kathrin Komp, 33–49. New York: Springer.

Glauser, Marcos. 2009. *Extranjerización del territorio paraguayo*. Asunción: BASE Investigaciones Sociales.

Glick Schiller, Nina. 2009. "A Global Perspective on Migration and Development." *Social Analysis* 53, no. 3: 14–37.

Glick Schiller, Nina, and Thomas Faist, eds. 2010. *Migration, Development, and Transnationalization: A Critical Stance*. New York: Berghahn Books.

Glick Schiller, Nina, and Noel Salazar. 2013. "Regimes of Mobility across the Globe." *Journal of Ethnic and Migration Studies* 39, no. 2: 183–200.

Go, Julian. 2009. "The 'New' Sociology of Empire and Colonialism." *Sociology Compass* 3, no. 5: 775–88.

Gómez-Barris, Macarena. 2012. "Andean Translations: New Age Tourism and Cultural Exchange in the Sacred Valley, Peru." *Latin American Perspectives* 39, no. 6: 68–78.

Gómez Martín, Carmen. 2016. "¿Por qué hablamos de una crisis mundial del refugio?" *Boletín Andina migrante*, no. 20, 2–9. http://hdl.handle.net/10469/11639.

Gonzalez, Sara. 2016. "Looking Comparatively at Displacement and Resistance to Gentrification in Latin American Cities." *Urban Geography* 37, no. 8: 1245–52.

Goodman, Simon, Ala Sirriyeh, and Simon McMahon. 2017. "The Evolving (Re) categorisations of Refugees throughout the 'Refugee/Migrant Crisis.'" *Journal of Community and Applied Social Psychology* 27, no. 2: 105–14.

Gordon, Todd, and Jeffery R. Webber. 2016. *Blood of Extraction: Canadian Imperialism in Latin America*. Black Point, N.S.: Fernwood.

Gotham, Kevin. 2005. "Tourism Gentrification: The Case of New Orleans' Vieux Carré (French Quarter)." *Urban Studies* 42, no. 7: 1099–121.

Gowan, Peter. 2009. "Crisis in the Heartland." *New Left Review* 55: 5–29.

Gravari-Barbas, Maria, and Sandra Guinand. 2017. "Introduction: Addressing Tourism-Gentrification Processes in Contemporary Metropolises." In *Tourism and Gentrification in Contemporary Metropolises: International Perspectives*, edited by Maria Gravari-Barbas and Sandra Guinand, 1–21. New York: Taylor and Francis.

Green, Paul. 2017. "Racial Hierarchies and Contradictory Moral Regimes in Lifestyle Destinations: Older, Western Residents in Ubud, Bali." *Asia and Pacific Migration Journal* 26, no. 2: 161–80.

Greffe, Xavier. 2011. "L'économie politique du patrimoine culturelle: De la médaille au rhizome." In *Le patrimoine: Moteur du développement* [Heritage: A driver of development], 928–36. Paris: International Council on Monuments and Sites. http://openarchive.icomos.org/1307/1/IV-3-Article6_Greffe.pdf.

Grosfoguel, Ramón. 2007. "The Epistemic Decolonial Turn: Beyond Political-Economy Paradigms." *Cultural Studies* 21, no. 2–3: 211–23.

Grosfoguel, Ramón, Laura Oso, and Anastasia Christou. 2015. "'Racism,' Intersectionality and Migration Studies: Framing Some Theoretical Reflections." *Identities: Global Studies in Culture and Power* 22, no. 6: 635–52.

Guerrero, Andrés. 1983. *Haciendas, capital y lucha de clases Andina: Disolución de la hacienda serrana y lucha política en los años 1960–64*. Quito: Editorial El Conejo.

Guerrero, Andrés. 2003. "The Administration of Dominated Populations under a Regime of Customary Citizenship: The Case of Postcolonial Ecuador." In *After Spanish Rule: Postcolonial Predicaments of the Americas*, edited by Mark Thurner and Andrés Guerrero, 272–309. Durham, N.C.: Duke University Press.

Guerrero Carrión, Trotsky. 2010. *1970, Inflexión del movimiento social Lojano*. Loja: Casa de la Cultura Ecuatoriana.

Hansen, Peo. 2016. "Refugee Keynesianism? EU Migration Crises in Times of Financial Austerity." In *Austere Histories in European Societies: Social Exclusion and the Contest of Colonial Memories*, edited by Stefan Jonsson and Julia Willén, 135–60. Abingdon, U.K.: Routledge.

Hansen, Peo, and Stefan Jonsson. 2011. "Demographic Colonialism: EU–African Migration Management and the Legacy of Eurafrica." *Globalizations* 8, no. 3: 261–76.

Harman, Graham. 2016. *Immaterialism: Objects and Social Theory.* Malden, Mass.: Polity.

Harvey, David. 1978. "The Urban Process under Capitalism: A Framework for Analysis." *International Journal of Urban and Regional Research* 2: 101–31.

Harvey, David. 1985. *The Urbanization of Capital: Studies in the History and Theory of Capitalist Urbanization.* Baltimore: Johns Hopkins University Press.

Harvey, David. 1990. *The Condition of Postmodernity.* Cambridge, Mass.: Blackwell.

Harvey, David. 2005. *A Brief History of Neoliberalism.* Oxford: Oxford University Press.

Harvey, David. 2010. *The Enigma of Capital and the Crises of Capitalism.* Oxford: Oxford University Press.

Harvey, Graham. 2014. Introduction to *The Handbook of Contemporary Animism,* edited by Graham Harvey, 1–12. London: Routledge.

Hayes, Matthew. 2014. "'We Gained a Lot over What We Would Have Had': The Geographic Arbitrage of America's Lifestyle Migrants to Cuenca, Ecuador." *Journal of Ethnic and Migration Studies* 40, no. 12: 1953–71.

Hayes, Matthew. 2015a. "Into the Universe of the Hacienda: Lifestyle Migration, Individualism and Social Dislocation in Vilcabamba, Ecuador." *Journal of Latin American Geography* 14, no. 1: 79–100.

Hayes, Matthew. 2015b. "'It Is Hard Being the Different One All the Time': Gringos and Racialized Identity in Lifestyle Migration to Ecuador." *Ethnic and Racial Studies* 38, no. 6: 943–58.

Hayes, Matthew. Forthcoming. "The Gringos of Cuenca: How Retirement Migrants Perceive Their Impact on Lower Income Communities." *Area.*

Hayes, Matthew, and Jesse Carlson. 2018. "Good Guests and Obnoxious Gringos: Cosmopolitan Ideals among North American Migrants to Cuenca, Ecuador." *American Journal of Cultural Sociology* 6, no. 1: 189–211. https://link.springer.com/article/10.1057/s41290-017-0025-y.

Hermida, Augusta, Carla Hermida, Natasha Cabrera, and Christian Calle. 2015. "La densidad urbana como variable de análisis de la ciudad: El caso de Cuenca, Ecuador." *EURE (Santiago)* 41, no. 124: 25–44.

Herrera, Gioconda. 2005. "Remesas, dinámicas familiares y estatus social: La emigración ecuatoriana desde la sociedad de origen." In *La migración, un camino entre el desarrollo y la cooperación,* edited by Nieves Zúñiga García-Falcés, 149–62. Madrid: Centro de Investigación para la Paz.

Herrera, Gioconda. 2012. "Género y migración internacional en la experiencia latinoamericana: De la visibilización del campo a una presencia selectiva." *Política y sociedad* 49, no. 1: 35–46.

Hill, Michael. 2008. "Inca of the Blood, Inca of the Soul: Embodiment, Emotion and Racialization in the Peruvian Mystical Tourist Industry." *Journal of the American Academy of Religion* 76, no. 2: 251–79.

Hirschkind, Lynn. 1980. "On Conforming in Cuenca." PhD diss., University of Wisconsin.

Hitchings, Russell, Susan Venn, and Rosie Day. 2016. "Assumptions about Later-Life Travel and Their Implications: Pushing People Around?" *Ageing and Society*. https://doi.org/10.1017/S0144686X16000738.

Hochschild, Arlie. 2012. *The Second Shift: Working Families and the Revolution at Home*. New York: Penguin.

Hochschild, Arlie. 2013. *The Outsourced Self: What Happens When We Pay Others to Live Our Lives for Us*. London: Picador.

Horgan, Mervyn, and Saara Liinamaa. 2017. "The Social Quarantining of Migrant Labour: Everyday Effects of Temporary Foreign Worker Regulation in Canada." *Journal of Ethnic and Migration Studies* 43, no. 5: 713–30.

Houtart, François. 2015. "L'Équateur en 2015: L'épuisement d'un modèle dans un contexte de crise mondiale." *AlterInfos América Latina*, October 15. http://www.alterinfos.org/spip.php?article7034.

Huete, Raquel. 2009. *Turistas que llegan para quedarse*. San Vicente del Raspeig, Spain: Publicaciones de la Universidad de Alicante.

Hughey, Matthew W. 2010. "The (Dis)similarities of White Racial Identities: The Conceptual Framework of 'Hegemonic Whiteness.'" *Ethnic and Racial Studies* 33, no. 8: 1289–309.

Hurtado, Osvaldo. (1977) 2010. *El poder político en el Ecuador*. Quito: Editorial Planeta del Ecuador.

Hurtado, Osvaldo. 2007. *Las costumbres de los Ecuatorianos*. Quito: Editorial Planeta del Ecuador.

Hylton, Forrest. 2007. "Medellín's Makeover." *New Left Review* 44: 70–89.

Ibarra, Hernán. 1992. "Indios y cholos en la formación de la clase trabajadora ecuatoriana." *En Historia* 23: 85–104.

Ibarra, Hernán. 2002a. "Gamonalismo y dominación en los Andes." *Iconos* 14: 137–47.

Ibarra, Hernán. 2002b. "Origen y decadencia del gamonalismo en la sierra ecuatoriana." *Anuario de Estudios Americanos* 59: 491–510.

Ibarra, Hernán. 2013. "Anotaciones sobre las diferencias étnicas y el mestizaje en Ecuador y Perú, 1950–1970." *Ecuador Debate* 88: 31–50.

Inter-American Development Bank. 2006. *Loan Proposal (EC-L1021): Rehabilitation of Downtown Areas and Land Management Support in Cuenca*. Washington, D.C.: World Bank Group. http://www.iadb.org/en/projects/project-description-title,1303.html?id=ec-l1021.

Inzulza-Contardo, Jorge. 2012. "'Latino Gentrification'? Focusing on Physical and Socioeconomic Patterns of Change in Latin American Inner Cities." *Urban Studies* 49, no. 10: 2085–107.

Inzulza-Contardo, Jorge. 2016. "Contemporary Latin American Gentrification? Young Urban Professionals Discovering Historic Neighbourhoods." *Urban Geography* 37, no. 8: 1195–214.

Isin, Engin. 2002. *On Being Political*. Minneapolis: University of Minnesota Press.

Jacobson, Matthew F. 1999. *Whiteness of a Different Color: European Immigrants and the Alchemy of Race.* Cambridge, Mass.: Harvard University Press.

Jamieson, Ross W. 2002. *Domestic Architecture and Power: The Historical Archeology of Colonial Ecuador.* New York: Kluwer.

Janoschka, Michael. 2009. "The Contested Spaces of Lifestyle Mobilities: Regime Analysis as a Tool to Study Political Claims in Latin American Retirement Destinations." *DIE ERDE* 140, no. 3: 1–20.

Janoschka, Michael, and Jorge Sequera. 2016. "Gentrification in Latin America: Addressing the Politics and Geographies of Displacement." *Urban Geography* 37, no. 8: 1175–94.

Janoschka, Michael, Jorge Sequera, and Luis Salinas. 2014. "Gentrification in Spain and Latin America—a Critical Dialogue." *International Journal of Urban and Regional Research* 38, no. 4: 1234–65.

Jones, Reece. 2016. *Violent Borders: Refugees and the Right to Move.* London: Verso.

Kaag, Mayke, and Annelies Zoomers. 2014. "The Global Land Grab Hype—and Why It Is Important to Move Beyond." In *The Global Land Grab: Beyond the Hype,* edited by Mayke Kaag and Annelies Zoomers, 1–13. London: Zed Books.

Karlgaard, Rich. 2004. "Outsource Yourself." *Forbes,* April 19. http://www.forbes.com/forbes/2004/0419/033.html.

Karlgaard, Rich. 2006. "Special Report: 150 Cheap Places to Live." *Forbes,* May 5. http://www.forbes.com/2005/10/31/karlgaard-broadband-telecommuting_cz_rk_1101liverich.html.

Katz, Stephen. 2000. "Busy Bodies: Activity, Aging, and the Management of Everyday Life." *Journal of Aging Studies* 14, no. 2: 135–52.

Katz, Stephen. 2005. *Cultural Aging: Life Course, Lifestyle and Senior Worlds.* Peterborough, Ont.: Broadview.

Keita, Shomarka O. Y., and Rick A. Kittles. 1997. "The Persistence of Racial Thinking and the Myth of Racial Divergence." *American Anthropologist* 99: 534–44.

King, Russell, Diana Mata-Codesal, and Julie Vullnetari. 2013. "Migration, Development, Gender and the 'Black Box' of Remittances: Comparative Findings from Albania and Ecuador." *Comparative Migration Studies* 1, no. 1: 69–96.

King, Russell, Anthony Warnes, and Allan M. Williams. 1998. "International Retirement Migration in Europe." *International Journal of Population Geography* 4, no. 2: 91–111.

King, Russell, Tony Warnes, and Allan Williams. 2000. *Sunset Lives: British Retirement Migration to the Mediterranean.* New York: Berg.

Kingman, Eduardo. 2004. "Patrimonio, políticas de la memoria e institucionalización de la cultura." *Íconos: Revista de Ciencias Sociales* 20: 26–34.

Kingman, Eduardo. 2006. *La ciudad y los otros. Quito 1860–1940. Hiegenismo, ornato y policía.* Quito: FLACSO Sede Ecuador.

Kingman, Eduardo. 2012. *San Roque: Indígenas urbanos, seguridad y patrimonio.* Quito: FLACSO Sede Ecuador.

Klaufus, Christien. 2009. *Constsruir la ciudad Andina: Planificación y auto-construcción en Riobamba y Cuenca.* Quito: FLACSO.

Klinenberg, Eric. 2001. "Dying Alone: The Social Production of Urban Isolation." *Ethnography* 2, no. 4: 501–31.

Knowles, Caroline. 2006. "Seeing Race through the Lens." *Ethnic and Racial Studies* 29, no. 3: 512–29.

Knowles, Caroline. 2015. *Young Londoners in Beijing.* London: Goldsmiths. http://research.gold.ac.uk/18166/1/Beijing1_9_15%20FINAL.pdf.

Knowles, Caroline. 2017. "Reframing Sociologies of Ethnicity and Migration in Encounters with Chinese London." *British Journal of Sociology* 68, no. 3: 454–73. https://doi.org/10.1111/1468-4446.12271.

Knowles, Caroline, and Douglas Harper. 2009. *Hong Kong: Migrant Lives, Landscapes, and Journeys.* Chicago: University of Chicago Press.

Korovkin, Tanya. 1998. "Commodity Production and Ethnic Culture: Otavalo, Northern Ecuador." *Economic Development and Cultural Change* 47, no. 1: 125–54.

Korpela, Mari. 2009a. *More Vibes in India.* Tampere, Finland: University of Tampere Press.

Korpela, Mari. 2009b. "When a Trip to Adulthood Becomes a Lifestyle: Western Lifestyle Migrants in Varanasi, India." In *Lifestyle Migration: Expectations, Aspirations, and Experiences,* edited by Karen O'Reilly and Michaela Benson, 15–30. Farnham, U.K.: Ashgate.

Korpela, Mari. 2014. "Lifestyle of Freedom? Individualism and Lifestyle Migration." In *Understanding Lifestyle Migration,* edited by Michaela Benson and Nick Osbaldiston, 27–46. New York: Palgrave Macmillan.

Kunz, Sarah. 2016. "Privileged Mobilities: Locating the Expatriate in Migration Scholarship." *Geography Compass* 10, no. 3: 89–101.

Kurasawa, Fuyuki. 2007. *The Work of Global Justice: Human Rights as Practices.* Cambridge: Cambridge University Press.

Kyle, David. 2000. *Transnational Peasants: Migrations, Networks, and Ethnicity in Andean Ecuador.* Baltimore, Md.: Johns Hopkins University Press.

Lacarrieu, Mónica. 2016. "'Mercados tradicionales' en el proceso de gentrificación/recualificación: Consensos, disputas y conflictos." *Alteridades* 26, no. 51: 29–41.

Lamont, Michèle. 2000. *The Dignity of Working Men.* Chicago: University of Chicago Press.

Lan, Pei-Chia. 2011. "White Privilege, Language Capital and Cultural Ghettoisation: Western High-Skilled Migrants in Taiwan." *Journal of Ethnic and Migration Studies* 37, no. 10: 1669–93.

Lardiés Bosque, Raul. 2011. "A pocos kilómetros, pero en otro país: El retiro de jubilado estadounidenses en Baja California, México." *Geographicalia* 59–60: 183–97.

Laslett, Peter. 1991. *A Fresh Map of Life: The Emergence of the Third Age.* Cambridge, Mass.: Harvard University Press.

Latour, Bruno. 2005. *Reassembling the Social: An Introduction to Actor-Network-Theory.* Oxford: Oxford University Press.

Lawson, Michelle. 2017. "Narrative Positioning and 'Integration' in Lifestyle Migration: British Migrants in Ariège, France." *Language and Intercultural Communication* 17, no. 1: 58–75.

Leaf, Alexander. 1973. "Every Day Is a Gift When You Are Over 100." *National Geographic* 143, no. 1: 92–119.

Lees, Loretta, Hyun Bang Shin, and Ernesto López-Morales. 2016. *Planetary Gentrification.* Cambridge: Polity.

Lees, Loretta, Tom Slater, and Elvin Wyly. 2008. *The Gentrification Reader.* London: Routledge.

Lehmann, Angela. 2014. *Transnational Lives in China: Expatriates in a Globalizing City.* New York: Palgrave Macmillan.

Leonard, Pauline. 2008. "Migrating Identities: Gender, Whiteness and Britishness in Post-Colonial Hong Kong." *Gender, Place, and Culture* 15: 45–60.

Levitt, Peggy, and Nina Glick Schiller. 2004. "Conceptualizing Simultaneity: A Transnational Social Field Perspective on Society." *International Migration Review* 38, no. 3: 1002–39.

Lewis, Amanda. 2004. "'What Group?' Studying Whites and Whiteness in the Age of 'Color-Blindness.'" *Sociological Theory* 22, no. 4: 623–46.

Ley, David. 1996. *The New Middle Class and the Remaking of the Central City.* Oxford: Oxford University Press.

Longino, Charles F. 1995. *Retirement Migration in America.* Houston, Tex.: Vacation.

López-Morales, Ernesto. 2010. "Real Estate Market, State-Entrepreneurialism, and Urban Policy in the 'Gentrification by Ground Rent Dispossession' of Santiago de Chile." *Journal of Latin American Geography* 9, no. 1: 145–73.

López-Morales, Ernesto, Hyun Bang Shin, and Loretta Lees. 2016. "Latin American Gentrifications: Introduction." *Urban Geography* 37: 1091–108.

Louveau, Frédérique. 2016. "Migrants européens dans la ville de Saint-Louis du Sénégal: Des stratégies hétérogènes pour négocier sa place dans la cité." *Autrepart* 77: 107–23.

Lugones, María. 2007. "Heterosexism and the Colonial/Modern Gender System." *Hypatia* 22, no. 1: 186–209.

Lundström, Catrin. 2014. *White Migrations: Gender, Whiteness and Privilege in Transnational Migration.* New York: Palgrave Macmillan.

Lundström, Catrin. 2017. "The White Side of Migration: Reflections on Race, Citizenship and Belonging in Sweden." *Nordic Journal of Migration Research* 7, no. 2. https://doi.org/10.1515/njmr-2017-0014.

Lundström, Catrin, and France Winddance Twine. 2011. "White Migrations: Swedish Women, Gender Vulnerabilities and Racial Privileges." *European Journal of Women's Studies* 18, no. 1: 67–86.

Mackie, Peter K., Rosemary Bromley, and Alison Brown. 2014. "Informal Traders and the Battlegrounds of Revanchism in Cusco, Peru." *International Journal of Urban and Regional Research* 38, no. 5: 1884–903.

Maher, Kristen Hill, and Megan Lafferty. 2014. "White Migrant Masculinities in Thailand and the Paradoxes of Western Privilege." *Social and Cultural Geography* 15, no. 4: 427–48.

Mancero Acosta, Mónica. 2012. *Nobles y cholos: Raza, género, y clase en Cuenca 1995–2005.* Quito: FLACSO Ecuador. http://www.flacsoandes.edu.ec/libros/digital/52542.pdf.

Manrique Gómez, Adrian. 2013. "Gentrificación de La Candelaria: Reconfiguraciones de lugar de residencia y consumo de grupos de altos ingresos." *Cuadernos de Geografía—Revista Colombiana de Geografía* 22, no. 2: 211–34.

Mantecón, Alejandro. 2008. *La experiencia del turismo: Un estudio sociológico sobre el proceso turístico-residencial.* Barcelona: Icaria editorial.

Marshall, Barbara L. 2015. "Anti-Ageing and Identities." In *Routledge Handbook of Cultural Gerontology,* edited by Julia Twigg and Wendy Martin, 210–16. London: Routledge.

Martínez, María de los Ángeles. 2013. "Bohemia y vanguardia: El modernismo en Cuenca." In *Alma mía: Simbolismo y modernidad, Ecuador 1900–1930,* edited by Alexandra Kennedy Troya and Rodrigo Gutiérrez Viñuales, 136–37. Quito: Fundación Museos de la Ciudad.

Masi de Casanova, Erynn, Leila Rodríguez, and Rocío Bueno Roldán. 2017. "Informed but Insecure: Employment Conditions and Social Protection among Paid Domestic Workers in Guayaquil." *Latin American Perspectives.* https://doi.org/10.1177/0094582X17717989.

Mata-Codesal, Diana. 2018. "Trickling Down or Brimming Over Gains from Remittances? Local Processes of Economic Levelling in Rural Highland Ecuador." *Migration and Development* 7, no. 1: 26–39.

Matarrita-Cascante, David, and Gabriela Stocks. 2013. "Amenity Migration to the Global South: Implications for Community Development." *Geoforum* 49: 91–102.

McHugh, Kevin E. 2000. "The 'Ageless Self'? Emplacement of Identities in Sun Belt Retirement Communities." *Journal of Aging Studies* 14, no. 1: 103–15.

McHugh, Kevin E. 2003. "Three Faces of Ageism: Society, Image and Place." *Ageing and Society* 23: 165–85.

MCPEC. 2011. "Agendas por la transformación productiva territorial: Provincia de Loja. Quito: Gobierno de Ecuador." https://www.scribd.com/document/245007041/Agenda-Territorial-Loja.

Meisch, Lynn A. 1995. "Gringas and Otavalenos: Changing Tourist Relations." *Annals of Tourism Research* 22, no. 2: 441–62.

Meisch, Lynn A. 2002. *Andean Entrepreneurs: Otavalo Merchants and Musicians in the Global Arena.* Austin: University of Texas Press.

Membrado, Joan Carles. 2013. "Sunny Spain: Migrantes del sol y urbanismo expansivo en el litoral mediterráneo español." *Ciudad y territorio: Estudios territoriales* 178: 687–708.

Middleton, Alan. 2003. "Informal Traders and Planners in the Regeneration of

Historic City Centres: The Case of Quito, Ecuador." *Progress in Planning* 59, no. 2: 71–123.

Mies, Maria. 1986. *Patriarchy and Accumulation on a World Scale: Women in the International Division of Labor.* New York: Zed Books.

Mignolo, Walter. 2000. *Local Histories/Global Designs: Coloniality, Subaltern Knowledge, and Border Thinking.* Princeton, N.J.: Princeton University Press.

Mignolo, Walter. 2011. *The Darker Side of Modernity: Global Futures, Decolonial Options.* Durham, N.C.: Duke University Press.

Miles, Ann. 2004. *From Cuenca to Queens: An Anthropological Story of Transnational Migration.* Austin: University of Texas Press.

Miles, Ann. 2015. "Health Care Imaginaries and Retirement to Cuenca, Ecuador." *Journal of Latin American Geography* 14, no. 1: 39–55.

Miles, Robert. 1993. *Racism after Race Relations.* London: Routledge.

Miles, Robert, and Malcolm Brown. 2003. *Racism.* 2nd ed. London: Routledge.

Mollett, Sharlene. 2014. "A Modern Paradise: Garifuna Land, Labor, and Displacement-in-Place." *Latin American Perspectives* 41, no. 6: 27–45.

Mollett, Sharlene. 2016. "The Power to Plunder: Rethinking Land Grabbing in Latin America." *Antipode* 48, no. 2: 412–32.

Mosisa, Abraham, and Steven Hipple. 2006. "Trends in Labor Force Participation in the United States." *Monthly Labor Review* 129 (October): 35–57. http://greencompletely.com/blogandstuff/myblog/docs/agingworkforce.pdf.

Mumford, Jeremy Ravi. 2012. *Vertical Empire: The General Resettlement of Indians in the Colonial Andes.* Durham, N.C.: Duke University Press.

Munnell, Alicia, and Matthew Rutledge. 2013. "The Effects of the Great Recession on the Retirement Security of Older Workers." *Annals of the American Academy of Political and Social Science* 650: 124–42.

Noroña, Maria Belén. 2006. "Seizing the Lake: Tourism, Identity and Power of the Indigenous Peoples of Quilotoa, Ecuador." PhD diss., University of Texas at Austin.

Oliver, Caroline. 2007. "Imagined Comunitas: Older Migrants and Aspirational Mobility." In *Going First Class? New Approaches to Privileged Travel and Movement,* edited by Vered Amit, 126–43. New York: Berghahn Books.

Oliver, Caroline. 2008. *Retirement Migration: Paradoxes of Aging.* New York: Routledge.

Omi, Michael, and Howard Winant. 1994. *Racial Formation in the United States: From the 1960s to the 1990s.* 2nd ed. London: Routledge.

Ong, Aihwa. 2006. *Neoliberalism as Exception: Mutations in Citizenship and Sovereignty.* Durham, N.C.: Duke University Press.

Ono, Mayumi. 2015. "Commoditization of Lifestyle Migration: Japanese Retirees in Malaysia." *Mobilities* 10, no. 4: 609–27.

O'Reilly, Karen. 2000. *The British on the Costa del Sol: Transnational Identities and Local Communities.* London: Routledge.

O'Reilly, Karen. 2007. "Intra-European Migration and the Mobility-Enclosure Dialectic." *Sociology* 41: 277–93.

O'Reilly, Karen. 2012. *International Migration and Social Theory*. London: Palgrave Macmillan.

O'Reilly, Karen. 2014. "The Role of the Social Imaginary in Lifestyle Migration: Employing the Ontology of Practice Theory." In *Understanding Lifestyle Migration: Theoretical Approaches to Migration and the Quest for a Better Way of Life*, edited by Michaela Benson and Nick Osbaldiston, 211–34. New York: Palgrave Macmillan.

O'Reilly, Karen, and Michaela Benson. 2009. "Lifestyle Migration: Escaping to the Good Life." In *Lifestyle Migration: Expectations, Aspirations, and Experiences*, edited by Michaela Benson and Karen O'Reilly, 31–50. Farnham, U.K.: Ashgate.

Ormond, Meghann, and Mika Toyota. 2016. "Confronting Economic Precariousness through International Retirement Migration: Japan's Old-Age 'Economic Refugees' and Germany's 'Exported Grannies.'" In *Tourism and Leisure Mobilities: Politics, Work, and Play*, edited by Jillian Rickly, Kevin Hannam, and Mary Mostafanezhad, 134–46. Abingdon, U.K.: Routledge.

Otero, Lorena. 1997. "U.S. Retired Persons in Mexico." *American Behavioral Scientist* 40, no. 7: 914–22.

Páez Barrera, Oswaldo. 2014. *Cartas desde Guápulo*. Quito: Universidad Internacional SEK.

Painter, Nell Irvin. 2010. *The History of White People*. New York: W. W. Norton.

Palomeque, Silvia. 1990. *Cuenca en el siglo XIX: La articulación de una región*. Quito: Abya-Yala.

Pástor, Carlos. 2014. *Ley de Tierras: El debate y las organizaciones campesinas*. Quito: La Tierra.

Payne, Eugene H. 1954. "Islands of Immunity: Medicine's Most Amazing Mystery." *Reader's Digest*, November.

Pedone, Claudia. 2008. "'Varones aventureros' vs. 'madres que abandonan': Reconstrucción de las relaciones familiares a partir de la migración ecuatoriana." *Revista Interdisciplinar da Movilidade Humana* 16, no. 30: 45–64.

Peraldi, Michel, and Lisa Terrazzoni. 2016. "Anthropologie des europeéns en Afrique: Mémoires coloniales et nouvelles aventures migratoires." *Cahiers d'études africaines* 221: 9–28.

Picard, Michel. 2003. "Touristification and Balinization in a Time of *Reformasi*." *Indonesia and Malay World* 31, no. 89: 108–18.

Pietri-Levy, Anne-Lise. 1993. *Loja: una provincia del Ecuador*. Quito: Ediciones del Banco Central del Ecuador.

Pinley Covert, Lisa. 2017. *San Miguel de Allende: Mexicans, Foreigners, and the Making of a World Heritage Site*. Lincoln: University of Nebraska Press.

Poma, José, and Sinda Castro. 2009. "Dinámicas económicas territoriales en Loja, Ecuador: ¿Crecimiento sustentable o pasajero?" https://idl-bnc-idrc .dspacedirect.org/bitstream/handle/10625/46660/133139.pdf.

Ponce, Juan, Iliana Olivié Aldasoro, and Mercedes Onofa. 2008. "Remittances for Development? A Case Study of the Impact of Remittances on Human

Development in Ecuador." *Elcano Newsletter* 48. http://biblioteca.ribei .org/1489/.

Prasad, Vijay. 2012. *The Poorer Nations: A Possible History of the Global South*. London: Verso.

Prebisch, Raúl. 1962. "The Economic Development of Latin America and Its Principal Problems." *Economic Bulletin for Latin America* 7, no. 1: 1–12.

Pribilsky, Jason. 2007. *La Chulla Vida: Gender, Migration, and the Family in Andean Ecuador and New York City*. Syracuse, N.Y.: Syracuse University Press.

Quashie, Hélène. 2016a. "Débuter sa carrière professionelle en Afrique: L'idéal d'insertion sociale des volontaires français à Dakar et Antananarivo (Sénégal, Madagascar)." *Cahiers d'études africaines* 221: 53–80.

Quashie, Hélène. 2016b. "Les migrants européens du littoral sénégalais (Petit Côte, Saloum): ouverture de l'économie touristique et entre-soi identitaire." *Autrepart* 77: 125–41.

Quijano, Aníbal. 2000. "Colonialidad del poder, eurocentrismo y América Latina." In *Colonialidad del saber, eurocentrismo y ciencias sociales*, edited by Edgardo Lander, 201–46. Buenos Aires: CLACSO-UNESCO.

Quijano, Aníbal. 2007. "Coloniality and Modernity/Rationality." *Cultural Studies* 21, no. 2–3: 168–78.

Rainer, Gerhard, and Matilde Malizia. 2014. "Los countries en el country: Migración de amenidad, vino de altura y urbanizaciones cerradas en Cafayate (Salta, Argentina)." *Journal of Latin American Geography* 13, no. 1: 39–66.

Rainer, Gerhard, and Matilde Malizia. 2015. "En búsqueda de lo rural: Migración de amenidad en los Valles Calchaquíes, Argentina." *Journal of Latin American Geography* 14, no. 1: 57–78.

Rebaï, Nasser. 2009. "Diversidad de las estrategias campesinas en la provincia del Azuay: Un punto de vista geográfico." *Ecuador Debate* 77: 173–84.

Rebaï, Nasser. 2015. "Émigration paysanne et vulnérabilité des territoires ruraux dans les Andes équatoriennes." *EchoGéo* 34. https://echogeo.revues .org/14420?lang=en.

Rey Pérez, Julia, Sebastián Astudillo Cordero, María Eugenia Siguencia, Juliana Forero, and Silvia Auquilla. 2017. *Paisaje urbano histórico. La aplicación de la recomendación sobre el paisaje urbano histórico (PUH) en Cuenca (Ecuador): Una nueva aproximación al patrimonio cultural y natural*. Cuenca: Universidad de Cuenca.

Reyes-Bueno, Fabián, José Tubio Sánchez, Juan Gracía Samaniego, David Miranda Barrós, Rafael Crecente Maseda, and Aminael Sánchez-Rodríguez. 2016. "Factors Influencing Land Fractioning in the Context of Land Market Deregulation in Ecuador." *Land Use Policy* 52: 144–50.

Rodriguez, Vicente, Gloria Fernandez-Mayoralas, and Fermina Rojo. 2004. "International Retirement Migration: Retired Europeans Living on the Costa del Sol, Spain." *Population Review* 43: 1–36.

Roediger, David. 1991. *Wages of Whiteness: Race and the Making of the American Working Class*. London: Verso.

Roediger, David. 2005. *Working toward Whiteness. How America's Immigrants Became White*. New York: Basic Books.

Roitman, Karem. 2009. *Race, Ethnicity, and Power in Ecuador: The Manipulation of Mestizaje*. Boulder, Colo.: First Forum Press.

Rojas, Eduardo. 1999. *Old Cities, New Assets: Latin America's Urban Heritage*. Washington, D.C.: Inter-American Development Bank.

Rosa, Hartmut. 2013. *Social Acceleration: A New Theory of Modernity*. New York: Colombia University Press.

Rowe, John W., and Robert L. Kahn. 1998. *Successful Aging*. New York: Pantheon.

Rudman, Debbie Laliberte. 2006. "Shaping the Active, Autonomous and Responsible Modern Retiree: An Analysis of Discursive Technologies and Their Links with Neo-Liberal Political Rationality." *Ageing and Society* 26, no. 2: 181–201.

Salazar, Noel, and Nelson Graburn. 2014. "Introduction: Towards an Anthropology of Tourism Imaginaries." In *Tourism Imaginaries: Anthropological Approaches,* ed. Noel Salazar and Nelson Graburn, 1–28. New York: Berghahn.

Santos, Boaventura de Sousa. 2014. *Epistemologies of the South: Justice against Epistemicide*. New York: Routledge.

Sassen, Saskia. 2001. *The Global City: New York, London, Tokyo*. Princeton, N.J.: Princeton University Press.

Sassen, Saskia. 2017. "Predatory Formations Dressed in Wall Street Suits and Algorithmic Math." *Science and Technology Studies* 22, no. 1: 6–20.

Scarpaci, Joseph L. 2005. *Plazas and Barrios: Heritage Tourism and Globalization in the Latin American Centro Histórico*. Tucson: University of Arizona Press.

Shin, Hyuan Bang. 2018. "Studying Global Gentrifications." In *Doing Global Urban Research,* edited by J. Harrison and M. Hoyler, 138–52. London: Sage.

Sigler, Thomas, and David Wachsmuth. 2016. "Transnational Gentrification: Globalisation and Neighbourhood Change in Panama's Casco Viejo." *Urban Studies* 53, no. 4: 705–22.

Slater, Tom. 2017. "Planetary Rent Gaps." *Antipode* 49, no. S1: 114–37.

Smith, Linda Tuhiwai. 2013. *Decolonizing Methodologies: Research and Indigenous Peoples*. London: Zed Books.

Smith, Neil. 1996. *The New Urban Frontier: Gentrification and the Revanchist City*. London: Routledge.

Spalding, Ana. 2013. "Lifestyle Migration to Bocas del Toro, Panama: Exploring Migration Strategies and Introducing Local Implications of the Search for Paradise." *International Review of Social Research* 3: 67–86.

Stacey, Judith. 1990. *Brave New Families: Stories of Domestic Upheaval in Late-Twentieth-Century America*. Berkeley: University of California Press.

Stacey, Judith. 1993. "Good Riddance to 'The Family': A Response to David Popenoe." *Journal of Marriage and Family* 55, no. 3: 545–47.

Stoler, Ann Laura. 1995. *Race and the Education of Desire: Foucault's History of Sexuality and the Colonial Order of Things*. Durham, N.C.: Duke University Press.

Sugrue, Thomas J. 2014. *The Origins of the Urban Crisis: Race and Inequality in Postwar Detroit*. Princeton, N.J.: Princeton University Press.

Sullivan, Shannon. 2014. *Good White People: The Problem with Middle-Class White Anti-Racism*. Albany: State University of New York Press.

Sunil, Thankam S., Vivian Rojas, and Don E. Bradley. 2007. "United States' International Retirement Migration: The Reasons for Retiring to the Environs of Lake Chapala, Mexico." *Ageing and Society* 27, no. 4: 489–510.

Swanson, Kate. 2007. "Revanchist Urbanism Heads South: The Regulation of Indigenous Beggars and Street Vendors in Ecuador." *Antipode* 39, no. 4: 708–28.

Swidler, Ann. 2001. *Talk of Love: How Culture Matters*. Chicago: University of Chicago Press.

Tang, Fengyan, Eunhee Choi, and Rachel Goode. 2013. "Older Americans Employment and Retirement." *Ageing International* 38, no. 1: 82–94.

Thompson, E. P. (1967) 1993. "Time, Work-Discipline and Industrial Capitalism." In *Customs in Common: Studies in Traditional Popular Culture*, 352–403. New York: New Press.

Toossi, Mitra. 2015. "Labor Force Projections to 2024: The Labor Force Is Growing, but Slowly." *Monthly Labor Review* 138. https://doi.org/10.21916/mlr.2015.48.

Townsley, Eleanor. 2001. " 'The Sixties' Trope." *Theory, Culture, and Society* 18, no. 6: 99–123.

Toyota, Mika, and Biao Xiang. 2012. "The Emerging Transnational 'Retirement Industry' in Southeast Asia." *International Journal of Sociology and Social Policy* 32, no. 11–12: 708–19.

Tuck, Eve, and K. Wayne Yang. 2012. "Decolonization Is Not a Metaphor." *Decolonization: Indigeneity, Education, and Society* 1, no. 1: 1–40.

Unidad Técnica de la Fundación Municipal El Barranco. 2009. *Cuenca: Proyectos de revitalización urbana, 2004–2009*. Cuenca: Municipio de Cuenca.

Unidad Técnica de la Fundación Municipal El Barranco. 2015. *Cuenca: Proyectos de revitalización urbana, 2010–2015*. Cuenca: Municipio de Cuenca.

Universidad de Cuenca. 2007. "La incidencia de las remesas en la economía del Azuay." *Boletín del observatorio económico del Azuay* 11: 69–79.

Urry, John. 1990. *The Tourist Gaze: Leisure and Travel in Contemporary Societies*. London: Sage.

U.S. Government Accountability Office. 2012. "Unemployed Older Workers: Many Experience Challenges Regaining Employment and Face Reduced Retirement Security." https://www.gao.gov/assets/600/590408.pdf.

U.S. Government Accountability Office. 2015. "Retirement Security: Most Households Approaching Retirement Have Low Savings." http://www.gao.gov/assets/680/670153.pdf.

Valentine, Gill. 2008. "Living with Difference: Reflections on Geographies of Encounter." *Progress in Human Geography* 32, no. 3: 323–37.

van den Hoonaard, Deborah K. 2002. "Life on the Margins of a Florida Retirement Community: The Experience of Snowbirds, Newcomers, and Widowed Persons." *Research on Aging* 24, no. 1: 50–66.

van Noorloos, Femke. 2011. "Residential Tourism Causing Land Privatization and Alienation: New Pressures on Costa Rica's Coasts." *Development* 54, no. 1: 85–90.

van Noorloos, Femke, and Griet Steel. 2016. "Lifestyle Migration and Socio-spatial Segregation in the Urban(izing) Landscapes of Cuenca (Ecuador) and Guanacaste (Costa Rica)." *Habitat International* 54, no. 1: 50–57.

Vásquez Armijos, Bolívar. 2009. *Vilcabamba: Fantasía o Realidad.* Loja, Ecuador: Impresión Pixeles.

Vaughan-Williams, Nick. 2015. "'We Are Not Animals!' Humanitarian Border Security and Zoopolitical Spaces in Europe." *Political Geography* 45: 1–10.

Velásquez, Teresa. 2018. "Tracing the Political Life of Kimsacocha: Conflicts over Water and Mining in Ecuador's Southern Andes." *Latin American Perspectives* 45, no. 5: 154–69.

Viteri, María Amelia. 2015. "Cultural Imaginaries in the Residential Migration to Cotacachi." *Journal of Latin American Geography* 14, no. 1: 119–38.

Wade, Peter. 2010. *Race and Ethnicity in Latin America.* 2nd ed. New York: Pluto Press.

Walsh, Katie. 2010. "Negotiating Migrant Status in the Emerging Global City: Britons in Dubai." *Encounters* 2: 235–55.

Walsh, Katie. 2012. "Emotion and Migration: British Transnationals in Dubai." *Environment and Planning D: Society and Space* 30, no. 1: 43–59.

Weismantel, Mary. 2001. *Cholas and Pishtacos: Stories of Race and Sex in the Andes.* Chicago: University of Chicago Press.

Weiß, Anja. 2005. "The Transnationalization of Social Inequality: Conceptualizing Social Positions on a World Scale." *Current Sociology* 53, no. 4: 707–28.

Weller, Christian. 2016. *Retirement on the Rocks: Why Americans Can't Get Ahead and How New Savings Policies Can Help.* New York: Palgrave Macmillan.

Winant, Howard. 1999. "Racial Democracy and Racial Identity." In *Racial Politics in Contemporary Brazil,* edited by Michael Hanchard, 98–115. Durham, N.C.: Duke University Press.

Winant, Howard. 2001. "White Racial Projects." In *The Making and Unmaking of Whiteness,* edited by Birgit Brander Rasmussen, Irene J. Nexica, Matt Wray, and Eric Klinenberg, 97–112. Durham, N.C.: Duke University Press.

Wong Cruz, Ketty. 2013. *La música nacional: Identidad, mestizaje y migración en el Ecuador.* Quito: Casa de la Cultura Ecuatoriana.

World Bank. 2006. *Global Economic Prospects: Economic Implications of Remittances and Migration.* Washington, D.C.: World Bank.

World Bank. 2008. *Remittances and Development: Lessons from Latin America.* Washington, D.C.: World Bank.

World Tourism Organization. 2016. *Tourism Highlights, 2016 Edition.* Madrid: World Tourism Organization. https://www.e-unwto.org/doi/pdf/10.18111/9789284418145.

Yeates, Nicola. 2012. "Global Care Chains: A State-of-the-Art Review and Future Directions in Care Transnationalization Research." *Global Networks* 12, no. 2: 135–54.

< **260** >

BIBLIOGRAPHY

Zaban, Hila. 2015. "Living in a Bubble: Enclaves of Transnational Jewish Immigrants from Western Countries in Jerusalem." *Journal of International Migration and Integration* 16, no. 4: 1003–21.

Zaban, Hila. 2016. "City of Go(l)d: Spatial and Cultural Effects of High-Status Jewish Immigration from Western Countries on the Baka Neighbourhood of Jerusalem." *Urban Studies* 54, no. 7: 1539–58. https://doi.org/0042098015625023.

Zeltzer, Nicholas D. 2008. "Foreign-Economic-Retirement Migration: Promises and Potential, Barriers and Burdens." *Elder Law Journal* 16, no. 1: 211–41.

Zoomers, Annelies. 2010. "Globalisation and the Foreignisation of Space: Seven Processes Driving the Current Global Land Grab." *Journal of Peasant Studies* 37, no. 2: 429–47.

Index

aging: active, 14, 37, 40, 47; cultural
   ideals of, 11, 14–15, 37, 40–41,
   190, 197–98; older workers, 52–53,
   224n11; successful, 4, 11, 12, 37, 40,
   47, 55, 197; in the United States, 6.
   See also retirement
Agrarian Development Law (1994),
   172
agrarian reform, 152, 161–69, 170–71
Agrarian Reform Law (1964), 162–63
Alejandro (research participant), 175,
   178–79
Alicia (research participant), 147
alienation, 89, 123
Amanda (research participant), 111
Ana (research participant), 139
Andrea (research participant), 82,
   225n4
antimodernity. *See* nostalgia: as
   critique of modernity
arrimados, 24, 163, 165–67, 231n4
authenticity, 88–89, 144–45, 160
autonomous vendors, 142–43
Azuay, Ecuador (province), 22–23,
   30, 158

Barry (research participant), 53–54
Bellah, Robert, 197, 223n3
Benjamin (research participant),
   73–75
Berta (research participant), 164,
   165, 169
blanco, el, 93, 94
Bourdieu, Pierre, 219

Brett (research participant), 76,
   78–81, 106, 197
buen vivir, 151, 164, 194

Cabrera, Marcelo, 131, 133
Camilo (research participant), 168
capitalism; and modernization, 87;
   and surplus accumulation, 12, 88,
   198; and transformation of space,
   20, 60–61, 184, 190–91
caserios, 151, 154
citizenship. *See under* latitudes
Clem (research participant), 53, 100
Colin (research participant), 35–37,
   76–78, 102, 123–24
colones, 170. See also *arrimados*
coloniality of power, 9, 24
colonial legacy: of Ecuador, 23–24; of
   geoarbitrage, 57–58, 59, 147, 188;
   of heritage preservation, 198–99;
   of latitudes, 11; of lifestyle migration, 7–11, 20, 113, 179–81, 186,
   226n3, 232n10
comerciantes autónomas, 142–43
Cuenca, Ecuador, 1, 21–23, 71–72;
   architecture, 69–72, 121–22;
   displacement of inhabitants,
   200–201, 204–5; European orientation, 27, 68–72, 87–88, 113,
   225n2; gentrification, 194–96;
   heritage preservation, 27–28, 119;
   history, 23–27, 87; landowning
   elites, 25–27, 71, 113, 119–20,
   121–22, 190, 227n4; lifestyle

of, 127–28; and Otavalo vendors, 129, 133, 228n11; revitalization of, 130–32, 137, 144–46; role as labor market, 128–29; touristification of, 135–36, 145; vendors' campaign against dislocation from, 133–35, 227n3

plaza seca, 116, 133, 138

precaristas. See *arrimados*

Quijano, Aníbal, 9, 24, 85–86, 234n12
Quito, Ecuador, 28
Quito Letter, 28, 127

racialization, 5, 13, 92
racial subjectification, 92, 226n1
Rafael (research participant), 169
Raúl (research participant), 138
Ray (research participant), 44–45
recession (2008). See financial crisis (2008)
refugees: moving north, 15, 222n9. *See also* "economic refugees"
remittances: of Ecuadorian migrants, 30, 192, 223n15
research methods: ethnography, 217–18, 219; interviews, 216–18
retirement: early, 51–52, 53; unaffordability of in North America, 6, 37–39, 40, 49–50, 52–54; and women, 47
Rick (research participant), 5–6, 197, 221n4
Robert (research participant), 39
Rodrigo (research participant), 174
Ron (research participant), 58
Rosita (research participant), 176

Sam (research participant), 43–44, 58
Sandy (research participant), 98, 110, 149–50, 158–60
San Joaquín (hacienda), 173–74
Scarlett (research participant), 69
Shelley (research participant), 51

Simone (research participant), 44–45, 73, 231n22
Sixties, the, 80–81
social distance, 219–20
social imaginaries, 65, 67, 71, 227n9. *See also* migrant imaginaries
Stan (research participant), 91–92, 100, 103–6
Steve (research participant), 99–100

tarjos, 166
third age, 14–15, 37, 61
Thompson, E. P., 166
touristification, 223n12; in Cuenca, Ecuador, 21, 29–30, 70, 137–38; in El Centro (Cuenca), 5–17, 136–37; in plaza San Francisco, 135–36, 145
Townsley, Eleanor, 80–81
transnationalism: in migration scholarship, 184–85; of real estate, 146–47, 172–74, 176–79, 233nn2–3. *See also* gentrification: global; latitudes
tranvía project (Cuenca), 145, 199–200, 227nn1–2, 228–29nn14–15, 233n7

ugly American, 104–5, 107–8, 227n8
unemployment: as cause of migration, 42–45; and older U.S. workers after 2006, 45–46
UNESCO designation: Cuenca, Ecuador, 21, 29, 127; El Centro (Cuenca), 125, 134

Valentino (research participant), 168–69, 174
Vilcabamba, Ecuador: gentrification of, 171–74, 176–78, 180–81, 231nn5–6; geography of, 153–55, 157; hacienda system, 157–58; inhabitants migrating from, 175–76, 178–79, 181; landowning elites, 173–74, 232n10; land reform in, 161–69, 170–71; and lifestyle migrants, 150–53, 156,

(continued from page ii)

VOLUME 13
*El Paso: Local Frontiers at a
Global Crossroads*
Victor M. Ortíz-González

VOLUME 12
*Remaking New York: Primitive
Globalization and the Politics of
Urban Community*
William Sites

VOLUME 11
*A Political Space: Reading the
Global through Clayoquot Sound*
Warren Magnusson and
Karena Shaw, Editors

VOLUME 10
*City Requiem, Calcutta: Gender
and the Politics of Poverty*
Ananya Roy

VOLUME 9
*Landscapes of Urban Memory:
The Sacred and the Civic in India's
High-Tech City*
Smriti Srinivas

VOLUME 8
*Fin de Millénaire Budapest:
Metamorphoses of Urban Life*
Judit Bodnár

VOLUME 7
Latino Metropolis
Victor M. Valle and Rodolfo D. Torres

VOLUME 6
*Regions That Work: How Cities and
Suburbs Can Grow Together*
Manuel Pastor Jr., Peter Dreier,
J. Eugene Grigsby III, and
Marta López-Garza

VOLUME 5
*Selling the Lower East Side:
Culture, Real Estate, and Resistance
in New York City*
Christopher Mele

VOLUME 4
*Power and City Governance:
Comparative Perspectives on
Urban Development*
Alan DiGaetano and
John S. Klemanski

VOLUME 3
*Second Tier Cities: Rapid Growth
beyond the Metropolis*
Ann R. Markusen, Yong-Sook Lee,
and Sean DiGiovanna, Editors

VOLUME 2
*Reconstructing Chinatown: Ethnic
Enclave, Global Change*
Jan Lin

VOLUME 1
The Work of Cities
Susan E. Clarke and Gary L. Gaile

Matthew Hayes is the Canada Research Chair in Global and International Studies at St. Thomas University, Fredericton, New Brunswick.

CPSIA information can be obtained
at www.ICGtesting.com
Printed in the USA
FSHW022224200219
55815FS

9 781517 904920